# The Stewardship of God's Riches

## Readings in Economics

Edited by Ray Notgrass

Cover and Interior Design
Mary Evelyn Notgrass

ISBN: 978-1-933410-98-2

Published in the United States by Notgrass Company.

**Notgrass Company**
**370 S. Lowe Avenue, Suite A**
**PMB 211**
**Cookeville, Tennessee 38501**

**1-800-211-8793**
**books@notgrass.com**
**www.notgrass.com**

# Table of Contents

Introduction .................................................................................................................... vii

I, Pencil *Leonard Read (1958)* ...................................................................................... 1
The Wealth of Nations (excerpts) *Adam Smith (1776)* .............................................. 5
Socialism, Capitalism, and the Bible *Ronald H. Nash (1985)* ................................ 12
What Makes for Success? *Dave Thomas (1996)* ...................................................... 18
Christianity, the Market, and Beyond *John Davenport (1981)* ................................ 29
Economic Justice for All (excerpts) *U.S. Catholic Bishops (1986)* ......................... 37
Letter 4 of Letters from a Farmer in Pennsylvania *John Dickinson (1768)* ............ 43
The Legacy of the 1936 Election *Amity Shlaes (2007)* ............................................ 46
Politics, Economics, and Education in the 21st Century *John Fund (1998)* ............ 51
Three Cheers for Capitalism *Steve Forbes (1993)* .................................................. 57
The Entrepreneur As American Hero *Walter E. Williams (2005)* ............................ 61
The Market and Human Values *John Davenport (1975)* .......................................... 66
High Technology and Judeo-Christian Values: Mind, Not Money, Drives the Economy
    *Warren T. Brookes (1984)* ................................................................................ 71
Free to Choose: A Conversation with Milton Friedman (2006) ................................ 79
American Free Trade Policy: Rhetoric or Reality? (1989) ........................................ 85
Free Trade Under Attack: What Americans Can Do *Murray L. Wiedenbaum (1984)* ... 90
Market Entrepreneurs: Building Empires of Service *Burton W. Folsom Jr. (1997)* ... 98
American Small Business: The Quiet Giant *John E. Sloan (1984)* ......................... 104
Socialism, Free Enterprise, and the Common Good *Robert A. Sirico (2007)* ....... 110
Labor Unions in a Free Market *Ernest van den Haag (1979)* ............................... 115
The Legitimate Role of Government in a Free Society *Walter E. Williams (2000)* ... 123
The Deficit and Our Obligation to Future Generations *James M. Buchanan (1987)* ... 127
The Greatest Story Never Told: Today's Economy in Perspective *Patrick Toomey (2008)* ... 134
Solving the Problem of Poverty *Steve Mariotti (1998)* .......................................... 138
A Prescription for American Health Care *John C. Goodman (2009)* ..................... 143
How Detroit's Automakers Went from Kings of the Road to Roadkill
    *Joseph B. White (2009)* ..................................................................................... 147
Ecology and the Economy: The Problems of Coexistence *James L. Buckley (1980)* ... 154
I Must See the Things; I Must See the Men *Russell Kirk (1987)* ........................... 163
Speech on the Economic Bailout Proposal *George W. Bush (2008)* ...................... 170
The Innate Power of the Individual *Kent C. Nelson (1997)* ................................... 174
What Makes for Success? *Kemmons Wilson (1997)* ............................................. 178


Index of Titles and Authors ..................................................................................... 181
Image Credits ............................................................................................................ 182

# Introduction

*The Stewardship of God's Riches* is a compilation of documents, speeches, and essays that help the reader understand what the field of economics means for us in a practical way. It includes material from two Nobel Prize recipients, nationally-recognized economists, highly successful business leaders, renowned political and economic writers, and people who consider the spiritual dimensions of economic activity. It is designed to be used in conjunction with the text *Exploring Economics*. The student who is using that text will find readings in this volume assigned at the end of many of the lessons. We hope that these readings will help the student to appreciate the importance of economics and to develop a grasp of workable solutions to many of the economic questions we face.

Several entries are taken from *Imprimis*, the monthly speech journal published by Hillsdale College. The title is pronounced im-PRY-mis. It comes from the Latin and means "in the first place." Hillsdale is a private, liberal arts college in Michigan that accepts no government money of any kind, not even Federal loans and grants to students. The college decided some years ago that it did not want to deal with the strings that are attached to accepting Federal money. Each month, *Imprimis* presents the essence of a speech given at a recent Hillsdale-sponsored function. The publication is offered free of charge, and it is also available on the Internet at www.hillsdale.edu. Several years of *Imprimis* issues are archived on the website.

Hillsdale provides a valuable service with *Imprimis* by presenting thoughtful, relevant, conservative thinking; by offering the publication free; and by generously giving permission for the material to be reproduced without charge provided that the appropriate credit line is given. The *Imprimis* material is copyrighted by Hillsdale College and is used here by permission of Hillsdale. Occasionally a speech will include a few comments that are inappropriate; but generally *Imprimis* is worth reading every month. I strongly encourage anyone who is interested in government and politics to subscribe to it or to read it online.

In editing the entries in this volume, I have left out some sections that I thought best to omit. These are indicated by ellipses. I have also added some explanations that are enclosed in brackets. For the most part I have left variations in spelling and the citations of other works as they appear in the originals.

*Ray Notgrass*

# The Stewardship of God's Riches

# I, Pencil
## Leonard Read (1958)

*Leonard Read (1898-1983) established the Foundation for Economic Education in 1946 (www.fee.org). This organization promotes individual liberty, free markets, and property rights. Read wrote this essay in 1958. The* Imprimis *introduction to the essay invites the reader to "Wonder at the countless bits of human know-how and natural materials spontaneously organized by our global market economy into the making of a simple wooden pencil. . . . And wonder, most of all, at the everyday miracles made possible by a political and economic system that dares to have faith in free men."*

December 1983 *Imprimis*

I am a lead pencil—the ordinary wooden pencil familiar to all boys and girls and adults who can read and write. (My official name is "Mongol 482." My many ingredients are assembled, fabricated, and finished by Eberhard Faber Pencil Company, Wilkes-Barre, Pennsylvania.)

Writing is both my vocation and my avocation; that's all I do.

You may wonder why I should write a genealogy. Well, to begin with, my story is interesting. And, next, I am a mystery—more so than a tree or a sunset or even a flash of lightning. But, sadly, I am taken for granted by those who use me, as if I were a mere incident and without background. This supercilious attitude relegates me to the level of the commonplace. This is a species of the grievous error in which mankind cannot too long persist without peril. For, as a wise man observed, "We are perishing for want of wonder, not for want of wonders" (Chesterton).

I, Pencil, simple though I appear to be, merit your wonder and awe, a claim I shall attempt to prove. In fact, if you can understand me—no, that's too much to ask of anyone—if you can become aware of the miraculousness which I symbolize, you can help save the freedom mankind is so unhappily losing. I have a profound lesson to teach. And I can teach this lesson better than can an automobile or an airplane or a mechanical dishwasher because—well, because I am seemingly so simple.

Simple? Yet, not a single person on the face of this earth knows how to make me. This sounds fantastic, doesn't it? Especially when it is realized that there are about one and one-half billion of my kind produced in the U.S.A. each year.

Pick me up and look me over. What do you see? Not much meets the eye—there's some wood, lacquer, the printed labeling, graphite lead, a bit of metal, and an eraser.

## Innumerable Antecedents

Just as you cannot trace your family tree back very far, so is it impossible for me to name and explain all my antecedents. But I would like to suggest enough of them to impress upon you the richness and complexity of my background.

My family tree begins with what in fact is a tree, a cedar of straight grain that grows in Northern California and Oregon. Now contemplate all the saws and trucks and rope and the countless other gear used in harvesting and carting the cedar logs to the railroad siding.

Think of all the persons and the numberless skills that went into their fabrication: the mining of ore, the making of steel and its refinement into saws, axes, motors; the growing of hemp and bringing it through all the stages to heavy and strong rope; the logging camps with their beds and mess halls, the cookery and the raising of all the foods. Why, untold thousands of persons had a hand in every cup of coffee the loggers drink!

The logs are shipped to a mill in San Leandro, California. Can you imagine the individuals who make flat cars and rails and railroad engines and who construct and install the communication systems incidental thereto? These legions are among my antecedents.

Consider the millwork in San Leandro. The cedar logs are cut into small, pencil-length slats less than one-fourth of an inch in thickness. These are kiln dried and then tinted for the same reason women put rouge on their faces. People prefer that I look pretty, not a pallid white. The slats are waxed and kiln dried again. How many skills went into the making of the tint and the kilns, into supplying the heat, the light and power, the belts, motors, and all the other things a mill requires? Sweepers in the mill among my ancestors? Yes, and included are the men who poured the concrete for the dam of a Pacific Gas & Electric Company hydroplant which supplies the mill's power! Don't overlook the ancestors present and distant who have a hand in transporting sixty carloads of slats across the nation from California to Wilkes-Barre!

## Complicated Machinery

Once in the pencil factory—$4,000,000 in machinery and building, all capital accumulated by thrifty and saving parents of mine—each slat is given eight grooves by a complex machine, after which another machine lays leads in every other slat, applies glue, and places another slat atop—a lead sandwich, so to speak. Seven brothers and I are mechanically carved from this "wood-clinched" sandwich.

My "lead" itself—it contains no lead at all—is complex. The graphite is mined in Ceylon. Consider these miners and those who make their many tools and the makers of the paper sacks in which the graphite is shipped and those who make the string that ties the sacks and those who put them aboard ships and those who make the ships. Even the lighthouse keepers along the way assisted in my birth—and the harbor pilots.

The graphite is mixed with clay from Mississippi in which ammonium hydroxide is used in the refining process. Then wetting agents are added such as sulfonated tallow—animal fats chemically reacted with sulfuric acid. After passing through numerous machines, the mixture finally appears as endless extrusions—as from a sausage grinder—cut to size, dried, and baked for several hours at 1,850 degrees Fahrenheit. To increase their strength and smoothness the leads are then treated with a hot mixture which includes candelilla wax from Mexico, paraffin wax, and hydrogenated natural fats.

My cedar receives six coats of lacquer. Do you know all of the ingredients of lacquer? Who would think that the growers of castor beans and the refiners of castor oil are a part of it? They are. Why, even the processes by which the lacquer is made a beautiful yellow involves the skills of more persons than one can enumerate!

Observe the labeling. That's a film formed by applying heat to carbon black mixed with resins. How do you make resins and what, pray, is carbon black?

My bit of metal—the ferrule—is brass. Think of all the persons who mine zinc and copper and those who have the skills to make shiny sheet brass from these products of nature. Those black rings on my ferrule are black nickel. What is black nickel and how is it applied? The complete story of why the center of my ferrule has no black nickel on it would take pages to explain.

Then there's my crowning glory, inelegantly referred to in the trade as "the plug," the part man uses to erase the errors he makes with me. An ingredient called "factice" is what does the erasing. It is a rubber-like product made by reacting rape seed oil from the Dutch East Indies with sulfur chloride. Rubber, contrary to the common notion, is only for binding purposes. Then, too, there are numerous vulcanizing and accelerating agents. The pumice comes from Italy; and the pigment which gives "the plug" its color is cadmium sulfide.

## Vast Web of Know-How

Does anyone wish to challenge my earlier assertion that no single person on the face of this earth knows how to make me?

Actually, millions of human beings have had a hand in my creation, no one of whom even knows more than a very few of the others. Now, you may say that I go too far in relating the picker of a coffee berry in far off Brazil and food growers elsewhere to my creation; that this is an extreme position. I shall stand by my claim. There isn't a single person in all these millions, including the president of the pencil company, who contributes more than a tiny, infinitesimal bit of know-how. From the standpoint of know-how the only difference between the miner of graphite in Ceylon and the logger in Oregon is in the type of know-how. Neither the miner nor the logger can be dispensed with, any more than can the chemist at the factory or the worker in the oil field—paraffin being a by-product of petroleum.

Here is an astounding fact: Neither the worker in the oil field nor the chemist nor the digger of graphite or clay nor any who mans or makes the ships or trains or trucks nor the one who runs the machine that does the knurling on my bit of metal nor the president of the company performs his singular task because he wants me. Each one wants me less, perhaps, than does a child in the first grade. Indeed, there are some among this vast multitude who never saw a pencil nor would they know how to use one. Their motivation is other than me. Perhaps it is something like this: Each of these millions sees that he can thus exchange his tiny know-how for the goods and services he needs or wants. I may or may not be among these items.

## No Human Master Mind

There is a fact still more astounding: The absence of a master mind, of anyone dictating or forcibly directing these countless actions which bring me into being. No trace of such a person can be found. Instead, we find the Invisible Hand at work. This is the mystery to which I earlier referred.

It has been said that "only God can make a tree." Why do we agree with this? Isn't it because we realize that we ourselves could not make one? Indeed, can we even describe a tree? We cannot, except in superficial terms. We can say, for instance, that a certain molecular configuration manifests itself as a tree. But what mind is there among men that could even record, let alone direct, the constant changes in molecules that transpire in the life span of a tree? Such a feat is utterly unthinkable!

I, Pencil, am a complex combination of miracles; a tree, zinc, copper, graphite, and so on. But to these miracles which manifest themselves in Nature an even more extraordinary miracle has been added: the configuration of creative human energies—millions of tiny know-hows configurating naturally and spontaneously in response to human necessity and desire and in the absence of any human master-minding! Since only God can make a tree, I insist that only God could make me. Man can no more direct these millions of know-hows to bring me into being than he can put molecules together to create a tree.

The above is what I meant when writing, "If you can become aware of the miraculousness which I symbolize, you can help save the freedom mankind is so unhappily losing." For, if one is aware that these know-hows will naturally, yes, automatically, arrange themselves into creative and productive patterns in response to human necessity and demand—that is, in the absence of governmental or any other coercive master-minding—then one will possess an absolutely essential ingredient for freedom: a faith in free men. Freedom is impossible without this faith.

Once government has had a monopoly of a creative activity such, for instance, as the delivery of the mails, most individuals will believe that the mails could not be efficiently delivered by men acting freely. And here is the reason: Each one acknowledges that he himself doesn't know how to do all the things incident to mail delivery. He also recognizes that no other individual could do it. These assumptions are correct. No individual possesses enough know-how to perform a nation's mail delivery any more than any individual possesses enough know-how to make a pencil. Now, in the absence of a faith in free men—in the unawareness that millions of tiny know-hows would naturally and miraculously form and cooperate to satisfy this necessity—the individual cannot help but reach the erroneous conclusion that the mail can be delivered only by governmental "master-minding."

## Testimony Galore

If I, Pencil, were the only item that could offer testimony on what men can accomplish when free to try, then those with little faith would have a fair case. However, there is testimony galore; it's all about us and on every hand. Mail delivery is exceedingly simple when compared, for instance, to the making of an automobile or a calculating machine or a grain combine or a milling machine, or to tens of thousands of other things.

Delivery? Why, in this area where men have been left free to try, they deliver the human voice around the world in less than one second; they deliver an event visually and in motion to any person's home when it is happening; they deliver 150 passengers from Seattle to Baltimore in less than four hours; they deliver gas from Texas to one's range or furnace in New York at unbelievably low rates and without subsidy; they deliver each four pounds of oil from the Persian Gulf to our Eastern Seaboard—halfway around the world—for less money than the government charges for delivering a one-ounce letter across the street!

## Leave Men Free

The lesson I have to teach is this: Leave all creative energies uninhibited. Merely organize society to act in harmony with this lesson. Let society's legal apparatus remove all obstacles the best it can. Permit these creative know-hows freely to flow. Have faith that free men will respond to the Invisible Hand. This faith will be confirmed. I, Pencil, seemingly simple though I am, offer the miracle of my creation as testimony that this is a practical faith, as practical as the sun, the rain, a cedar tree, the good earth.

# The Wealth of Nations (excerpts)
## Adam Smith (1776)

*The publication of* An Inquiry into the Nature and Causes of the Wealth of Nations *by the Scottish philosopher Adam Smith is usually cited as the beginning of the modern study of economics. The excerpts below highlight some of Smith's main points in the book.*

The annual labour of every nation is the fund which originally supplies it with all the necessaries and conveniences of life which it annually consumes, and which consist always either in the immediate produce of that labour, or in what is purchased with that produce from other nations.

According therefore as this produce, or what is purchased with it, bears a greater or smaller proportion to the number of those who are to consume it, the nation will be better or worse supplied with all the necessaries and conveniences for which it has occasion.

But this proportion must in every nation be regulated by two different circumstances; first, by the skill, dexterity, and judgment with which its labour is generally applied; and, secondly, by the proportion between the number of those who are employed in useful labour, and that of those who are not so employed. Whatever be the soil, climate, or extent of territory of any particular nation, the abundance or scantiness of its annual supply must, in that particular situation, depend upon those two circumstances.

*Adam Smith*

The abundance or scantiness of this supply, too, seems to depend more upon the former of those two circumstances than upon the latter. Among the savage nations of hunters and fishers, every individual who is able to work, is more or less employed in useful labour, and endeavours to provide, as well as he can, the necessaries and conveniences of life, for himself, or such of his family or tribe as are either too old, or too young, or too infirm to go a-hunting and fishing. Such nations, however, are so miserably poor that, from mere want, they are frequently reduced, or, at least, think themselves reduced, to the necessity sometimes of directly destroying, and sometimes of abandoning their infants, their old people, and those afflicted with lingering diseases, to perish with hunger, or to be devoured by wild beasts. Among civilised and thriving nations, on the contrary, though a great number of people do not labour at all, many of whom consume the produce of ten times, frequently of a hundred times more labour than the greater part of those who work; yet the produce of the whole labour of the society is so great that all are often abundantly supplied, and a workman, even of the lowest and poorest order, if he is frugal and industrious, may enjoy a greater share of the necessaries and conveniences of life than it is possible for any savage to acquire.

The causes of this improvement, in the productive powers of labour, and the order, according to which its produce is naturally distributed among the different ranks and conditions of men in the society, make the subject of the first book of this Inquiry. . . .

The greatest improvement in the productive powers of labour, and the greater part of the skill, dexterity, and judgment with which it is anywhere directed, or applied, seem to have been the effects of the division of labour.

The effects of the division of labour, in the general business of society, will be more easily understood by considering in what manner it operates in some particular manufactures. It is commonly supposed to be carried furthest in some very trifling ones; not perhaps that it really is carried further in them than in others of more importance: but in those trifling manufactures which are destined to supply the small wants of but a small number of people, the whole number of workmen must necessarily be small; and those employed in every different branch of the work can often be collected into the same workhouse, and placed at once under the view of the spectator. In those great manufactures, on the contrary, which are destined to supply the great wants of the great body of the people, every different branch of the work employs so great a number of workmen that it is impossible to collect them all into the same workhouse. We can seldom see more, at one time, than those employed in one single branch. Though in such manufactures, therefore, the work may really be divided into a much greater number of parts than in those of a more trifling nature, the division is not near so obvious, and has accordingly been much less observed.

To take an example, therefore, from a very trifling manufacture; but one in which the division of labour has been very often taken notice of, the trade of the pin-maker; a workman not educated to this business (which the division of labour has rendered a distinct trade), nor acquainted with the use of the machinery employed in it (to the invention of which the same division of labour has probably given occasion), could scarce, perhaps, with his utmost industry, make one pin in a day, and certainly could not make twenty. But in the way in which this business is now carried on, not only the whole work is a peculiar trade, but it is divided into a number of branches, of which the greater part are likewise peculiar trades. One man draws out the wire, another straights it, a third cuts it, a fourth points it, a fifth grinds it at the top for receiving the head; to make the head requires two or three distinct operations; to put it on is a peculiar business, to whiten the pins is another; it is even a trade by itself to put them into the paper; and the important business of making a pin is, in this manner, divided into about eighteen distinct operations, which, in some manufactories, are all performed by distinct hands, though in others the same man will sometimes perform two or three of them. I have seen a small manufactory of this kind where ten men only were employed, and where some of them consequently performed two or three distinct operations. But though they were very poor, and therefore but indifferently accommodated with the necessary machinery, they could, when they exerted themselves, make among them about twelve pounds of pins in a day. There are in a pound upwards of four thousand pins of a middling size. Those ten persons, therefore, could make among them upwards of forty-eight thousand pins in a day. Each person, therefore, making a tenth part of forty-eight thousand pins, might be considered as making four thousand eight hundred pins in a day. But if they had all wrought separately and independently, and without any of them having been educated to this peculiar business, they certainly could not each of them have made twenty, perhaps not one pin in a day; that is, certainly, not the two hundred and fortieth, perhaps not the four thousand eight hundredth part of what they are at present capable of performing, in consequence of a proper division and combination of their different operations.

In every other art and manufacture, the effects of the division of labour are similar to what they are in this very trifling one. . . .

This division of labour, from which so many advantages are derived, is not originally the effect of any human wisdom, which foresees and intends that general opulence to which it gives occasion. It is the necessary, though very slow and gradual consequence of a certain propensity in human nature which has in view no such extensive utility; the propensity to truck, barter, and exchange one thing for another. . . .

In civilised society [the individual] stands at all times in need of the cooperation and assistance of great multitudes, while his whole life is scarce sufficient to gain the friendship of a few persons. In almost every other race of animals each individual, when it is grown up to maturity, is entirely independent, and in its natural state has occasion for the assistance of no other living creature. But man has almost constant occasion for the help of his brethren, and it is in vain for him to expect it from their benevolence only. He will be more likely to prevail if he can interest their self-love in his favour, and show them that it is for their own advantage to do for him what he requires of them. Whoever offers to another a bargain of any kind, proposes to do this. Give me that which I want, and you shall have this which you want, is the meaning of every such offer; and it is in this manner that we obtain from one another the far greater part of those good offices which we stand in need of. It is not from the benevolence of the butcher, the brewer, or the baker that we expect our dinner, but from their regard to their own interest. We address ourselves, not to their humanity but to their self-love, and never talk to them of our own necessities but of their advantages. . . .

As it is by treaty, by barter, and by purchase that we obtain from one another the greater part of those mutual good offices which we stand in need of, so it is this same trucking disposition which originally gives occasion to the division of labour. In a tribe of hunters or shepherds a particular person makes bows and arrows, for example, with more readiness and dexterity than any other. He frequently exchanges them for cattle or for venison with his companions; and he finds at last that he can in this manner get more cattle and venison than if he himself went to the field to catch them. From a regard to his own interest, therefore, the making of bows and arrows grows to be his chief business, and he becomes a sort of armourer. Another excels in making the frames and covers of their little huts or movable houses. He is accustomed to be of use in this way to his neighbours, who reward him in the same manner with cattle and with venison, till at last he finds it his interest to dedicate himself entirely to this employment, and to become a sort of house-carpenter. In the same manner a third becomes a smith or a brazier, a fourth a tanner or dresser of hides or skins, the principal part of the clothing of savages. And thus the certainty of being able to exchange all that surplus part of the produce of his own labour, which is over and above his own consumption, for such parts of the produce of other men's labour as he may have occasion for, encourages every man to apply himself to a particular occupation, and to cultivate and bring to perfection whatever talent or genius he may possess for that particular species of business. . . .

As it is the power of exchanging that gives occasion to the division of labour, so the extent of this division must always be limited by the extent of that power, or, in other words, by the extent of the market. When the market is very small, no person can have any encouragement to dedicate himself entirely to one employment, for want of the power to exchange all that surplus part of the produce of his own labour, which is over and above his own consumption, for such parts of the produce of other men's labour as he has occasion for.

There are some sorts of industry, even of the lowest kind, which can be carried on nowhere but in a great town. A porter, for example, can find employment and subsistence in no other place. A village is by much too narrow a sphere for him; even an ordinary market town is scarce large enough to afford him constant occupation. In the lone houses and very small villages which are scattered about in so desert a country as the Highlands of Scotland, every farmer must be butcher, baker and brewer for his own family. In such situations we can scarce expect to find even a smith, a carpenter, or a mason, within less than twenty miles of another of the same trade. The scattered families that live at eight or ten miles distance from the nearest of them must learn to perform themselves a great number of little pieces of work, for which, in more populous countries, they would call in the assistance of those workmen. Country workmen are almost everywhere obliged to apply themselves to all the different branches of industry that have so much affinity to one another as to be employed about the same sort of materials. A country carpenter deals in every sort of work that is made of wood; a country smith in every sort of work that is made of iron. The former is not only a carpenter, but a joiner, a cabinet-maker, and even a carver in wood, as well as a wheel-wright, a plough-wright, a cart and waggon maker. The employments of the latter are still more various. It is impossible there should be such a trade as even that of a nailer in the remote and inland parts of the Highlands of Scotland. Such a workman at the rate of a thousand nails a day, and three hundred working days in the year, will make three hundred thousand nails in the year. But in such a situation it would be impossible to dispose of one thousand, that is, of one day's work in the year.

*Blacksmith*

As by means of water-carriage a more extensive market is opened to every sort of industry than what land-carriage alone can afford it, so it is upon the sea-coast, and along the banks of navigable rivers, that industry of every kind naturally begins to subdivide and improve itself, and it is frequently not till a long time after that those improvements extend themselves to the inland parts of the country. . . .

When the division of labour has been once thoroughly established, it is but a very small part of a man's wants which the produce of his own labour can supply. He supplies the far greater part of them by exchanging that surplus part of the produce of his own labour, which is over and above his own consumption, for such parts of the produce of other men's labour as he has occasion for. Every man thus lives by exchanging, or becomes in some measure a merchant, and the society itself grows to be what is properly a commercial society.

But when the division of labour first began to take place, this power of exchanging must frequently have been very much clogged and embarrassed in its operations. One man, we shall suppose, has more of a certain commodity than he himself has occasion for, while another has less. The former consequently would be glad to dispose of, and the latter to purchase, a part of this superfluity. But if this latter should chance to have nothing that the former stands in need of, no exchange can be made between them. The butcher has more meat in his shop than he himself can consume, and the brewer and the baker would each of them be willing to purchase a part of it. But they have nothing to offer in exchange, except the different productions of their respective trades, and the butcher is already provided with all the bread and beer which he has immediate occasion for. No exchange can, in this case, be made between them. He cannot be their merchant, nor they his customers; and they are all of them thus mutually less serviceable to one another. In order to avoid the inconveniency of such situations, every prudent man in every period of society, after the first establishment of the division of labour, must naturally have endeavoured to manage his affairs in such a manner as to have at all times by him, besides the peculiar produce of his own industry, a certain quantity of some one commodity or other, such as he imagined few people would be likely to refuse in exchange for the produce of their industry.

Many different commodities, it is probable, were successively both thought of and employed for this purpose. In the rude ages of society, cattle are said to have been the common instrument of commerce; and, though they must have been a most inconvenient one, yet in old times we find things were frequently valued according to the number of cattle which had been given in exchange for them. The armour of Diomede, says Homer, cost only nine oxen; but that of Glaucus cost an hundred oxen. Salt is said to be the common instrument of commerce and exchanges in Abyssinia; a species of shells in some parts of the coast of India; dried cod at Newfoundland; tobacco in Virginia; sugar in some of our West India colonies; hides or dressed leather in some other countries; and there is at this day a village in Scotland where it is not uncommon, I am told, for a workman to carry nails instead of money to the baker's shop or the alehouse.

In all countries, however, men seem at last to have been determined by irresistible reasons to give the preference, for this employment, to metals above every other commodity. Metals can not only be kept with as little loss as any other commodity, scarce anything being less perishable than they are, but they can likewise, without any loss, be divided into any number of parts, as by fusion those parts can easily be reunited again; a quality which no other equally durable commodities possess, and which more than any other quality renders them fit to be the instruments of commerce and circulation. The man who wanted to buy salt, for example, and had nothing but cattle to give in exchange for it, must have been obliged to buy salt to the value of a whole ox, or a whole sheep at a time. He could seldom buy less than this, because what he was to give for it could seldom be divided without loss; and if he had a mind to buy more, he must, for the same reasons, have been obliged to buy double or triple the quantity, the value, to wit, of two or three oxen, or of two or three sheep. If, on the contrary, instead of sheep or oxen, he had metals to give in exchange for it, he could easily proportion the quantity of the metal to the precise quantity of the commodity which he had immediate occasion for.

Different metals have been made use of by different nations for this purpose. Iron was the common instrument of commerce among the ancient Spartans; copper among the ancient Romans; and gold and silver among all rich and commercial nations. . . .

Those metals seem originally to have been made use of for this purpose in rude bars, without any stamp or coinage. Thus we are told by Pliny, upon the authority of Timaeus, an ancient historian, that, till the time of Servius Tullius, the Romans had no coined money, but made use of unstamped bars of copper, to purchase whatever they had occasion for. These bars, therefore, performed at this time the function of money.

The use of metals in this rude state was attended with two very considerable inconveniencies; first, with the trouble of weighing; and, secondly, with that of assaying them. In the precious metals, where a small difference in the quantity makes a great difference in the value, even the business of weighing, with proper exactness, requires at least very accurate weights and scales. The weighing of gold in particular is an operation of some nicety. In the coarser metals, indeed, where a small error would be of little consequence, less accuracy would, no doubt, be necessary. Yet we should find it excessively troublesome, if every time a poor man had occasion either to buy or sell a farthing's worth of goods, he was obliged to weigh the farthing. The operation of assaying is still more difficult, still more tedious, and, unless a part of the metal is fairly melted in the crucible, with proper dissolvents, any conclusion that can be drawn from it, is extremely uncertain. Before the institution of coined money, however, unless they went through this tedious and difficult operation, people must always have been liable to the grossest frauds and impositions, and instead of a pound weight of pure silver, or pure copper, might receive in exchange for their goods an adulterated composition of the coarsest and cheapest materials, which had, however, in their outward appearance, been made to resemble those metals. To prevent such abuses, to facilitate exchanges, and thereby to encourage all sorts of industry and commerce, it has been found necessary, in all countries that have made any considerable advances towards improvement, to affix a public stamp upon certain quantities of such particular metals as were in those countries commonly made

*Smelting Room, United States Mint, Philadelphia, c. 1876*

use of to purchase goods. Hence the origin of coined money, and of those public offices called mints; institutions exactly of the same nature with those of the aulnagers [government inspectors—RN] and stamp-masters of woolen and linen cloth. All of them are equally meant to ascertain, by means of a public stamp, the quantity and uniform goodness of those different commodities when brought to market. . . .

As every individual, therefore, endeavours as much as he can both to employ his capital in the support of domestic industry, and so to direct that industry that its produce may be of the greatest value; every individual necessarily labours to render the annual revenue of the society as great as he can. He generally, indeed, neither intends to promote the public interest, nor knows how much he is promoting it. By preferring the support of domestic to that of foreign industry, he intends only his own security; and by directing that industry in such a manner as its produce may be of the greatest value, he intends only his own gain, and he is in this, as in many other cases, led by an invisible hand to promote an end which was no part of his intention. Nor is it always the worse for the society that it was no part of it. By pursuing his own interest he frequently promotes that of the society more effectually than when he really intends to promote it. I have never known much good done by those who affected to trade for the public good. It is an affectation, indeed, not very common among merchants, and very few words need be employed in dissuading them from it. . . .

Every system which endeavours, either by extraordinary encouragements to draw towards a particular species of industry a greater share of the capital of the society than what would naturally go to it, or, by extraordinary restraints, force from a particular species of industry some share of the capital which would otherwise be employed in it, is in reality subversive of the great purpose which it means to promote. It retards, instead of accelerating, the progress of the society towards real wealth and greatness; and diminishes, instead of increasing, the real value of the annual produce of its land and labour.

All systems either of preference or of restraint, therefore, being thus completely taken away, the obvious and simple system of natural liberty establishes itself of its own accord. Every man, as long as he does not violate the laws of justice, is left perfectly free to pursue his own interest his own way, and to bring both his industry and capital into competition with those of any other man, or order of men. The sovereign is completely discharged from a duty, in the attempting to perform which he must always be exposed to innumerable delusions, and for the proper performance of which no human wisdom or knowledge could ever be sufficient; the duty of superintending the industry of private people, and of directing it towards the employments most suitable to the interest of the society. According to the system of natural liberty, the sovereign has only three duties to attend to; three duties of great importance, indeed, but plain and intelligible to common understandings: first, the duty of protecting the society from violence and invasion of other independent societies; secondly, the duty of protecting, as far as possible, every member of the society from the injustice or oppression of every other member of it, or the duty of establishing an exact administration of justice; and, thirdly, the duty of erecting and maintaining certain public works and certain public institutions which it can never be for the interest of any individual, or small number of individuals, to erect and maintain; because the profit could never repay the expense to any individual or small number of individuals, though it may frequently do much more than repay it to a great society. . . .

# Socialism, Capitalism, and the Bible
## Ronald H. Nash (1985)

*Ronald Nash received a doctorate from Syracuse University. He was a professor of philosophy and religion at Western Kentucky University, Reformed Theological Seminary in Maitland, Florida, and Southern Baptist Theological Seminary in Louisville, Kentucky. The author of numerous books, Nash died in 2006. This essay presents the idea that free market capitalism, not socialism, best accomplishes Biblical teachings.*

July 1985 *Imprimis*

In the Christian church today, one can find a small but growing army of Protestants and Roman Catholics who have entered into an uncritical alliance with the political Left. The so-called liberation theologians not only promote a synthesis of Marxism and Christianity, but attempt to ground their recommended restrictions of economic and political freedom on their interpretation of the biblical ethic. A growing number of my own religious fellowship (those theologically conservative Protestants known as evangelicals) appear to stop just short of the more radical pronouncements of the liberation thinkers. These evangelicals of the Left are convinced that the biblical ethic obliges them to condemn capitalism and endorse the politics of statism and the economics of socialism.

Many writings from the Christian Left illustrate what can be called the prooftext method. What these writers normally do is isolate some vague passage (usually one from the Old Testament) that pertains to an extinct culture situation or practice. They then proceed to deduce some complex economic or political program from that text.

My approach to the subject rejects the prooftext method and proceeds via three main steps. First, a Christian should acquire a clear and complete picture of the Christian worldview. What basic views about God, humankind, morality, and society are taught or implied by Scripture? Second, he should put his best effort into discovering the truth about economic and political systems. He should try to clarify what capitalism and socialism really are (not what the propagandists say they are); he should try to discover how each system works or, as in the case of socialism, whether it can work. He should identify the strengths and weaknesses of each system. Third, he should compare his economic options to the standard of biblical morality, and ask which system is more consistent with the entire Christian worldview.

## Creator and Freedom; Morality and Sin

We can begin, then, by noting several relevant aspects of the biblical worldview:

1. Certainly the biblical worldview implies that since God is the creator of all that exists, He ultimately is the rightful owner of all that exists. Whatever possessions a human being may acquire, he holds them temporarily as a steward of God and is ultimately accountable to God for how he uses them. However omnipresent greed and avarice may be in the human race, they are clearly incompatible with the moral demands of the biblical worldview.

2. The biblical worldview also contains important claims about human rights and liberties. All human beings have certain natural rights inherent in their created nature and have certain moral obligations to respect the rights of others. The possibility of human freedom is not a gift of government but a gift from God.

The Old Testament tended to focus on the economic and social dimensions of freedom. But gradually, as one moves into the New Testament, a more spiritual dimension of freedom assumes dominance. Freedom in the New Testament is deliverance from bondage to sin and is available only to those who come to know God's truth through Christ and enter into a saving relationship with Christ.

Some interesting parallels between the biblical account of spiritual freedom and political-economic freedom should be noted. For one thing, freedom always has God as its ultimate ground. For another, freedom must always exist in relationship to law. The moral law of God identifies definite limits beyond which human freedom under God should not pass. Liberty should never be turned into license.

3. The moral system of the Bible is another key element of the Christian worldview. While the Ten Commandments do not constitute the entire biblical ethic, they are a good place to begin. But it is important to notice other dimensions of the biblical ethic that have relevance for our subject. For example, Christians on the Left insist that the biblical ethic condemns individual actions and social structures that oppress people, harm people and favor some at the expense of others. I agree. Where I disagree, however, is with the next step taken by the Leftists. They claim that capitalism inevitably and necessarily encourages individual actions and produces social structures that oppress and harm people. On this point, they are dead wrong. Fortunately, the question as to which system actually harms or helps different classes of people is an empirical and not a normative matter. The Leftists simply have their facts wrong.

4. One final aspect of the Christian worldview must be mentioned: the inescapable fact of human sin and depravity. No economic or political system that assumes the essential goodness of human nature or holds out the dream of a perfect earthly society can possibly be consistent with the biblical worldview.

## Peaceful or Violent Exchange?

Now we must examine the three major economic systems that compete for attention: capitalism, socialism and somewhere between, the hybrid known as interventionism or the mixed economy.

One dominant feature of capitalism is economic freedom, the right of people to exchange things voluntarily, free from force, fraud, and theft. Socialism, on the other hand, seeks to replace the freedom of the market with a group of central planners who exercise control over essential market functions. There are degrees of socialism as there are degrees of capitalism in the real world. But basic to any form of socialism is distrust of or contempt for the market process and the desire to replace the freedom of the market with some form of centralized control. Generally speaking, as one moves along the continuum of socialism to capitalism, one finds the following: the more freedom a socialist allows, the closer his position is to interventionism; the more freedom an interventionist allows, the closer his position is to capitalism. The crux is the extent to which human beings will be permitted to exercise their own choices in the economic sphere of life.

I will say nothing more about that deplorable economic system known as interventionism, a hopeless attempt to stop on a slippery slope where no stop is possible. The only way the half-hearted controls of the interventionist can work is if they become the total controls of the socialist. Anything less will result in the kind of troubled and self-damaging economy we have had for the past several decades in the United States.

I shall attempt to get a clearer fix on the real essence both of capitalism and socialism and then see which is more compatible with the biblical worldview. The best starting point for this comparison is a distinction made most recently by the American economist, Walter Williams. According to Williams, there are two and only two ways in which something may be exchanged. He called them *the peaceful means of exchange and the violent means of exchange.*

The peaceful means of exchange may be summed up in the phrase, "If you do something good for me, then I'll do something good for you." When capitalism is understood correctly, it epitomizes the peaceful means of exchange. The reason people exchange in a real market is because they believe the exchange is good for them. They take advantage of an opportunity to obtain something they want more in exchange for something they desire less. Capitalism then should be understood as a voluntary system of relationships that utilizes the peaceful means of exchange.

But exchange can also take place by means of force and violence. In this violent means of exchange, the basic rule of thumb is: "Unless you do something good for me, I'll do something bad to you." This turns out to be the controlling principle of socialism. Socialism means far more than centralized control of the economic process. It entails the introduction of coercion into economic exchange in order to facilitate the attainment of the goals of the elite who function as the central planners. One of the great ironies of Christian socialism is that its proponents in effect demand that the State get out its weapons and force people to fulfill the demands of Christian love. Even if we fail to notice any other contrast between capitalism and socialism, we already have a major difference to relate to the biblical ethic. One system stresses voluntary and peaceful exchange while the other depends on coercion and violence.

Some Christian socialists object to the way I have set this up. They profess contempt for the more coercive forms of state-socialism on exhibit in communist countries. They would like us to believe that a more humane, non-coercive kind of socialism is possible. They would like us to believe that there is a form of socialism, not yet tried anywhere on earth, where the central ideas are cooperation and community and where coercion and dictatorship are precluded. But they provide very little information about the workings of this more utopian kind of socialism, and they ignore the fact that however humane and voluntary their socialism is supposed to become after it has been put into effect, it will take massive amounts of coercion and theft to get things started.

## Socialist Falsehoods, Capitalist Facts

To that paradox, add one more: the fact that socialists need capitalism in order to survive. Unless socialists make allowance for some free markets which provide the pricing information that alone makes rational economic activity possible, socialist economies would have even more problems than those for which they are already notorious. Consequently, socialism is a gigantic fraud which attacks the market at the same time it is forced to utilize the market process.

But critics of the market try to shift attention away from their own embarrassing problems to claims that capitalism must be abolished or restricted because it is unjust or because it restricts important human freedoms. Capitalism is supposed to be unchristian because it allegedly gives a predominant place to greed and other unchristian values. It is alleged to increase poverty and the misery of the poor while, at the same time, it makes a few rich at the expense of the many. Socialism, on the other hand, is portrayed as the economic system of people who really care for the less fortunate members of society. Socialism is represented as the economics of compassion. Socialism is also recommended on the ground that it encourages other basic Christian values such as community.

If these claims were true, they would constitute a serious problem for anyone anxious to show that capitalism is compatible with the biblical ethic. But, of course, the claims are not true. People who make such charges have their facts wrong or are aiming at the wrong target. The "capitalism" they accuse of being inhumane is a caricature. The system that in fact produces the consequences they deplore turns out to be not capitalism, but interventionism.

Capitalism is not economic anarchy. It recognizes several necessary conditions for the kinds of voluntary relationships it recommends. One of these presuppositions is the existence of inherent human rights, such as the right to make decisions, the right to be free, the right to hold property, and the right to exchange what one owns for something else. Capitalism also presupposes a system of morality. Capitalism should be thought of as a system of voluntary relationships within a framework of laws which protect people's rights against force, fraud, theft, and violations of contracts. "Thou shalt not steal" and "Thou shalt not lie" are part of the underlying moral constraints of the system. Economic exchanges can hardly be voluntary if one participant is coerced, deceived, defrauded, or robbed.

## Allowing for Human Weakness

Once we grant that consistency with the biblical doctrine of sin is a legitimate test of political and economic systems, it is relatively easy to see how well democratic capitalism scores in this regard. The limited government willed to Americans by the Founding Fathers was influenced in large measure by biblical considerations about human sin. If one of the more effective ways of mitigating the effects of human sin in society is dispersing and decentralizing power, the conservative view of government is on the right track. So too is the conservative vision of economics.

The free market is consistent with the biblical view of human nature in another way. It recognizes the weaknesses of human nature and the limitations of human knowledge. No one can possibly know enough to manage a complex economy. No one should ever be trusted with this power. However, in order for socialism to work, socialism requires a class of omniscient planners to forecast the future, to set prices and to control production. In the free market system, decisions are not made by an omniscient bureaucratic elite but made across the entire economic system by countless economic agents.

At this point, of course, collectivists will raise another set of objections. Capitalism, they will counter, may make it difficult for economic power to be consolidated in the hands of the state; but it only makes it easier for vast concentrations of wealth and power to be vested in the hands of private individuals and companies. But the truth turns out to be something quite different from this widely accepted myth. It is not the free market that produces monopolies; rather it is governmental intervention with the market that creates the conditions that encourage monopoly.

As for another old charge, that capitalism encourages greed, the truth is just the reverse. The mechanism of the market neutralizes greed as selfish individuals are forced to find ways of servicing the needs of those with whom they wish to exchange. As we know, various people often approach economic exchanges with motives and objectives that fall short of the biblical ideal. But no matter how base or selfish a person's motives may be, so long as the rights of the other parties are protected, the greed of the first individual cannot harm them. As long as greedy individuals are prohibited from introducing force, fraud, and theft into the exchange process, their greed must be channeled into the discovery of products or services for which people are willing to exchange their holdings. Every person in a market economy has to be other-directed.

## New Religion of the Left

Finally, some examples of the way in which attempts to ground American liberalism and interventionism or Latin American liberationism on the Bible involve serious distortions of the biblical message.

For instance, consider how radical American evangelicals on the Left abuse the biblical notion of justice. The basic idea in the Old Testament notion of justice is righteousness and fairness. But it is essential to the Leftist's cause that he read into biblical pronouncements about justice, contemporary notions of distributive justice. When the Bible says that Noah was a just man, it does not mean that he would have voted the straight Democratic ticket. It means simply that he was a righteous man.

Likewise, many Christians on the Left seek to reinterpret Jesus' earthly mission in exclusively economic and political terms. In their view, Jesus came primarily to deliver those who were poor and oppressed in a material sense. But every member of the human race is poor in the sense of being spiritually bankrupt. Jesus came to end our spiritual poverty by making available the righteousness that God demands and that only God can provide.

It is heresy to state that God's love for people varies in proportion to their wealth and social class. It is nonsense to suggest that all the poor are good and all the rich are evil. Once we eliminate the semantic game-playing by which some refer to a non-coercive voluntary utopian type of socialism, it becomes clear that socialism is incompatible with a truly free society. Edmund Opitz has seen this clearly:

> As History's vice-regent, the Planner is forced to view men as mass; which is to deny their full stature as persons with rights endowed by the Creator, gifted with free will, possessing the capacity to order their own lives in terms of their convictions. The man who has the authority and the power to put the masses through their paces, and to punish nonconformists, must be ruthless enough to sacrifice a person to a principle . . . a commissar who believes that each person is a child of God will eventually yield to a commissar whose ideology is consonant with the demands of his job.

And so, Opitz concludes, "Socialism needs a secular religion to sanction its authoritarian politics, and it replaces the traditional moral order by a code which subordinates the individual to the collective." All of this is justified in the cause of improving economic well-being and in the name of compassion.

## The Choice I Make

I think I have said enough to allow me, at least, to make a reasoned choice between capitalism and socialism on the basis of each system's compatibility to the biblical worldview. The alternative to free exchange is violence. Capitalism is a mechanism that allows natural human desires to be satisfied in a nonviolent way. Little can be done to prevent human beings from wanting to be rich. But what capitalism does is channel that desire into peaceful means that benefit many besides those who wish to improve their own situation.

Which choice then should I, as a Christian, make in the selection between capitalism and socialism? Capitalism is quite simply the most moral system, the most effective system, and the most equitable system of economic exchange. When capitalism, the system of free economic exchange, is described fairly, there can be no question that it, rather than socialism or interventionism, comes closer to matching the demands of the biblical ethic.

*Produce Market in Belize, Central America*

# What Makes for Success?
## Dave Thomas (1996)

---

*Dave Thomas (1932-2002) started working in a restaurant when he was twelve and became a millionaire when he was 35. He founded the Wendy's restaurant chain in 1969. In this speech Thomas shared the principles that guided his life and business.*

July 1996 *Imprimis*

There are all kinds of success and all kinds of ways to achieve it. I know bus drivers who are as successful as bankers. I know anonymous computer programmers who are now more successful than some of the biggest sports celebrities. I also know glamorous Hollywood stars and leading political figures who are failures. Sometimes you can spot true success. Sometimes you can't. Success can take many forms, but one thing's for sure: There are certain ingredients that are necessary in any recipe for success, and they may be applied by anyone.

In other words, success comes through doing the right things—developing proper skills, attitudes, and values. As I've thought this through from an ordinary guy's perspective (which, above all else, I am; Lord knows, I'm no scholar), I have come to identify twelve ingredients. We know them as "character traits" or "values" or "virtues." People have been making lists of these ingredients ever since the Bible was written—and even before then. I've seen lists that are longer and some that are shorter, but twelve feels just about right to me. They are the ones that have made the most sense and have proved most valuable in my walk through life. But I should warn you, making lists is not enough to achieve success. You have to show people what success is. For example, I don't think that we really need to define generosity; we need to show what it means to be more generous—with our time, our talents, and our treasures.

My list of ingredients for success is divided into four basic groups:

*Inward*—these have to do with getting your own act together successfully.

*Outward*—these are all about treating people right.

*Upward*—these are skills you need to know if you want to go beyond just doing an okay job and truly excel.

*Onward*—these are attitudes you need to have in order to put yourself second and other people first. I think that onward values may be the toughest and the most rewarding values of all.

Added on to these ingredients are some others. Since I'm a hamburger cook, I call them "toppings." They are the pickles and onions of how I look at success:

Anything is possible within the laws of God and man.

You can't cut corners on quality.

Give back—early and often.

When you help someone, you really help yourself.

Pay attention to the basics.

You can't make much progress walking forward if you don't keep your balance, and that means balance in every part of your life.

Have a sense of urgency about most things you do, and you won't end up as the caboose.

Focus on only one thing at a time, and on just a few things in a lifetime.

Don't waste time trying to do things you know nothing about: Either learn the basics or steer clear.

Remember that life is short and fragile. Live it as if you don't know if you are going to be around for the next breath.

Don't take the people of our nation—or their freedom—for granted.

Be yourself—don't take yourself too seriously.

Do the right thing—even when it may seem like the hardest thing in the world.

Put more into life than you get out of it.

## Inward: Getting Your Own Act Together

Success starts inside. Unless your own attitude and beliefs are right, you can never be a success. That goes for being successful in raising your family or helping to lead your church or synagogue or just making a buck. People never really have their act together unless they are honest, they believe in something, and they develop basic discipline.

## Honesty

Many good people may look at honesty backwards. They think that it's okay if they don't come forward with the whole truth until someone challenges them with the right questions. But honesty doesn't mean hiding in the weeds; it means stepping out and telling the whole truth. Honesty means being sincere. It also means being fair in all your dealings with others.

Honesty is the number-one ingredient for success. I learned this the way most people do: through trial and error. I was born out of wedlock in New Jersey in 1932. A Michigan couple adopted me just after I was born. My adopted mother died when I was only five, but I had the good fortune to have a wonderful adoptive grandmother, Minnie Sinclair, who looked out for my welfare and helped shape my beliefs. I did not discover that I was adopted for many years, and, I have to admit, this made me angry and resentful for some time. I wish I had known from the beginning.

Yet after I learned the truth, I didn't always share it with others. One day, an African-American Wendy's manager buttonholed me and said, "Dave, when you gave your speech today, you left out the part about being adopted. Why did you do that? I always related to that because I was adopted myself." The comment hit home. From that point on, I made it a practice to be fully honest—and proud—about my past.

## Faith

Honesty doesn't come from out of nowhere. It is a product of your moral convictions. But what do you do when your convictions are challenged? It is faith that gives you the strength to go on believing. Though I am a Christian, I respect the religions of others, and I think that they play a vital role in our society. But I don't support convictions or cults that are negative and lead only to hatred and fanaticism. Faith must be positive.

Live your faith. Don't wear it on your sleeve; roll up both sleeves and do something about it. When I was eleven years old, my adoptive grandmother took me to Michigan's Gull Lake to be baptized by immersion. I really felt that I was accepted by God when I was baptized. But what I remember most about my baptism was that my Grandma Minnie made it happen. For her, Christianity meant more than doctrine you talked about on Sundays. It meant working hard in a restaurant, seeing to the lodgers she rented rooms to, tending a big garden, doing the canning, and taking care of the farm animals every morning. And it meant teaching her grandson about faith.

At night we would listen to a gospel radio station that broadcast out of Chicago, and on Sundays before church we would listen to shows like the *Cato Tabernacle* out of Indianapolis. The public praying and singing part of her faith might not have stuck with me all that much, but I got baptized into the roll-up-your-sleeves kind of faith of Grandma Minnie. And I believe in it to this day.

## Discipline

Routine lies at the heart of discipline. Routine is what keeps us focused on the main things in life. But routine doesn't have to mean boring. Unless you have a strong, healthy routine, I doubt that you can live a successful life. Discipline means keeping things and people in their proper places. For example, I think that taxpayers should discipline their politicians so that they don't get too uppity! Children need discipline, too—plenty more than most of them get—and that's the fault of their parents. Discipline means direction—clear and firm direction—not physical or mental abuse. Discipline helps you keep track of your own thinking and also keeps such thinking simple and to the point so that you don't mess up by dreaming up fancy, big-shot thoughts when you shouldn't.

Roy Tuggle, one of the pioneers of the modern restaurant business, is a classic in discipline as far as I'm concerned. When he was fourteen years old, Roy—the sixth of twelve children—left Ravenna, Kentucky, during the Great Depression. With only two years of school under his belt, nine pennies in his pocket, and cardboard soles in his shoes, he hopped a freight train to Columbus, Ohio. After unloading stoves and refrigerators and working as a dishwasher, he became a fry cook. By sheer will and discipline he built his career and a great restaurant business while he and his wife Mary raised their family.

When Roy started out, hamburgers were only a nickel and a small restaurant operator had to scrimp for every penny. Years later, when Roy sold his business, he became a millionaire. But the dollar signs never changed Roy. He's never been driven by money. As you'll hear Roy often put it today, "I never wanted to be the richest man in the graveyard," to which I'll generally chime in, "You got it, Roy. You've never seen a hearse with luggage racks." Roy's is the kind of discipline that keeps success from going to your head once you have had the good fortune to achieve your goals.

## Outward: Treating People Right

Success may start inside, but it doesn't mean anything until you draw other people into the picture. The key is whether you are going to be fair to other folks—will you treat people right? If you are to treat people right, you have to master three fundamentals: caring, teamwork, and support. Most of us are lucky enough to learn these basic ideas from our parents and should be pros at them by the time we are in nursery school. (But I have met some Ph.D.s and millionaires who have never learned the words or have forgotten what they mean, and I bet that you know people like that, too.) Not taking people for granted is a great way to steer a straight outward course and to do right by your fellow human beings.

## Caring

Caring is the rock that love is built upon. Caring is feeling what another person feels. Some people call it "empathy." Genuinely caring about people usually leads to success. And really successful people widen the circle of people they care about more and more as they grow older. Mary Kay Ash, founder of Mary Kay Cosmetics, once told me something I'll never forget. She said the one suggestion she got in life that helped her most was to "pretend that every single person you meet has a sign around his or her neck that says, 'Make me feel important.'"

Why aren't we just nice to people? One year, shortly before Christmas, I went to a Wendy's restaurant in Albuquerque to film a television program about adoption with two youngsters. The little girl, who was about seven, had a fresh scar where her father had walloped her with a beer bottle. That scar wasn't going to go away. As we ate lunch along with a friend of mine, the girl and her older brother, who was about nine, finally started to look us in the eyes, and that was none too easy for them. We talked about how important it is to stick together when you don't have other family. And then the boy said: "I don't want to be adopted with her. Just look at her ugly scar!"

It may seem cruel, but he was right. The boy knew his sister's appearance would turn off many possible adoptive parents. And before you condemn him, think back for a minute: Were you any less selfish when you were nine? I doubt that I was. My friend—who is smart in a low-key way and who made it big-time by building a big business over the years—reached into his wallet and pulled out two crisp one hundred dollar bills. "You kids," he said in a real quiet voice, "don't have any money to buy Christmas presents. It's plain to see that. So I want you to buy some Christmas presents, but there's a catch. You can't buy anything for yourself. Think hard about what your brother or sister might like or need and buy that instead. Finally, you have to write me a letter about what you got each other."

That five-minute course in caring outdid the best universities anywhere. The brother and sister made up. In January, my friend received a letter reporting what they bought each other, and he sent a copy to me. Then we learned that they had been adopted by a family. As I hear it, they're quite a team, and their new parents are proud to have them—because of the way that they care for each other and for lots of other reasons, too.

## Teamwork

Teamwork is the starting point for treating people right. Most people think that teamwork is only important when competing against other teams. But competition is only part of the picture. In most things we do in life, people have to work with rather than against each other to get something done. Win-win situations and partnerships are the most important results of teamwork. The best teams in the world are the ones that help people become better and achieve more than they ever thought they could on their own.

One place people learn teamwork from is their families. Children get their first lesson watching how their parents behave toward each other. So, if you're a parent, you are also a teacher of teamwork—for good or ill—every day. Your sons and daughters learn from what you do. For me, the people I've worked with have become my family, too. Throughout my career, my "second family" has taught me a whole lot about teamwork.

There are little teams and there are big teams. Your community is a team, for example. My daughter Pam organizes volunteer work for the city of Columbus, so she knows a lot about how to get different kinds of teams to work together, on projects ranging from recreation centers to hospital boards. Teams can work together, and teams can compete, too, even when they are not rivals. Why aren't Pam's kids jealous when she spends so much of her time on community work? There is a simple answer: The kids are all involved in community work themselves, and they have been from an early age. Pam and her husband, Steve, endorse it and encourage it. The community team isn't a rival or an opponent of the family team—it's an extension of it. Neat idea, don't you think?

## Support

Many people believe that support is something you give to someone you feel sorry for or that it means propping someone up who would fail unless you were there to give him a boost. But that's not the way I see it. Support is the boost you give someone who can help himself but who needs a partner to open a window or to push aside a roadblock. Support isn't a bunch of reckless advice, either. It's real help—commitment and effort. Support is "teamwork plus." Support is also sharing feelings and insights with other people. It's helping others with their level of awareness and making your own awareness stronger at the same time.

The best way to get support is to give it. Wendy's President Gordon Teter likes to remind people of a saying that Jack Mollenkopf, his college coach at Purdue, often used: "Meet me halfway, and it's amazing what can happen." It is amazing what can be done when you treat people with respect. Respect goes both ways, too. Just as the players need it from the coach, the coach needs it from the players.

Support is also easier if things aren't too complicated. Gordon believes in what he calls "The Law of the Lowest Common Denominator," and it has nothing to do with arithmetic. It goes like this: "The simpler you can keep it, the better you can execute it." It's that way for a department and its boss, for a congregation and its minister, and for a volunteer group and its chairperson. If you want to give and get support, it's a lot more likely to come and keep coming if the rules are simple and clear.

## Upward: Going for Excellence and Beyond

When you have your own act together and get along well with others, you're ready to reach for another goal, that of excellence. Nothing is as tricky in the world of success as excellence. From our earliest days, we are taught that it is snazzy, glossy, bigger than life. It's that three seconds of glory when a major leaguer puts one out of the park or a figure skater completes a triple jump, not the constant training or workouts. But that's just false. Most people think excellence in business is sitting at a big desk and making power decisions, but true excellence is really the years beforehand making little and big decisions and learning from mistakes when things go wrong.

No one can excel in everything. In fact, excellence in any one little thing is hard enough. And don't forget: It's easy to become selfish when you "go for the gold." The graveyards of the world are loaded with people who lost it all at the same time they thought they were winning it all.

## Motivation

Without a doubt, motivation is a key ingredient of success. Know what motivates you, and prove to yourself that this motivation is honest and worthwhile. But don't let too many different things motivate you, or you'll be tangled up in a maze of all kinds of conflicts. Stay focused. Figure out what your motivations are going to be in the next step of your life before you arrive at it. Keep dreaming, but don't daydream. And don't do anything just to earn praise, or you are likely to short-change yourself in the end. Look at success firsthand so that you really know how it works and what it costs to achieve.

It may be corny, but I'm big on lapel pins. Some people hand out business cards; I give away lapel pins. Wendy's gives out pins to employees, and to customers, too—they're just as much a part of the family as anyone else. As I said, I don't believe in wearing your beliefs on your sleeve; but I do believe in wearing them on your lapel. Yep, I'm one of those guys who'll wear an American flag pin on my lapel from time to time; it shows I'm proud to be an American. In the same way, by wearing Wendy's lapel pins, our employees show they're proud to be a part of the Wendy's team. Does having a little symbol that means they're part of the Wendy's family motivate employees to work a little harder, or customers to come in more often? A little bit, I'll bet. And success in life is made up of a lot of little things that keep you motivated and that motivate others too.

## Creativity

Creativity means change, but if you don't use common sense when you change things around, you are likely to end up farther behind than when you started. Not everybody can be creative. Accept it as a fact of life that if you aren't creative yourself your challenge is to learn how to work with people who are. And being creative doesn't always mean doing new things. Sometimes, it's using a creative idea that worked in one instance and applying it to another. I'm a disciple of reality. Successful creative dreams have to be realistic—within man's laws as well as God's—and within the realm of common sense.

What makes people creative? Sometimes, it's having your life shaken up. George Valassis is a pal of mine. For nineteen years he worked as an advertising salesman for his father's brother. One day his uncle decided to retire and his cousin took over the business. The cousin fired him. Without warning, George lost a modest though comfortable job, and he realized then and there that job security could vanish like a puff of smoke. So, he put his nineteen years of experience to use in order to come up with an innovative idea. He knew that advertisers like Procter and Gamble and General Foods were having a really tough time delivering coupons to customers quickly, so he came up with the idea of inserting books filled with coupons in newspapers. To this day, when you open the Sunday edition of your newspaper and see a book of coupons inside, you're looking at what the ad industry calls a "Valassis Insert." George sold the company he built for big bucks. If he hadn't gotten fired, would he have come up with this great idea? George doesn't think so. To this day, he says he just played the hand he was dealt. Pretty creative though, wasn't it?

## Leadership

Everybody is saying that we need to stop putting leaders on pedestals. I'm not so sure. The real problem is finding leaders who truly deserve to keep their pedestals. What knocks off more leaders than anything else is failing to practice what they preach. Of all the things leaders are supposed to do, nothing is more important than setting a good example. Ben Franklin had it right when he wrote in *Poor Richard's Almanac*, "Well done is better than well said." I don't think we should do away with pedestals; we ought to be putting a lot more "little people"—people who have really achieved something—on them so that ordinary folks have a better, clearer idea of who's doing the job and who's setting the pace.

J. B. Fuqua is a titan of industry who built a huge conglomerate and broadcast empire. J. B. is also a guy who still knows the meaning of being humble. Born to a poor family, his mother died when he was two months old, and his grandparents adopted him. When J. B. was out on his own and wanted to learn about radio electronics, the only library he knew about was Duke University's. The library staff decided to loan him the books he needed even though he was not a student. It wasn't a bad deal for Duke: After J. B. hit the bull's-eye in his own companies, he invested $15 million in the Duke University business school, helping put it in the front ranks of all business schools in the U.S.

First and foremost, J. B. is a leader. In addition to the donations he's made to Duke, he's donated $4 million to train managers in Russia and Ukraine as these nations attempt to put at least a few true free enterprise principles into practice. And then there's the $10 million that he's giving to Prince Edward County, Virginia, to help turn around the educational system for youngsters in kindergarten through twelfth grade. It will be a model of doing the right thing for rural school systems throughout the United States.

It's not the money that makes J. B. successful as a leader. It's the fact that he won't let go. J. B. will tell you that leadership doesn't stop with giving but begins there. He's well past retirement age, yet you'll find him all over—from Farmville to Kiev—giving to others, passing on his own experience and wisdom. J. B.'s style is real leadership—letting go in the doing, but not letting go in the guiding.

## Onward: Putting Yourself Second and Others First

If going upward and reaching for excellence is where success gets tricky, going onward by putting yourself second and others first is where success really gets tough. Most books on success tell you that you have really "arrived" when you win the race. That's wrong. Truly successful people are the ones who help others cross the finish line. People who make this last big step toward success really have three things: responsibility, courage, and generosity. Onward is the direction Success Soldiers follow—Christian or any other kind.

## Responsibility

We try to teach children responsibility, and that's good, but, as I have already said, most of us don't learn the full meaning of responsibility until we are older and have gained solid experience, made some decisions, and learned from our mistakes—not the simple mistakes we make when "following orders" but mistakes we make when trying to do something really hard or trying to excel. Making these sorts of mistakes teaches us judgment, and it helps toughen our backbone.

Mature responsibility means realizing that no single person can be responsible for everything. You can't be successful if you are stumbling around trying to juggle the whole world on your shoulders. Responsible people refuse to take shortcuts, even though they are almost always available. They make sure that others with duties act responsibly, too. And they use whatever recognition or honor they may have earned not to further their own ends but on behalf of good causes. Instead of stealing the limelight, they allow it to shine upon a good cause.

My son Kenny says that the most important piece of advice I ever gave him came in 1979 as the two of us were driving over the Oakland Park Bridge in Ft. Lauderdale. He was thinking about becoming a Wendy's franchisee. I gave him my opinion; I was against it. I didn't come out and say why, but my feeling was that he wasn't ready for that kind of responsibility, and I didn't want to see him fail. When he told me his mind was made up, I said, "Don't ever forget how you got here, and don't ever let yourself become complacent." Kenny went on to become pretty successful in the restaurant business. He says my advice really helped him. But I could have summed up everything I said that day in just two words: Be responsible.

## Courage

We tend to make courage too dramatic. Courage is often doing something simple, unpleasant, or boring again and again until we get it down pat. People who are physically challenged and who have the determination to get around their handicaps are great examples because their courage makes them test their limits every day in a way that the rest of us write off as small-time or insignificant. Lois Gruenbaum grew up in Cleveland and went to work in a hospital kitchen when she was fifteen. During World War II, she became a nurse's aide and worked in an army hospital. After a shift, she would say to herself, "Hey, things are bad, but there's always someone who is worse off. All you need to do is find out what you can and can't do and then go ahead and do what you can do."

Great lesson—Lois learned it not long before she needed to put it to use. In 1955, she was diagnosed with cancer. Operation after operation followed, but the cancer always came back. Finally, she lost one leg and half of the pelvic bone and was forced to drag herself around on crutches. She came home from the hospital faced with the challenge of taking care of her husband, a seven-year-old, a four-year-old, and two-year-old twins. She says she cut a deal with the Lord: "I promised that if He let me live to raise my children, I would not vegetate. I would be a contributing person." It was a good deal. Forty years later, the family is flourishing, and Lois is one of the most active and happy people you could ever hope to meet. And there are thousands of such quiet, unsung heroes in every town. I'll bet you know lots of people with the courage of Lois Gruenbaum.

## Generosity

A person who has modest means and won't share may be considered stingy. But rich people can give 'til they're purple and still not be truly generous. You have to give of yourself, not just of your wallet. One of the things I'm proudest about in the Wendy's family is that so many franchisees make significant donations to the community—and they contribute leadership as well as dollars. Another old friend, the late Kenny King, was a generous guy who had a real knack for how he gave. He really took pleasure in it, was modest about it, and often gave anonymously. But even more important was the fact that he really tried to learn what giving was all about. Whether he was giving people moral or financial support, he would always say, "I'm really getting a lot more out of this than you are." I can't tell you how many times he said that same thing to me. Later, when I tried to do for others what Kenny had done for me, I learned what he meant. When you give people help and understanding, you truly learn what they are like. And those who understand others better are certainly the most likely to succeed. The giving and the getting become all mixed up—which is great.

## The Proud Beggar

In February of 1991, I had to travel to Memphis. It wasn't a trip I wanted to make. There's a church there I'll never forget; you don't forget places where you say good-bye to your best friends. It's plenty bigger than Calvary Church in Kalamazoo where I had my first memories of going to church. In fact, it's a cathedral—the Cathedral of the Immaculate Conception. It looks Spanish and it's mighty big and fancy. On the day I was there, every seat was filled, and a huge crowd stood outside. A lot of other people—not just me—had lost a friend.

> Oh, Danny boy, the pipes, the pipes are calling,
> From glen to glen and down the mountainside,
> The summer's gone—all the roses falling,
> 'Tis you, 'tis you must go, and I must bide.

A song you'd expect to hear in an Irish pub, not in a cathedral. You wouldn't expect it to be sung by a Metropolitan Opera soprano like Marguerite Piazza either. Maybe you'd think that it was honoring an Irish cardinal, but who would expect that it was in memory of a Lebanese entertainer of humble origins? Many eyes were tearing before the music started, but when they heard the first notes of that song—Danny Thomas's theme song for decades— everybody choked up. A little girl and an older couple near me were crying, and I don't know what sound seemed bigger to my ears—the crying or the music.

Danny was a great friend. He was one heck of a showman. But, most of all, he was a success—not just as an entertainer but as a human being. An obsession drove him—the St. Jude's Children's Hospital in Memphis. He'd do anything for that hospital. No man or woman I know ever got over every inch of the false pride that we are all born with more than Danny Thomas did. He called himself the "Proud Beggar."

If Danny Thomas hadn't forgotten a promise, St. Jude would never have been built. Back in 1943, Danny was still playing five-dollar-a-week gigs. His wife was pregnant with their first child, Marlo, and they needed money to raise a family. Danny's uncle by marriage was a butcher who offered him a job cutting meat, but he wanted to stay in show business. Danny stopped at a church and, according to the Catholic tradition, prayed to St. Jude for direction. He promised he would show his gratitude if guided to the right path: Should he be a comedian or a butcher? Not much later, Danny's act was booked at Chez Paris in Chicago. He had made it to the big time. The booking lasted for five years, and it helped launch his television career.

Until well into his stint at Chez Paris, Danny had forgotten all about his promise. Forgetting to make good on a promise was about the worst thing a person could do, in Danny's book. When he finally remembered, he went to see an old friend, Cardinal Stritch, and he asked what he should do. The cardinal told him that there were already enough churches and enough statues in the world. Recalling his first parish in Memphis, he proposed the idea of starting a children's hospital there.

That's what Danny did. He built the best children's hospital in the world. Why is the place named after St. Jude? St. Jude is the saint in charge of impossible acts. Danny felt that "no child should die in the dawn of life," so he declared a personal war against the killer diseases that strike the young. He started funding the hospital in Memphis in 1957. Great names in medicine led the research. Plenty of impossible things were made possible because Danny stuck to his mission like a bulldog. In 1962, only 4 percent of the victims of acute lymphocytic leukemia survived the disease; in 1991, 73

*St. Jude Children's Research Hospital in Memphis, Tennessee*

percent survived. Only 7 percent of patients with non-Hodgkin lymphoma recovered; now, about 80 percent do. The list goes on and on. When people tell you about the "impossible," just think of St. Jude's Hospital.

In 1991, Danny Thomas was promoting his new book, the proceeds of which were earmarked for St. Jude. He always did fund-raising for the hospital before taking on jobs that would put money in his own pocket. One night, worn out, he got home late. At 2:30 a.m., a massive heart attack killed him. He was not buried in some grassy cemetery. He was laid to rest in a mausoleum inside St. Jude's Hospital. All around the mausoleum, Danny's favorite sayings are inscribed—sayings like: "Blessed is the man who knows why he was born," and "He who denies his heritage has no heritage." Danny gave of himself. He taught others to give of themselves, too, and to forget their selfish side. I remember his response to a donor who had put down a large hunk of change: "The deepest thank-you I can offer is to pray that you and yours will never need the help of St. Jude's."

Well done, Danny boy!

Danny Thomas's example is worth remembering anytime the temptation arises for "me" to take over "we." Everything that made him a success was based on simple principles:

Keep your word. Danny kept his word to God.

Let a good cause that's bigger than you take over your life. What is your St. Jude? There ought to be one. Think about it, and support it.

Don't get scared by the word impossible. In fact, get together the best talents you can find to tackle the impossible.

Do it through people. Danny got people to work together. That's the way it should be, isn't it?

Whether you are passing the hat for a good cause, defending your beliefs, teaching your children, helping your community, or starting a business, be a proud beggar. Real proud.

# Christianity, the Market, and Beyond
## John Davenport (1981)

*John Davenport graduated from Yale in 1926. He was a writer and economic journalist who worked at* Barron's Weekly *and* Fortune *magazines and wrote for many other publications. He wrote* The U.S. Economy *in 1964. Davenport died in 1987 at the age of 82. In this essay Davenport demonstrated the importance of Christianity in guiding our economic decisions.*

March 1981 *Imprimis*

. . . On the face of it, religion and economics would seem to have little to do with each other; and when they do get mixed up together, most of us do not like it. For instance, we resent the fact that gentlemen of the cloth on occasion have preached socialist doctrine. Nor are we quite comfortable when, as more recently, they take the opposite tack, implying that to be part of the "moral majority" we should have opposed the Panama Canal treaty or should be favorably disposed to whatever private enterprise may do or may not do. To separation of church and state we are inclined to add a strong wall of separation between religion and any particular set of economic views. Render unto Caesar the things that are Caesar's and to God what belongs to God.

Yet as a practical matter we cannot completely compartmentalize religion, politics and economics, and certainly the Founding Fathers did not do so. The Declaration speaks of men being endowed by their Creator with certain inalienable rights, and refers to the laws of nature and of nature's God. The U.S. set sail with certain moral presuppositions flying at its masthead, and these in turn would seem to have had something to do with belief in the limitation of secular government power. Given that limitation it followed, though it was never overtly stated, that the U.S. would develop not according to some master economic plan but through an economy based on private property and the operation of what we call the free market. Had we done otherwise, had we believed in a totally planned economy, our forefathers might well have crossed the Alleghenies. But I suspect we might still be trying to reach Hillsdale or be stuck on the Great Plains without reaching California and the broad Pacific!

There has been therefore, I would suggest, a kind of trilogy working through our affairs in which religion and certain ethical values or standards, a certain view of government, and a certain practical way of carrying on the world's work, flowed together like the tributaries of the Mississippi to produce a great nation. The problem we face today, and of this seminar, is whether this fortunate confluence of ideals and ideas can be maintained in an age of rapid technological advance and in an increasingly secular society. Is it true as a previous speaker, Edmund Opitz, has argued, that religion and capitalism are fundamentally not enemies but friends, and that in Winston Churchill's phrase we still stand for what in the darkest hour of the war he called Western Christian civilization? Or is there some fatal conflict afoot in our society and in its underlying philosophic strata? Attending the great Chicago Exposition of 1893, old Henry Adams began to ponder the seemingly divergent lines of force symbolized for him in the Dynamo and the Virgin. How reconcile the genii of electricity with his beloved Mont St. Michel and Chartres? How reconcile the coming of atomic fission, the computer, mass markets and [television], with the Cross?

Before trying to answer these questions analytically it will repay us, I believe, to turn back the pages of history to events which long predate the founding of our still fortunate Republic, and to reexamine the flow of ideas and developments which have brought us to our present posture of doubt and uncertainty. Among the more amazing phenomena of history is how from humble beginnings the teachings of Christianity in a matter of a few generations came to sweep the decaying Roman Empire and the world of antiquity—"the glory that was Greece and the grandeur that was Rome." Many explanations have been offered for this phenomenon but the most eloquent statement of Christianity's role in history that I know is contained in the final pages of Walter Lippmann's *The Good Society*, a book which I recommend to you. Writes Lippmann, looking back over the centuries: "To the masses of the Western world the news that all men are more than things was proclaimed by the Christian gospel and was celebrated in its central mysteries. . . . For in the recognition that there is in each man a final essence—that is to say, an immortal soul—which only God can judge, a limit was set up on the dominion of men over men. . . . Toward this conviction men have fought their way in the long ascent out of the morass of barbarism. Upon this rock they have built the rude foundations of the Good Society."

An extraordinary statement considering that Lippmann, so far as I know, was not himself a devout churchman and considering that the rise of Christianity is associated in the pages of Gibbon and others with the coming of the so-called Dark Ages, in which the civilizations of the ancient world disappeared in an era marked by war, pestilence, and crass superstition where, at best, Christianity offered a City of God to be found in the next world but certainly not in this. Yet modern scholarship has, I believe, tended to refine if not overthrow the view that the Middle Ages were an age of darkness unrelieved till the escape from Christian teachings in the glorious Renaissance of the fourteenth century. William Carroll Bark of Stanford University has suggested that some of the liberties we prize today owe their origin fully as much to "barbaric" German tribes as to Rome itself. Christopher Dawson has shown that the Dark Ages were not so dark even when it came to technological progress. One of the perennial mysteries of history is why the Greeks and later the Romans, possessed as they were of enormous advances in mathematics and abstract philosophy, rarely applied such learning to mechanical contrivances. One possible answer is the presence and acceptance of slavery. If you have plenty of slaves about you are not apt to be interested in the modern dishwasher!

Now the Christian Church at times tolerated slavery as we Americans, the product of the Civil War, have reason to know. But the mindset of the Christian doctrine was against the slave society, and the scholars to whom I am referring make much of the fact that as slavery diminished, men were forced to pay some attention to how drudging work in the fields and the towns could be alleviated. In the days of bread and circuses Roman chariots were drawn by traces and a yoke which had the misfortune of nearly strangling the horse when he was trying to respond to the whip of his master. The Middle Ages saw the introduction of the simple device of the horse collar, a tiny advance by our standards but one which multiplied horsepower many times over. To this period we owe the rotation of crops, the development of the wheeled plow, and the widespread use of the windmill for draining swamps, and the water mill for grinding wheat. The monasteries were not just devoted to prayer. As the rule of St. Benedict put it: "If the brothers, whether from necessity or poverty, are obliged to go out to harvest crops themselves, let them not be distressed, for it is when they live by the work of their hands that they will in truth be monks." The building of cathedrals involved the use of hydraulic jacks, levers, and all manner of building tools. Meanwhile trade, at first local and sporadic, expanded. The late Middle Ages saw the rise of the guilds and the artisans. As Dawson has pointed out, Christianity differed from all other Eastern religions in its dual emphasis on the divine and the practical. "Deliverance is to be obtained not by a sheer disregard of physical existence and a concentration of the intellect on pure Being, but by creative activity that affects every part of the corporate nature of man."

Finally, it should be emphasized that while we owe the preservation of the great intellectual works of classical antiquity to the Arabs and to the East, still when the writings of Plato and Aristotle were brought back to Europe, they were put to good use. It is fashionable today to ridicule the Schoolmen [medieval academics] for arguing as to how many angels could dance on the point of a pin. In point of fact we owe to them, and especially to Aquinas, the reconciliation of faith and reason. The flowering of modem science in the seventeenth century is usually associated with the rise of inductive as against deductive reasoning. But Alfred North Whitehead, in his *Science and the Modern World*, surely one of the more profound histories of thought, points out that the mere observation of facts will never create true science. There must be method and hypothesis into which the facts will flow. There must likewise be faith that there is an order in nature and in the universe that can be discovered, for "without this belief the incredible labors of scientists would be without hope." In the medieval view God at least was rational, and this belief in its turn affected all that was to come. In explaining the modern world of high technology Whitehead states, "My explanation is that the faith in the possibility of science, generated antecedently to the development of modern scientific theory, is *an unconscious derivative from medieval theology.*"

What is true is that until the Christianity of the Schoolmen rid itself of the particular cosmology of Aristotle in which the earth was conceived to be the center of the universe and until men began to apply their minds to what Galileo called "the irreducible and stubborn facts" of nature, modern scientific advance was impossible. And what is true is that the Christian Church for far too long resisted this breakout, giving rise to the Inquisition and many other atrocities which those who today still call themselves Christians, whether Catholic or Protestant, would prefer to forget about. Yet in the end the breakout occurred and I read in the papers that the Catholic Church is even now reconsidering its indictment of Galileo over three hundred years ago for his apostasy in declaring that the earth moved around the sun, not vice versa, a small but significant act of penance for its apostasy in seeking to bottle up for far too long man's Promethean spirit of inquiry and of confusing the humble teachings of Christ with the literal interpretation of Genesis [Editor's note: In 1992 the Roman Catholic Church admitted its mistake in condemning Galileo].

In any case, having paid our respects to medievalism it is only a truism to say that we cannot understand the achievements and the perplexities of modernity without saluting what Whitehead calls the Century of Genius—that time span including the late sixteenth and seventeenth centuries which brought to fruition the insights of Copernicus, Kepler, Galileo, Harvey, and Francis Bacon, not to mention in literature the penning of *Don Quixote* and

*Hamlet.* In this period man was freed from the illusion that physically speaking he is the center of the universe. In this period and with Harvey's discovery of the circulation of the blood, modern medicine with all its blessings to the human condition took its start. In this period the foundations were laid for Newtonian physics, with its twin concepts of mass and energy, which allowed man not just to bow to the laws of nature but to tame and manipulate nature to his own desired ends. And from this period arose two problems with which modern man has ever since had to cope.

The first is the philosophical problem deriving especially from Descartes (i.e., "I think therefore I am") of how the inner spirit of man and the world of sentient consciousness can be reconciled with the "night view" of science out there, the world of colorless and soundless atoms whirling on in their apparently purposeless configurations. I shall come back to this problem—what Whitehead calls the fatal "bifurcation" in our thinking—at the end of this lecture. The second and more practical problem arising from the Renaissance was how, in the light of advancing science and technology, man should reorder his political and economic life. It is on this latter problem that I wish to concentrate first. For it cannot be assumed that the largely agricultural economy of the Middle Ages would survive the Century of Genius intact, nor did it. On the contrary the new world opened up by the Renaissance led on directly to the industrial revolution and the Satanic mills of William Blake and to something more fundamental. That something is the division of labor and the ever widening markets which have made modern progress possible.

The man who most clearly grasped the significance of this enormous change—the change inherent in the fact that men might be producing goods not in exchange for those of his neighbors, but for far-distance consumers—was of course Adam Smith whose *Wealth of Nations* was published in the same year as the Declaration of Independence. In the very first sentence of that seminal tract Smith points out that nothing has contributed more to man's material advancement than the division of labor, and there follows the famous illustration of the making of a pin where if one man makes the pin head another the shaft, we obtain larger output than if a single artisan should try to fashion the whole of this lowly but useful commodity. But if this is true then some means must be found for integrating the work of many hands. Smith's answer and the answer of the whole libertarian tradition in economics is that this integration is best achieved through the free play of wages, prices and profits—the signaling system whereby scarce resources, material and human, are allocated to their appointed task. This plus Smith's insight that in following their own self-interest men frequently produce larger social results than any one man could have foreseen is the foundation stone of what we today call the enterprise economy. Again to quote Walter Lippmann's *Good Society*: "The market is not something invented by businessmen and speculators for their profit, or by the classical economists for their intellectual pleasure. The market is the only possible method by which labor that has been analyzed into separate specialities can be synthesized into useful work. . . . The division of labor and its regulation in markets are two inseparable aspects of the same process of producing wealth, and the failure to understand that truth is a sure sign of a failure to understand the technical principle of production in the modern world."

The man who least understood this principle is, of course, Karl Marx who, coming on scene nearly a century after Adam Smith, sought to turn libertarian economics on its head. Building on the false labor theory of value, traces of which are to be found in both Smith and Ricardo, he indicted the profit motive as simply a means of exploitation of the worker by greedy capitalists. Building on a materialistic view of the world which may be helpful to the natural sciences, and mixing this up with the ruminations of Hegel, he devised the system of dialectical materialism in which history is inevitably determined by economic forces. The rule of the bourgeoisie creates a rising proletariat. The proletariat in their turn seize and socialize the means of production through the power of the state. The state then "withers away," and we have the perfect communist society ruled by the principle of, "From each according to his abilities, to each according to his need."

The prospect is at first dazzling, and unfortunately the promise of socialism if not of Marxism has at one time or another had wide influence in the thinking of men who call themselves Christians, not to mention those who don't, as represented by members of the famous British Fabian Society, H. G. Wells, Bernard Shaw, the Webbs, the original formulators of the welfare if not the socialist state. Nor should we underrate the appeal of what is sometimes called Christian socialism to men of the cloth and to missionaries who have sought to carry the Gospel to far off lands in Africa and elsewhere. The Gospels are there to remind us of the condition of the poor, but despite enormous advances under capitalism, the poor are still with us. The Gospels appeal to our sense of justice, but the market rewards men not according to their abstract merit but according to what other men—ultimately the consumer—think of their product: hence higher salaries paid to, say, movie stars and much lower pay to the ditch digger who may be equally deserving. The Christian message is one of peace on earth, good will toward men. The market depends, for its proper function, on competition.

Yet, granting these enticements for condemning modern capitalism or for looking for some better way of organizing the world's work, the evidence is overwhelming that so far at least that better way has not been found. On the contrary all those glittering promises of the Marxian dialectic have turned to dust and ashes. And this for two reasons: one practical, one more profound. The practical reason as developed in our time by Ludwig von Mises, whose master works are collected here at Hillsdale, is that once the state has seized the means of production, once the pricing system has been abandoned, there is no way of knowing what should be produced, in what quantities, and for what purpose. It is told of Lenin that on assuming power in Russia in 1917 he confidently expected that somewhere in the book of Marx there must be a blueprint for guiding production into the proper channels. There is no such blueprint. As Mises demonstrated long ago, rational socialist calculation is impossible. And events have more than proved that insight. The present Russian state is very good at making guns and rockets where priorities are set by military dictate. It has no way of determining what people need and want: the consumer, who is every man, becomes a shabby non-entity.

But beyond this, of course, the Russian "experiment" drives home a more profound if obvious lesson, namely that where the state acquires economic power over men's lives, that power is not apt to "wither away." On the contrary, with every attempt to enforce five-year or ten-year plans on a society, that power expands geometrically, and tends to reach into every department of life, with a consequent loss of liberty itself. In the communal societies as envisaged by Robert Owen and briefly by our Puritan forefathers there was at least a modicum of voluntary collaboration though these experiments foundered for want of motivation. But under a Marxist dispensation such collaboration is what "withers away" and the K.G.B. with its "knock at the door" takes over. In the end the practice of intellectual and religious freedom is at hazard. It is no happenstance that Marx declared that religion is the "opium of the people." For religion and especially Christianity assumes that men are free to choose not just between this or that economic good but free to choose between this or that mode of conduct and this or that belief. The practice of virtue, charity, compassion assumes freedom of the will. Where exercise of such freedom is endangered, the spirit of Christianity is bound to resist, as Solzhenitsyn has grandly shown.

We may conclude then that, whatever its defects, the market economy based on private property and entailing the widespread diffusion of economic power and decision-making is the indispensable condition of the free and humane society. The question remains whether if this condition is satisfied we can assume that all will be well. On this point so-called economic science gives little guidance and indeed raises more questions than it answers. For as economics has freed itself from the nursery strings of moral philosophy, and has become a separate discipline, it has, following the lead of the natural sciences, sought to free itself of all value judgments. Economics, as defined by Mises and Lionel Robbins, is the study of human behavior or choice when faced by scarce means that can be put to alternative uses. It passes no judgment on whether those choices are good or bad. If a boy takes to drugs instead of pursuing his education that is indeed a lamentable happening. But it is not the business of the economist to say so. His business is that if an individual or government chooses A, then B follows. With respect to the value of that choice the economist is neutral.

Now this is a permissible and no doubt useful position. For we all gain by knowing the results of alternative lines of action and their probable consequences. I have sometimes wondered, however, just how far it can be carried. Libertarian economists in particular are the staunch defenders of freedom, no one more so than Ludwig von Mises. Yet freedom is, after all, a value—one of the most precious known to man—and it is precisely on the basis that it annuls freedom that we condemn the collectivist state. Moreover, and more importantly, the achievement of individual freedom inevitably raises the question of freedom for what and to what ends? This is the question which modern economics studiously avoids, and if you ask why, you may as likely as not be told that whereas free choice may be taken as an "objective" fact or scientific datum, the ends to which men put freedom are at best "subjective." If this means only that deliberate choice is a psychological phenomenon differing from the hard measurable facts of nature, well and good. But if this means that the ends men choose are no better than human whim, we are in difficulties. For this entails the proposition common in our day that if "you do your thing and I do mine," then all will be for the best. In fact all will not be for the best, for we are plunged into a world of complete moral relativism, lacking any standards by which to judge human conduct.

Yet such relativism will not, I suspect, even sustain the normal workings of the market, let alone its other shortcomings. The simplest economic exchange requires good faith on the part of both buyer and seller, i.e., honesty. The New York Stock Exchange would be out of business tomorrow if the broker could not trust his client to make good on a contract initiated by a telephone call, and without formal papers, to buy or sell securities. The whole complex fabric of modern economic life, involving as it does transactions that span the oceans, is built on certain assumptions as to what is wrong and what is right, what is permissible and what is nonpermissible. Even our efforts to curb the overwhelming power of government involve in the end certain moral presuppositions. What is the worst that can be said of inflation brought on by the reckless spending of government and the easy accommodation of same by central banks? Not just that such practices will inevitably drive prices upward. The telling indictment of inflation is that it is a form of theft executed, as Keynes reminded us, by a process that only one man in a thousand can understand. What is the strongest argument against the ever-spreading dominion of the welfare state? Not that it is often inefficient, but that it cannot make good on its promises. Harry Scherman, former head of the Book of the Month Club, once wrote a book titled *The Promises Men Live By*. It will bear rereading at a time when economics, celebrating free choice, washes its hands of what choices are made.

Let me repeat that this is not a criticism of modern economic method. It is simply to argue that if economics perhaps rightly shuns the problem of value, then it must step aside to make way for those disciplines which have always made judgments of value their business, notably ethics and what used to be called moral philosophy. And this is the path which some fully at home in economics and stout defenders of the market have taken. F. A. Hayek, for one, reminds us that any free society must be grounded in a certain moral "consensus." He even argues in his monumental *Constitution of Liberty* for the need of a "meta-legal" system which stands above all man-made laws and even above all man-made constitutions. Meta-legal? That is a strange phrase to be issuing from the pen of our foremost libertarian thinker. For it seems to open the door to speculations (speculo, speculate—to observe) that reach beyond the normal purview of science—the meta-physics of Aristotle, for instance, which dealt with such unhandy subjects as the "Unmoved Mover" or God. Or with the affirmations of the Old Testament prophets that a God and not always a jealous God exists.

What we are looking for in any case is at the least a standard by which actions can be judged. If we cast such a standard in purely moral terms we run the danger of cheap moralistic preachment. Turn then for a moment to aesthetics. It is the business of the artist to render his vision of the outside world in terms of color, and at the moment there seem to be precious few standards for judging the result. Two ropes hanging from the ceiling, if they express the artist's feelings, are said to be art no less than the *Mona Lisa*. But in fact standards of art remain which declare that the one is meaningless and the other beautiful, and that it is the business of aesthetics to differentiate between the two. Or turn back again to science, whose method is experimental and empiric following always where the so-called facts lead. Yet in this question, as we have seen, there is a hidden assumption, that somewhere out there Truth exists—a truth which makes the whole pursuit of knowledge meaningful. Truth, Beauty and Goodness—we shall not go far without them.

It would be my contention that the Judeo-Christian tradition has something to offer in this search for standards in the world in which we find ourselves. This and one thing more. You will recall that in delineating the challenge which science and technology let loose in the modern world I referred not just to its practical consequences—the division of labor and the necessity for the market but its deeper spiritual consequences. From the time of Descartes forward modern man has been troubled by what Whitehead called the "bifurcation" in our thinking wherein the sentient self seems to be trapped in its own world of consciousness while "out there" exists a mindless and purposeless world of material being taking the form of colorless non-sentient atoms, molecules, electrons or what you will, comprehensible only to the sweep of mathematical equations. Indeed in the view of modern behaviorists such as B. F. Skinner that is the only world that exists and all our inner perceptions of color, imagination, memory, love, and free will are simply brain patterns responding to outside stimuli. Man is in the end an automaton or robot.

Yet this view of our condition breaks down on the most cursory examination. There is no way that brain cells can, so to speak, "ooze out" the variegated world of color and shape which we see at first hand, and with which, it must be added, scientific examination begins (we perceive the color red before we locate the light wave causing it). It is the contention of Whitehead that this modern view of nature, however necessary as a framework to scientific advance, is fundamentally an abstraction from reality, a partial view but by no means the whole truth. The whole truth must include the world from which science starts, the everyday phenomenon of experience. The late W. E. Hocking, Whitehead's associate, reinforces this insight. It is his contention that Christianity, through its "willful curbing of self-will" (as well as by its exclusion of polytheism, which saw a capricious god behind every tree), had much to do with launching Western science on its momentous voyage of discovery. But if science is based on the "will to truth" we cannot exclude will and purpose from our final view of reality. To do so is to engage in a spurious metaphysics that is no part of the mathematical and experimental method. It follows that religion which set the stage for scientific advance may also provide the key to solving modern man's dilemma.

For as against naive materialism religion affirms man's spirituality and freedom to choose, and posits a God endowed with compassion and purpose. Its major affirmation is,

to be sure, based on faith, but as Hocking observes, "faith is as natural as breathing" and, indeed, we practice it in a small way every time we cross the street or entrust ourselves to a Boeing 707. Is it really common sense to believe, as economists among others believe, that the mark of man is *purposive* action, yet to deny Purpose to an unfolding universe, so that in the end man becomes simply a blip on a vast and impersonal radar screen? What we are reaching for in any case is not just a standard of conduct but a metaphysics (after physics) which synthesizes and reconciles our total experience. Let us hope that this seminar and the re-emphasis of Christian teaching at Hillsdale will speed this process of reconciliation, and that like Virgil and Dante after descending into the Inferno, we shall emerge again to glimpse the stars.

# Economic Justice for All (excerpts)
## Pastoral Letter on Catholic Social Teaching and the U.S. Economy
## U.S. Catholic Bishops (1986)

*In 1986 the Roman Catholic Bishops of the United States published this pastoral letter, intended to teach Catholics the bishops' perspectives on the economy. The letter raised many issues and concerns and suggested some policies and programs. The excerpts presented here emphasize the six elements of what the bishops called a just economic system and also include a few of the many perspectives and specific proposals made in the letter regarding economic life, including poverty, employment, agriculture, and American participation in the global economy. The entire letter, including footnotes, runs to over 56,000 words and about 89 single-spaced pages. It can be found at www.osjspm.org/economic_justice_for_all.aspx. The paragraphs were numbered in the original document, but those numbers and footnotes are omitted here.*

Brothers and Sisters in Christ:

We are believers called to follow Our Lord Jesus Christ and proclaim his Gospel in the midst of a complex and powerful economy. This reality poses both opportunities and responsibilities for Catholics in the United States. Our faith calls us to measure this economy, not by what it produces but also by how it touches human life and whether it protects or undermines the dignity of the human person. Economic decisions have human consequences and moral content; they help or hurt people, strengthen or weaken family life, advance or diminish the quality of justice in our land. . . .

The pastoral letter is not a blueprint for the American economy. It does not embrace any particular theory of how the economy works, nor does it attempt to resolve disputes between different schools of economic thought. Instead, our letter turns to Scripture and to the social teaching of the Church. There, we discover what our economic life must serve, what standards it must meet. Let us examine some of these basic moral principles.

[1] Every economic decision and institution must be judged in light of whether it protects or undermines the dignity of the human person. The pastoral letter begins with the human person. We believe the person is sacred—the clearest reflection of God among us. Human dignity comes from God, not from nationality, race, sex, economic status, or any human accomplishment. We judge any economic system by what it does *for* and *to* people and by how it permits all to *participate* in it. The economy should serve people, not the other way around.

[2] Human dignity can be realized and protected only in community. In our teaching, the human person is not only sacred but social. How we organize our society—in economics and politics, in law and policy—directly affects human dignity and the capacity of individuals to grow in community. The obligation to "love our neighbor" has an individual dimension, but it also requires a broader social commitment to the common good. We have many partial ways to measure and debate the health of our economy: Gross National Product, per capita income, stock market prices, and so forth. The Christian vision of economic life

looks beyond them all and asks, Does economic life enhance or threaten our life together as a community?

[3] All people have a right to participate in the economic life of society. Basic justice demands that people be assured a minimum level of participation in the economy. It is wrong for a person or a group to be excluded unfairly or to be unable to participate or contribute to the economy. For example, people who are both able and willing, but cannot get a job are deprived of the participation that is so vital to human development. For, it is through employment that most individuals and families meet their material needs, exercise their talents, and have an opportunity to contribute to the larger community. Such participation has a special significance in our tradition because we believe that it is a means by which we join in carrying forward God's creative activity.

[4] All members of society have a special obligation to the poor and vulnerable. From the Scriptures and church teaching, we learn that the justice of a society is tested by the treatment of the poor. The justice that was the sign of God's covenant with Israel was measured by how the poor and unprotected—the widow, the orphan, and the stranger—were treated. The kingdom that Jesus proclaimed in his word and ministry excludes no one. Throughout Israel's history and in early Christianity, the poor are agents of God's transforming power. "The Spirit of the Lord is upon me, therefore he has anointed me. He has sent me to bring glad tidings to the poor" (Luke 4:18). This was Jesus' first public utterance. Jesus takes the side of those most in need. In the Last Judgment, so dramatically described in St. Matthew's Gospel, we are told that we will be judged according to how we respond to the hungry, the thirsty, the naked, the stranger. As followers of Christ, we are challenged to make a fundamental "option for the poor"—to speak for the voiceless, to defend the defenseless, to assess life styles, policies, and social institutions in terms of their impact on the poor. This "option for the poor" does not mean pitting one group against another, but rather, strengthening the whole community by assisting those who are the most vulnerable. As Christians, we are called to respond to the needs of *all* our brothers and sisters, but those with the greatest needs require the greatest response.

[5] Human rights are the minimum conditions for life in community. In Catholic teaching, human rights include not only civil and political rights but also economic rights. As Pope John XXIII declared, "all people have a right to life, food, clothing, shelter, rest, medical care, education, and employment." This means that when people are without a chance to earn a living, and must go hungry and homeless, they are being denied basic rights. Society must ensure that these rights are protected. In this way, we will ensure that the minimum conditions of economic justice are met for all our sisters and brothers.

[6] Society as a whole, acting through public and private institutions, has the moral responsibility to enhance human dignity and protect human rights. In addition to the clear responsibility of private institutions, government has an essential responsibility in this area. This does not mean that government has the primary or exclusive role, but it does have a positive moral responsibility in safeguarding human rights and ensuring that the minimum conditions of human dignity are met for all. In a democracy, government is a means by which we can act together to protect what is important to us and to promote our common values.

These six moral principles are not the only ones presented in the pastoral letter, but they give an overview of the moral vision that we are trying to share. This vision of economic life cannot exist in a vacuum; it must be translated into concrete measures. Our pastoral letter spells out some specific applications of Catholic moral principles. We call for a new national commitment to full employment. We say it is a social and moral scandal that one of every seven Americans is poor, and we call for concerted efforts to eradicate poverty. The fulfillment of the basic needs of the poor is of the highest priority. We urge that all economic policies be evaluated in light of their impact on the life and stability of the family. We support measures to halt the loss of family farms and to resist the growing concentration in the ownership of agricultural resources. We specify ways in which the United States can do far more to relieve the plight of poor nations and assist in their development. We also reaffirm church teaching on the rights of workers, collective bargaining, private property, subsidiarity, and equal opportunity. . . .

We are always in need of . . . a change of heart. We are richly blessed, and as St. Paul assures us, we are destined for glory. Yet, it is also true that we are sinners; that we are not always wise or loving or just; that, for all our amazing possibilities, we are incompletely born, wary of life, and hemmed in by fears and empty routines. We are unable to entrust ourselves fully to the living God, and so we seek substituted forms of security in material things, in power, in indifference, in popularity, in pleasure. The Scriptures warn us that these things can become forms of idolatry. We know that, at times, in order to remain truly a community of Jesus' disciples, we will have to say "no" to certain aspects of our culture, to certain trends and ways of acting that are opposed to a life of faith, love and justice. Changes in our hearts lead naturally to a desire to change how we act. With what care, human kindness, and justice do I conduct myself at work? How will my economic decisions to buy, sell, invest, divest, hire, or fire serve human dignity and the common good? In what career can I best exercise my talents so as to fill the world with the Spirit of Christ? How do my economic choices contribute to the strength of my family and community, to the values of my children, to a sensitivity to those in need? In this consumer society, how can I develop a healthy detachment from things and avoid the temptation to assess who I am by what I have? How do I strike a balance between labor and leisure that enlarges my capacity for friendships, for family life, for community? What government policies should I support to attain the well-being of all, especially the poor and vulnerable? . . .

There are many signs of hope in U.S. economic life today:

- Many fathers and mothers skillfully balance the arduous responsibilities of work and family life. There are parents who pursue a purposeful and modest way of life and by their example encourage their children to follow a similar path. A large number of women and men, drawing on their religious tradition, recognize the challenging vocation of family life and child-rearing in a culture that emphasizes material display and self-gratification.

- Conscientious business people seek new and more equitable ways to organize resources and the workplace. They face hard choices over expanding or retrenching, shifting investments, hiring or firing.

- Young people choosing their life's work ask whether success and security are compatible with service to others.

- Workers whose labor may be toilsome or repetitive try daily to ennoble their work with a spirit of solidarity and friendship.

- New immigrants brave dislocations while hoping for the opportunities realized by millions who came before them.

These signs of hope are not the whole story. There have been failures—some of them massive and ugly:

- Poor and homeless people sleep in community shelters and in our church basements; the hungry line up in soup lines.

- Unemployment gnaws at the self-respect of both middle-aged persons who have lost jobs and the young who cannot find them.

- Hardworking men and women wonder if the system of enterprise that helped them yesterday might destroy their jobs and their communities tomorrow.

- Families confront major challenges: dwindling social supports for family stability; economic pressures that force both parents of young children to work outside the home; a driven pace of life among the successful that can sap love and commitment; lack of hope among those who have less or nothing at all. Very different kinds of families bear different burdens of our economic system.

- Farmers face the loss of their land and way of life; young people find it difficult to choose farming as a vocation; farming communities are threatened; migrant farm workers break their backs in serf-like conditions for disgracefully low wages.

And beyond our own shores, the reality of 800 million people living in absolute poverty and 450 million malnourished or facing starvation casts an ominous shadow over all these hopes and problems at home. . . .

The United States is among the most economically powerful nations on earth. In its short history the U.S. economy has grown to provide an unprecedented standard of living for most of its people. The nation has created productive work for millions of immigrants and enabled them to broaden their freedoms, improve their families' quality of life, and contribute to the building of a great nation. Those who came to this country from other lands often understood their new lives in the light of biblical faith. They thought of themselves as entering a promised land of political freedom and economic opportunity. The United States is a land of vast natural resources and fertile soil. It has encouraged citizens to undertake bold ventures. Through hard work, self-sacrifice, and cooperation, families have flourished; towns, cities and a powerful nation have been created.

But we should recall this history with sober humility. The American experiment in social, political, and economic life has involved serious conflict and suffering. Our nation was born in the face of injustice to native Americans, and its independence was paid for with the blood of revolution. Slavery stained the commercial life of the land through its first two hundred and fifty years and was ended only by a violent civil war. The establishment of women's suffrage, the protection of industrial workers, the elimination of child labor, the response to the Great Depression of the 1930s, and the civil rights movement of the 1960s all involved a sustained struggle to transform the political and economic institutions of the nation.

The U.S. value system emphasizes economic freedom. It also recognizes that the market is limited by fundamental human rights. Some things are never to be bought or sold. This conviction has prompted positive steps to modify the operation of the market when it harms vulnerable members of society. Labor unions help workers resist exploitation. Through their government, the people of the United States have provided support for education, access to food, unemployment compensation, security in old age, and protection of the environment. The market system contributes to the success of the U.S. economy, but so do many efforts to forge economic institutions and public policies that enable all to share in the riches of the nation. The country's economy has been built through a creative struggle; entrepreneurs, business people, workers, unions, consumers, and government have all played essential roles. . . .

The preeminent role of the United States in an increasingly interdependent global economy is a central sign of our times. The United States is still the world's economic giant. Decisions made here have immediate effects in other countries; decisions made abroad have immediate consequences for steelworkers in Pittsburgh, oil company employees in Houston, and farmers in Iowa. U.S. economic growth is vitally dependent on resources from other countries and on their purchases of our goods and services. Many jobs in U.S. industry and agriculture depend on our ability to export manufactured goods and food.

In some industries the mobility of capital and technology makes wages the main variable in the cost of production. Overseas competitors with the same technology but with wage rates as low as one-tenth of ours put enormous pressure on U.S. firms to cut wages, relocate abroad, or close. U.S. workers and their communities should not be expected to bear these burdens alone.

All people on this globe share a common ecological environment that is under increasing pressure. Depletion of soil, water and other natural resources endangers the future. Pollution of air and water threatens the delicate balance of the biosphere on which future generations will depend. The resources of the earth have been created by God for the benefit of all, and we who are alive today hold them in trust. This is a challenge to develop a new ecological ethic, that will help shape a future that is both just and sustainable. . . .

*Government has a moral function: protecting human rights and securing basic justice for all members of the commonwealth.* Society as a whole and in all its diversity is responsible for building up the common good. But it is the government's role to guarantee the minimum conditions that make this rich social activity possible, namely, human rights and justice. This obligation also falls on individual citizens as they choose their representatives and participate in shaping public opinion.

More specifically, it is the responsibility of all citizens, acting through their government, to assist and empower the poor, the disadvantaged, the handicapped, and the unemployed. Government should assume a positive role in generating employment and establishing fair labor practices, in guaranteeing the provision and maintenance of the economy's infrastructure, such as roads, bridges, harbors, public means of communication, and transport. It should regulate trade and commerce in the interest of fairness. Government may levy the taxes necessary to meet these responsibilities, and citizens have a moral obligation to pay those taxes. The way society responds to the needs of the poor through its public policies is the litmus test of its justice or injustice. The political debate about these policies is the indispensable forum for dealing with the conflicts and tradeoffs that will always be present in the pursuit of a more just economy.

The primary norm for determining the scope and limits of governmental intervention is the "principle of subsidiarity" cited above. This principle states that, in order to protect basic justice, government should undertake only those initiatives which exceed the capacities of individuals or private groups acting independently. Government should not replace or destroy smaller communities and individual initiative. Rather it should help them contribute more effectively to social well-being and supplement their activity when the demands of justice exceed their capacities. These does not mean, however, that the government that governs least, governs best. Rather it defines good government intervention as that which truly "helps" other social groups contribute to the common good by directing, urging, restraining, and regulating economic activity as "the occasion requires and necessity demands". This calls for cooperation and consensus building among the diverse agents in our economic life, including government. The precise form of government involvement in this process cannot be determined from abstract. It will depend on an assessment of specific needs and the most effective ways to address them. . . .

With the rapid pace of technological change, continuing education and training are even more important today than in the past. Businesses have a stake in providing it, for skilled workers are essential to increase productivity. Labor unions should support it, for their members are increasingly vulnerable to displacement and job loss unless they continue to develop their skills and their flexibility on the job. Local communities have a stake as well, for their economic well-being will suffer serious harm if local industries fail to develop and are forced to shut down.

The best medicine for the disease of plant closings is prevention. Prevention depends not only on sustained capital investment to enhance productivity through advanced technology but also on training and retraining of workers within the private sector. In circumstances where plants are forced to shut down, management, labor unions, and local communities must see to it that workers are not simply cast aside. Retraining programs will be even more urgently needed in these circumstances. . . .

At times we will be called upon to say no to the cultural manifestations that emphasize values and aims that are selfish, wasteful, and opposed to the Scriptures. Together we must reflect on our personal and family decisions and curb unnecessary wants in order to meet the needs of others. There are many questions we must keep asking ourselves: Are we becoming ever more wasteful in a "throw-away" society? Are we able to distinguish between our true needs and those thrust on us by advertising and a society that values consumption more than saving? All of us could well ask ourselves whether as a Christian prophetic witness we are not called to adopt a simpler lifestyle, in the face of the excessive accumulation of material goods that characterizes an affluent society.

Husbands and wives, in particular, should weigh their needs carefully and establish a proper priority of values as they discuss the questions of both parents working outside the home and the responsibilities of raising children with proper care and attention. At times we will be called as individuals, as families, as parishes, as Church, to identify more closely with the poor in their struggle for participation and to close the gap of understanding between them and the affluent. By sharing the perspectives of those who are suffering, we can come to understand economic and social problems in a deeper way, thus leading us to seek more durable solutions. . . .

The Church has always held that the first task and responsibility for education lies in the hands of parents: they have the right to choose freely the schools or other means necessary to educate their children in the faith. The Church also has consistently held that public authorities must ensure that public subsidies for the education of children are allocated so that parents can freely choose to exercise this right without incurring unjust burdens. This parental right should not be taken from them. We call again for equitable sharing in public benefits for those parents who choose private and religious schools for their children. Such help should be available especially for low-income parents. Though many of these parents sacrifice a great deal for their children's education, others are effectively deprived of the possibility of exercising this right. . . .

# Letter 4 of
# Letters from a Farmer in Pennsylvania
## John Dickinson (1768)

*In 1767 the British Parliament passed the Townshend Acts that imposed taxes on the American colonies for the purpose of raising revenue. Many Americans believed that Parliament could enact taxes to regulate trade but not simply to raise revenue. Later that year, Pennsylvania attorney John Dickinson began publishing a series of letters in opposition to the Townshend Acts. In the letters he expressed the objections that many colonists had to paying taxes imposed on them by the British government. The taxes called for in the Townshend Acts were eventually repealed, except for the tax on tea.*

My dear Countrymen,

An objection, I hear, has been made against my second letter, which I would willingly clear up before I proceed. "There is," say these objectors, "a material difference between the Stamp Act and the late act for laying a duty on paper, etc. that justifies the conduct of those who opposed the former, and yet are willing to submit to the latter. The duties imposed by the Stamp Act were internal taxes; but the present are external, and therefore the parliament may have a right to impose them."

To this I answer with a total denial of the power of parliament to lay upon these colonies any "tax" whatever.

This point, being so important to this, and to succeeding generations, I wish to be clearly understood.

To the word "tax," I annex that meaning which the constitution and history of England require to be annexed to it; that is—that it is an imposition on the subject, for the sole purpose of levying money.

In the early ages of our monarchy, certain services were rendered to the crown for the general good. These were personal: But in process of time, such institutions being found inconvenient, gifts and grants of their own property were made by the people, under the several names of aids, tallages, talks, taxes and subsidies, etc. These were made, as may be collected even from the names, for public

*John Dickinson*

service upon "need and necessity." All these sums were levied upon the people by virtue of their voluntary gift. Their intention was to support the national honor and interest. Some of those grants comprehended duties arising from trade; being imports on merchandizes. These Lord Chief Justice Coke classes under "subsidies," and "parliamentary aids." They are also called "customs." But whatever the name was, they were always considered as gifts of the people to the crown, to be employed for public uses.

Commerce was at a low ebb, and surprising instances might be produced how little it was attended to for a succession of ages. The terms that have been mentioned, and, among the rest, that of "tax," had obtained a national, parliamentary meaning, drawn from the principles of the constitution, long before any Englishman thought of imposition of duties, for the regulation of trade.

Whenever we speak of "taxes" among Englishmen, let us therefore speak of them with reference to the principles on which, and the intentions with which, they have been established. This will give certainty to our expression, and safety to our conduct: But if, when we have in view the liberty of these colonies, we proceed in any other course, we pursue a juno indeed, but shall only catch a cloud.

In the national, parliamentary sense insisted on, the word "tax" was certainly understood by the congress at New York, whose resolves may be said to form the American "bill of rights."

The third, fourth, fifth, and sixth resolves, are thus expressed.

III. "That it is inseparably essential to the freedom of a people, and the undoubted right of Englishmen, that NO TAX be imposed on them, except with their own consent, given personally, or by their representatives."

IV. "That the people of the colonies are not, and from their local circumstances, cannot be represented in the house of commons in Great Britain."

V. "That the only representatives of the people of the colonies, are the persons chosen therein by themselves; and that NO TAXES ever have been, or can be constitutionally imposed on them, but by their respective legislatures."

VI. "That all supplies to the crown, being free gifts of the people, it is unreasonable, and inconsistent with the principles and spirit of the British constitution, for the people of Great Britain to grant to his Majesty the property of the colonies."

Here is no distinction made between internal and external taxes. It is evident from the short reasoning thrown into these resolves, that every imposition "to grant to his Majesty the property of the colonies," was thought a "tax"; and that every such imposition, if laid any other way, than "with their consent, given personally, or by their representatives," was not only "unreasonable, and inconsistent with the principles and spirit of the British constitution," but destructive "to the freedom of a people."

This language is clear and important. A "tax" means an imposition to raise money. Such persons therefore as speak of internal and external "taxes," I pray may pardon me, if I object to that expression, as applied to the privileges and interests of these colonies. There may be internal and external impositions, founded on different principles, and having different tendencies; every "tax" being an imposition, though every imposition is not a "tax." But all taxes are founded on the same principle; and have the same tendency.

External impositions, for the regulation of our trade, do not "grant to his Majesty the property of the colonies." They only prevent the colonies acquiring property, in things not necessary, in a manner judged to be injurious to the welfare of the whole empire. But the last statute respecting us, "grants to his Majesty the property of the colonies," by laying duties on the manufactures of Great Britain which they must take, and which she settled them, on purpose that they should take.

What tax can be more internal than this? Here is money drawn, without their consent, from a society, who have constantly enjoyed a constitutional mode of raising all money among themselves. The payment of this tax they have no possible method of avoiding; as they cannot do without the commodities on which it is laid, and they cannot manufacture these commodities themselves. Besides, if this unhappy country should be so lucky as to elude this act, by getting parchment enough, in the place of paper, or by reviving the ancient method of writing on wax and bark, and by inventing something to serve instead of glass, her ingenuity would stand her in little stead; for then the parliament would have nothing to do but to prohibit such manufactures, or to lay a tax on hats and woolen cloths, which they have already prohibited the colonies from supplying each other with; or on instruments and tools of steel and iron, which they have prohibited the provincials from manufacturing at all: And then, what little gold and silver they have, must be torn from their hands, or they will not be able, in a short time, to get an ax for cutting their firewood, nor a plough for raising their food. In what respect, therefore, I beg leave to ask, is the late act preferable to the Stamp Act, or more consistent with the liberties of the colonies? For my own part, I regard them both with equal apprehension; and think they ought to be in the same manner opposed.

[Dickinson closed with a Latin phrase which translated:]
We have a statute, laid up for future use, like a sword in the scabbard.

A Farmer

# The Legacy of the 1936 Election
## Amity Shlaes (2007)

*Amity Shlaes, a graduate of Yale, is an economics writer. She has worked for* Bloomberg *magazine and the* Wall Street Journal. *Her book,* The Forgotten Man: A New History of the Great Depression, *was published in 2007. In this speech she focused on the 1936 presidential election and its impact on the growth of federal spending.*

September 2007 *Imprimis*

What makes the current field of [presidential] candidates so timid? It is clear listening to figures from both parties this year that they still believe Social Security is untouchable. This despite the fact that bringing Social Security into solvency is a relatively easy task. When it comes to the more serious fiscal burdens upon our grandchildren, the candidates are likewise timid. This despite the fact that those burdens only become heavier as we delay. We speak of 2008 as an election year, but it is also the year when the tide of Social Security cash begins to recede with the retirement of Baby Boomers.

But where is the origin of the problem? Traditionally historians have focused on the slow rise of American progressivism over the past century and a half. I'm going to do something different, and undertake an almost artificial exercise. Here I will compress history and argue that this destructive hesitation comes out of a single political campaign, the presidential campaign of 1936. This campaign marked the virtual end of old-fashioned American federalism and the rise of a new kind of politics. It was 1936 more than any other campaign that created modern interest groups and taught us that Washington should subsidize them. Pinning blame on a single campaign (and its run up) may seem facile. Still, the story is well worth telling.

**The Run Up**

In 1932, total federal spending was still only five percent of gross domestic product. Spending by states and local governments represented by contrast ten percent of GDP. Even well into the Depression, it was to state and local governments that many looked for a means to recovery. There was no big tax redistribution. The word "liberalism" still signified a belief in individual liberty rather than paternalistic government. Nor did American workers view themselves so much as a class in those years. They viewed themselves as moving up and down the economic ladder. Even our greatest union, the American Federation of Labor, was more of a craft and trade union than a class union. But all this was soon to change.

In his 1932 campaign, Franklin D. Roosevelt had talked about helping someone he called "the forgotten man." He was thinking of the poorest man, or as he put it—invoking the time of the pharaohs—"the man at the bottom of the economic pyramid." His speechwriter, Ray Moley, had inserted the phrase into an address on The Lucky Strike Hour. Moley wrote to his sister Nell that he didn't know where the phrase came from. But in fact it did have a provenance. It came from an essay (and later a book) written decades before, called The

Forgotten Man. Written by a famous Yale professor named William Graham Sumner, this essay defined "the forgotten man" differently.

Sumner employed an algebra to explain what he meant: A and B want to help X, he wrote. This is the charitable impulse. The problem arises when A and B band together and pass a law that coerces C into co-funding their project for X. Sumner identified C as the forgotten man. He is the man who works, the man who prays, the man who pays his own bills, the man who is "never thought of."

But this did not matter to Roosevelt, who of course won handily in 1932 without thinking much about the phrase again. He spent the next few years trying to help the poor through the now famous New Deal measures. But three years into his presidency, his efforts were still failing. The New Deal was having mixed results. Unemployment in May 1935 stood at what we today would compute to 20.1 percent—a large share of Americans were still forgotten men. The Brookings Institution wrote a nearly 1,000-page report on the New Deal's centerpiece, the National Recovery Administration, concluding that it "on the whole retarded recovery." The Dow was stuck in the low hundreds, nowhere near even the 250 it had been in 1930 under Hoover, well into the downturn. As a result, in July 1935—the year before the 1936 election—Roosevelt made a decision to give up on trying to help the general economy. Instead, he decided to refine his definition of "the forgotten man." No longer would this man be simply the poor person at the bottom of the economic pyramid. The forgotten man would now be the member of certain defined constituency groups—groups like senior citizens, farmers, writers and artists, and union members.

## Federal Largesse

Critical to FDR's plan was to invent ways to alter the bonds of towns and individuals with their states and establish bonds with Washington, D.C. One of the first important institutions through which this was accomplished was an old office that we rarely talk about anymore, the Public Works Administration or PWA. The PWA was placed under the control of Secretary of the Interior Harold L. Ickes—father of Harold M. Ickes, the prominent Democratic strategist who has worked with Bill and Hillary Clinton. The PWA's role was to fund buildings, bridges, and other structures in towns and villages all over America.

The PWA went to counties and towns to offer them a combination of grants and loans to build schools or dams or power plants, or any kind of public buildings. PWA regional offices sent all bids for structures back to the national office, where Ickes reviewed them. Then, every week, with a manila envelope, he went to the White House and Roosevelt looked them over personally, just as he looked, say, over his stamp collection in the evenings.

On the local end, the experience was a pleasant one for mayors or officers of the county. They were able to allocate the cash, to pick the architect and even the contractors. The money made them feel empowered.

The scale of the spending of the PWA was unprecedented. Its budget was $3 billion in its first few years, or half the size of the federal budget in any given year. Ickes himself was stunned by the magnitude: "It helped me to estimate its size," he wrote, "by figuring that if we had it all in currency and should load it into trucks, we could set out with it from Washington, D.C., for the Pacific Coast, shovel off one million dollars at every milepost," and at the end "still have enough left to build a fleet of battle ships." It is hard now, when we have become accustomed to imperious Washington bureaucrats, to imagine the high of the brand new experience Ickes was enjoying. Riding up and down the East Coast and across the country on a train with the President—in special cars with a new luxury that Ickes in his diary calls "cooled air"—he felt that his job gave him the ability to reshape the country. And indeed, the pyramid image appeared again: people called Ickes a pharaoh. And in fact, the PWA

enabled him to be like a pharaoh—simultaneously grandiose and petty. On each PWA structure were placed the words: "Harold L. Ickes, Secretary of the Interior."

There were more than 3,000 counties in the United States, and all but 33 of them received a PWA project. Many received several. At Michigan State University alone—just up the road from Hillsdale—nine PWA buildings went up.

What did the country think of it all? The critic Frederick A. Gutheim wrote an article at the end of the 1930s complaining that the entire PWA produced "not one architectural masterpiece." But that in a way was

*Public Library in Brown County, Wisconsin*
*Built by the PWA, 1939*

the point. Roosevelt knew that masterpieces were not what was needed for his purpose. On the contrary, a masterpiece from Washington might stand out too much in small town America. This was a task of ingratiation.

The goal was to make the towns feel that the buildings were theirs, to get people used to Washington's hand being involved in projects that formerly were entirely local. Relatedly, Ickes was attacked on all sides for the pickiness with which he reviewed PWA projects. But Roosevelt told Ickes that he did not mind. "This slowness did not displease him," Ickes wrote. "On the contrary, he said to me, 'I do not want you to move any faster.'" The extra months that the process took were extra months of activity that held the eye, evidence that Roosevelt the candidate was doing something.

With this advertisement campaign in place, Roosevelt went on to connect with all his targeted groups. The Wagner Act, the Public Utilities Law, the Social Security Law, and the Works Progress Administration—WPA, not to be confused with PWA—were all passed in great haste, beginning in the summer of 1935. Senator Arthur Vandenberg of Michigan was so aghast at the scale of WPA spending that he decried the "four or five billion worth of lost liberty."

The WPA served much the same purpose as the PWA. Many here will recall those humble, high quality WPA guidebooks to cities, states and regions. They were another way of making the new federal role seem less threatening. Just like the building projects of the PWA, they symbolized a new relationship between the federal government and the counties and localities, from which states are cut out.

The WPA also developed a direct form of propaganda: writings and theater that supported the New Deal. In October 1935, the Agency announced that it was producing a play in New York about agriculture called Triple A Plowed Under (Triple A was a New Deal agency). The WPA also produced Power, a Marxist play that caricatured private-sector utilities executives as old men who exploit American households. The New Deal produced some real art—we all remember the compelling photo of the migrant mother by Dorothea Lange. But it also produced pure propaganda.

It is hard for us now to overestimate how welcome it was for so many journalists, photographers, artists, sculptors, and actors, to be on the Washington payroll. There was no Hatch Act in those days, no federal law precluding political activity by government officials. The WPA was the equivalent of Congress or the White House today moving, after a market crash, to put the staffers of Slate and Google on its payroll as bloggers.

Even by the end of 1935, what the federal government was doing was so changed that it would have been scarcely recognizable to someone from the minimalist 1920s. Washington spent $5.6 billion for the year, double the level of 1930—and this was before the first Social Security check was cut.

## Interest Group Politics

It is worthwhile to pause and consider what all these New Deal programs were doing. They were not bringing the economy back to health. Indeed, they frightened participants in the economy. Utilities, for example, were seeing increased use of electricity, even in the Depression. But utility stocks were not booming because Roosevelt was attacking utility companies as enemies of "the forgotten man." In fact, Ickes was giving towns power plants in exchange for their commitment to use government power instead of private power. The Dow, as mentioned before, was still in the 100s. Unemployment was still through the roof—19 percent in March 1936. Nonetheless, Roosevelt saw what his work at identifying groups to receive federal largesse would do: it would get votes. He continued to reach out to the mythical figure of "the forgotten man" through the spring, summer, and fall of 1936. Interestingly, people especially preferred the projects that were not for the poorest—the ones that instead helped the middle class along, not with relief, but with work and entitlements. This foreshadowed our own attitudes today.

Toward the end of the 1936 campaign, near the elections, Roosevelt moved into a frenzy, reaching out even to those groups he might have neglected before. He announced a $2 million expansion at Virginia State College, a black institution. In late October of 1936, days before the vote, he told an audience at Howard University that there are "no forgotten men and no forgotten races." By the last days of the election Roosevelt therefore had cemented his party's position vis-à-vis his revised "forgotten man"—now a member of a group, not an individual. The job of everyone in the "unforgotten" groups henceforward would be to pay for the larger Washington that in turn would pay for the "forgotten" ones.

In 1936, federal spending moved to nine percent of GDP, up from two-and-a-half percent in 1929. If the gift to the 1932 electorate had been liquor—with the promise of Prohibition's repeal—federal spending was the gift in this election cycle. Historian Jim Couch of the University of North Alabama has shown the precision of the targeting of this money as a way of buying votes. He documents that Roosevelt poured money into battleground states and gave short shrift to safe states, including those of the poor South. Richard Vedder of the University of Ohio has data that suggests that the creation of jobs was also targeted politically. Reckoning unemployment rates month-by-month for 1930 to 1939, he found that though the average for 1935 or 1936 is between 15 and 20 percent, there is one month where unemployment dropped to 13.9 percent: November 1936, the month of the election. It went below that, and then rose again.

In other words, it is true that FDR was at his most popular in 1936, taking 46 of 48 states; but that fact cannot be credited entirely to his radio voice. Nor to the heroic popularity of an ailing president leading a nation through World War II—as we now, anachronistically, remember the 1930s elections. That would come later. In 1936, Roosevelt's was also the popularity of a leader who had invented a new way to reward the constituencies that he needed to win.

* * *

The overall lesson of this is that we can continue to respect many aspects of Roosevelt's presidency today. But we shouldn't have false nostalgia about it. After all, it was Roosevelt's political machinations in the 1936 campaign—symbolized by the PWA—that gave us the "earmarks" that bedevil Congress today, on both sides of the political aisle. Action is more important today because of our fiscal challenge—the new forgotten men are the grandchildren who will pay if we do not give up some of that costly nostalgia. . . .

When I was writing my book on the Great Depression, I kept thinking back to William Graham Sumner, who originated the idea of "the forgotten man." Sumner was a Victorian who died in 1910. But I continued to hear him in the background as I studied Roosevelt and Ickes, and what Sumner said continued to apply—both to the 1930s and to our current political life. He spoke prophetically about the voter who was not included in preferred interest groups—the man or woman who everyone fails to think about. He spoke of the forgotten voter for whom there is "no provision in the great scramble" for federal largesse. Our elections are not good elections until they welcome back that voter, too.

*Franklin D. Roosevelt*

# Politics, Economics, and Education in the 21st Century
## John Fund (1998)

*John Fund is a political journalist who has been associated with* The Wall Street Journal *for many years. He has contributed to many print, electronic, and Internet media and has authored or co-authored several books. Here Mr. Fund makes some predictions about politics and the economy in the 21st century and emphasizes the need for Americans to make educated choices in their lives.*

May 1998 *Imprimis*

Since its founding in 1887, the *Wall Street Journal* has refused to endorse political candidates. The lone exception occurred in 1928, when the paper championed Herbert Hoover. "Never again!" the editors vowed, for they had rediscovered the wisdom of our founder, Charles Dow, who once said, "Politicians, properly observed, will often disappoint. Ideas, properly understood, seldom will." . . . I want to take this opportunity to remind those individuals who have been deeply disappointed by recent political events that the long-term outlook is much brighter than they may realize.

## The Cyberspace Economy

Look, for example, at the economy. Despite the predictions of many economists, the largest and fastest growing market in the world in the next twenty years is not going to be in China. It is going to be in cyberspace. We are about to witness incredible technological developments that will make it very difficult for traditional nation-states to "capture" income, to tax heavily, and to enforce burdensome regulations. Just as communism in the East failed to survive the technological revolution of the last half of the 20th century, big bureaucratic governments in the West will fail to survive the advances of the first half of the 21st century.

"Cybercash" and encryption will protect and conceal assets, and nation-states will find it increasingly difficult to tax at punitive rates. Welfare states will lose their most talented citizens through mass desertion if they don't adopt common sense economic policies. Jim Davidson, chairman of the National Taxpayers Union, recalls that in the Middle Ages there were "march regions"—areas bordering two or more kingdoms—that won favorable tax rates from governments, just as the Cayman Islands, Bermuda, and the Bahamas are doing today.

In the next century, more and more technologically savvy individuals will also choose to set up shop where their capital is best treated. It will thus be impossible for tax collectors to penalize successful entrepreneurs because goods will be made in one country, sold in a second, financed in a third, by investors living in a fourth, whose profits are sent to a fifth, which is a tax haven.

## The Global Tax Revolt

In the 21st century, governments will surrender power to citizens, not because they want to, but because they must. This long-term trend is inspired by what I call Fund's Law: "Governments will always do the right thing—after they have exhausted all other possibilities."

America will institute a flat tax, a national sales tax, or some other version of radical tax reform, not because Washington, D. C., wants it, but because the tax system is on the verge of collapse. I have examined the private studies of the size of the "underground economy." Believe it or not, they frighten even me, and I am an ardent advocate of laissez-faire!

In every nation, people have had enough of Robin Hood-style income redistribution and of confiscatory taxes on wages, savings, investment, and entrepreneurship. A global tax revolt is brewing. To prevent it from boiling over, governments will, as a last resort, finally turn to the free market.

## New Attitudes

There are three new public attitudes emerging that constitute another longterm trend. First, the next generation will not regard government as a "good buy." Even today, if government were a consumer product on the store shelf, it would probably be recalled as defective and its manufacturer sued for false advertising. People will look to private instead of public alternatives to fulfill their needs. Does this sound improbable? Consider this: Ten years ago, it was the kiss of death for a politician to express even mild concern about Social Security funding. Now, members on both sides of the aisle in Congress are talking openly about the "inevitability" of privatizing the entire pension system. Moreover, a decade ago, educational choice was a "wacky" idea proposed by the "rightwing fringe." Now, it has gained so much credibility among liberals as well as conservatives that it can be called "mainstream" and it has captured the partial support of Democratic senators Daniel Patrick Moynihan and Joseph Lieberman.

The second attitude is that politicians should be held accountable. Voters are tired of candidates who make promises on the campaign trail only to break them once they are elected to office. For the same reason, proposals to institute "direct democracy" through such legislation as term limits and initiative, referendum, and recall will gather momentum in the next century.

The third attitude concerns values. People are telling pollsters that the single greatest threat to future generations is the decline of morals and ethical standards. Fortunately, these individuals aren't content merely to voice their fears; they are doing something about them. In other words, they are leading a moral counterrevolution. They are buying millions of copies of values-oriented texts like William Bennett's *Book of Virtues*. They are founding thousands of home school cooperatives and hundreds of new private schools. They are joining dozens of traditionalist groups like Promise Keepers, Focus on the Family, and the Christian Coalition. And in towns and cities across the land, they are rebuilding the "little platoons" of family, church, and community that are the basis of the free society.

Does this mean that Americans are becoming more intolerant? Certainly not. We have always enjoyed a reputation for being a tolerant sort. For more than 200 years, we have prospered with a "live and let live" philosophy. Our famous "melting pot" society allows for all kinds of differences in lifestyle and opinion and even a good deal of outright eccentricity.

But what is changing, and changing dramatically, is Americans' consensus on personal responsibility. From time to time, the Times Mirror Corporation conducts a national poll asking, in effect, "Do you believe success in life is largely determined by forces outside of a person's control?" Twenty years ago, 50 percent of the respondents said "yes." Today, only 33 percent answer affirmatively.

There is a growing consensus that personal responsibility is important. Indeed, most Americans believe that if it were assumed a little more often it might even result in a lot less sin. Think about how this will play out in terms of politics, economics, and the culture at large. Political candidates who encourage people to think of themselves as victims will lose votes. Economic programs like welfare, that promote dependence, will be cut or even scrapped.

## The Reins of Power

I do not mean to paint a rosy picture in which the 21st century fulfills every promise of Paradise. Many serious problems will still exist, and many sound reforms will suffer defeat, if only because of another law, named after Grover Norquist, president of Americans for Tax Reform. Norquist's Law is: "Rarely do institutions surrender the reins of power voluntarily." Well, we know who has the power right now. It is labor unions, the academic elite, public employees, and big government. These groups have had the power for most of this century, and they will fight every attempt to wrest it from them.

However, I am optimistic that we can restore power to individuals. One of the best places to start is in education. It is here that we may see the essence of the problem of big government, which is insidiously making a silent bargain with the next generation—in dumbing down the curriculum, in teaching "self-esteem" over knowledge, in challenging established notions of truth and virtue, and in convincing children that their parents are not to be trusted. It is an insidious bargain that encourages young people to stop thinking for themselves in exchange for living in a world in which they will never be held accountable and will never be expected to care for themselves.

Of course, no one ever discusses this bargain in such bald terms. But it exists all the same; public schools are allowing students to graduate from high school and college without mastering basic skills or meeting academic requirements that were once the minimum standard for junior high students. Is this an accident? Of course not. It is the intention of big government to eliminate educational standards and to discourage citizens from thinking for themselves.

## Statism and Paternalism

If such an intention doesn't sound like a serious threat, please recall the example of communism, which springs from the same deadly combination of statism and paternalism. It was one of the most meaningful experiences of my entire life when, in 1984 (the year British novelist George Orwell made infamous), I visited East Germany. You remember East Germany—the Berlin Wall, the border guards, the secret police, the bread lines, the burnt out and crumbling buildings?

That was the Germany I went to visit. I was accompanied by a friend from the American Embassy. On our tour, we stopped by the Museum of History in East Berlin. It was an amazing place. I learned things there I never thought I would learn. For example, I learned that television was invented by an East German in 1956. While we were at the museum, a small group of teenage girls approached us. They were about fourteen or fifteen years old, and they hailed from a small town in the remote countryside. This was their first trip to the capital. They asked us what time it was. Clearly, they knew the answer. They wanted to have a conversation. We were the first Westerners they had ever met.

My first question to them was, "How did you know we were from the West?" They replied, "It was simple. We looked at your shoes and noticed that they weren't made of plastic." For some time, we exchanged anecdotes and impressions about East Berlin until their chaperone arrived to break things up. She was a stern-looking woman . . . [who] told the girls, "The museum is closing. It is time to go." It wasn't, but we were clearly a subversive influence.

Three hours later my friend and I were shopping in a downtown department store. What was an East German department store like? Imagine Wal-Mart without the inventory. All of the furniture and most of the other items there were "just for show." But the same teenage girls were there—without their chaperone, who had either decided to trust them or who was just tired of them. My friend and I had been in the capital for three days, so we volunteered to be their tour guides.

We showed them our passports; they showed us their identity papers and told us a little about what it was like to live in a small town in East Germany. One of the girls told us, for example, the economy was so run-down that, when she lost an air valve on a bicycle tire, there was no way to replace it. People didn't have much money, but what was worse, there was nothing on which to spend it.

Our travel visas expired at midnight, so by dusk we were on our way back to the glittering lights of West Berlin. The girls came along to the train station to bid us farewell. They had never seen the Berlin Wall, but they knew it was close. They gradually slowed their pace and stopped on a street corner just before we reached the railyard. One said, "You know, we really shouldn't go any further. We are not Berliners. If we are stopped, the guards will ask us why we are so close to the border zone."

As we stood in the growing darkness, a feeling of incredible sadness came over me. Here I was, in my mid-twenties, free as a bird. I wasn't rich, but I could go anywhere in the world from that street corner. They could not go another one hundred yards. Their world ended at the Wall. They could not go any further.

They were trapped in a human zoo. My friend and I were just tourists wandering through their grounds and by their cages. To keep the conversation going, because I didn't want to part from them, I asked what they wanted to be when they grew up. One said a beautician, one said a nurse, and one said a teacher. But the oldest and wisest, whose name was Monica, looked up at me with the most sorrowful face I have ever seen and said very slowly, "It doesn't matter what we become when we grow up. They will always treat us like children."

*They will always treat us like children.* That sentence really defines Soviet communism in its waning years. There were very few knocks in the dead of night; people were rarely taken away to the gulag. There were very few summary executions. Instead, there was an insufferable and widespread paternalism. It was a dark cloud hanging over citizens. It weighed down their spirits and prevented them from maturing. Worst of all, it kept them from becoming that which was best within them.

We parted almost tearfully. Monica and I exchanged addresses, and every year or so a postcard would come from her, and I would send some little trinket in the mail. She wrote that she had applied to a university, but she was rejected for her unacceptable views. She managed to get a job in a veterinarian's office.

Five years later, in 1989, Monica turned nineteen and the Berlin Wall came crashing down. I watched the first television broadcast that showed wave upon wave of East Germans crossing over into the West for their first taste of freedom, and I wondered if Monica and her friends were in one of those waves.

At about 10:00 a.m. the next day, the telephone rang. AT&T, already trying to introduce the consumer culture to East Germans, had set up a cellular phone service. As an incentive, they gave prospective customers the opportunity to make a phone call anywhere in the world for free. Monica called me. Her first words were, "John, this is Monica. I am over the Wall." We talked for a few minutes, and I was reminded of our last conversation on a street corner in East Berlin. I said, "Well, does this mean that your country has grown up, and you are no longer going to be treated as children?"

She responded with a laugh, "I think my entire country has graduated from kindergarten to high school overnight."

*Belin Wall*

## Acting Like Children

Over the course of the next year, I learned that Monica had made it into medical school. Today, she is completing her internship. A happy ending, to be sure, but one with a bittersweet quality. In 1994, Monica and her fiance came to the United States for a vacation. She had only one request: She wanted to speak to an American high school civics class about her experiences growing up in East Germany. Very reluctantly, I arranged for her to speak to just such a class at a high school in California. It was my alma mater, and I had spoken there a number of times since my graduation.

I didn't enjoy these experiences. Each time I met a new generation of America's youth, I discovered firsthand that things were getting worse. The students were learning little or nothing, discipline was practically unheard of, and respect was nonexistent. On the last occasion, I was so distressed that I vowed never to return. But I swallowed my doubts and arranged a talk for Monica. It was a disaster. The students weren't openly disrespectful, but they whispered constantly during her remarks and now and then a spitwad would rocket across the room. Even the quiet students were simply uninterested.

Finally, Monica opened the session up to questions. A girl asked, "Why in the world would someone want to build a wall in the middle of a city?" She clearly had no understanding why this had happened or what historical forces were at work, even after Monica had told her story.

As we walked out of the classroom, I tried to explain to Monica that not all young Americans were like this. She looked at me, and once again I saw that same sad, pensive face I remembered from a street corner in East Berlin. She said, "John, please don't explain anymore. I've been in America for three weeks now, and I've learned that this is a great and wonderful country. But because you have never lost your freedom, because you have never been conquered, because you have never had all your possessions taken from you, you are now willing to surrender your freedom, independence, and autonomy by inches. You simply don't notice it, but, one inch at a time, it slips away." She continued, "Those students in there—I feel sorry for them. No matter what they do when they grow up, many of them will always be acting like children."

*Acting like children.* Is that to be the description of our society? I hope not. As I noted earlier, there are so many historical and technological trends working in our direction. But what about our young people? Does it matter if they can run a computer if they don't have an understanding of what this country is all about? Do they really have the ability to think for themselves? We are told that jobs in the future will be marvelous—unskilled workers can get jobs in supermarkets and because of electronic scanners won't have to add or subtract. But that is not the America we want. It is not the America we had; it is not the America we have now.

We have a personal and moral responsibility to ensure that everyone in this country receives a sound education. We can't simply worry about the school across the street either; we have to worry about the schools across the nation. What makes for a good school? It doesn't take a panel of experts or millions of dollars to figure it out. . . . It takes good parental involvement in the early years. It takes a no-nonsense approach to basics. It takes discipline. It takes love. It takes concern for the individual student. It takes personal responsibility—on the part of students, parents, teachers, and administrators.

## Thinking for Ourselves

And it takes freedom. The public school monopoly has to be ended, and genuine competition has to be restored. The National Education Association's number one priority isn't quality education. It is its members' financial and political power. American Federation of Teachers President Al Shanker, who was one of this century's best labor union presidents, once openly admitted, "I will begin to care about the quality of children's education in this country when they start paying union dues." Now, this may shock you, but it really shouldn't surprise you.

Since 1962, when teachers were first allowed to unionize, the public school system has been a system that benefits and answers to the producers of education, not the consumers. Eighty-eight percent of the schools in America are public schools, and 75 percent of the teachers are union members.

The good news is that in the last few years people have started to make a distinction between teachers and teacher unions. The NEA can no longer get away with saying that its interests are the interests of the nation.

And this brings us back to the story of Monica. She came back to America in 1996. I took her to several charter schools that, although they are still public schools, are free of a lot of bureaucratic regulation. She came back with a much different impression. So there is hope.

One of the greatest gifts we can give to succeeding generations is the ability to think for themselves, and that means challenging the government monopoly of thought in education directly. It will be a struggle. All it takes is a trip to the ruins of the Berlin Wall to remind us that governments never give up power voluntarily. It is up to us to reassert our rights and recover our responsibilities.

# Three Cheers for Capitalism
## Steve Forbes (1993)

*Steve Forbes (born in 1947) is president and chief executive officer of Forbes Inc. and editor-in-chief of* Forbes *business magazine. He was a candidate for the Republican presidential nomination in 1996 and 2000. Here Mr. Forbes emphasizes the importance of the freedom to make choices in the capitalist system.*

September 1993 Imprimis

Living in the 1990s, we are uniquely able to judge what the American economy has achieved in the 20th century, For this reason, we ought to give three cheers for capitalism. By the term, I mean "democratic capitalism," which is as fundamentally different from the "managed capitalism" of modern-day central planners as it is from the "state capitalism" of old-style fascists, socialists, and communists.

Capitalism works better than any of us can conceive. It is also the only truly *moral* system of exchange. It encourages individuals to freely devote their energies and impulses to peaceful pursuits, to the satisfaction of others' wants and needs, and to constructive action for the welfare of all. The basis for capitalism is not greed. You don't see misers creating Wal-Marts and Microsofts.

Think about it for a moment. Capitalism is truly miraculous. What other system enables us to cooperate with millions of other ordinary people—whom we will never meet but whom we will gladly provide with goods and services—in an incredible, complex web of commercial transactions? And what other system perpetuates itself, working every day, year in, year out, with no single hand guiding it?

Capitalism is a moral system if only because it is based on *trust*. When we turn on a light, we assume that there will be electricity. When we drive into a service station, we assume that there will be fuel. When we walk into a restaurant, we assume that there will be food. If we were to make a list of all the basic things that capitalism provides—things that we take for granted—it would fill an encyclopedia.

## How to Become Successful Capitalists

How do we become successful capitalists? The answer sounds simple, but it is often overlooked in places where you would think they would know better. (I am referring, of course, to government, the media, and our most elite business schools and economics departments.) We succeed as capitalists by offering goods and services that others are willing to buy. Many capitalists do not make correct assumptions about what to offer and fail, but that is as it should be. There is no guarantee of success in any area of life, including business—there is always risk. The particular advantage of capitalism is that failed businesses don't necessarily equal a failed economy; they make way for successful businesses.

But even the most successful businesses can't afford to forget about market principles. AT&T is a case in point. In the 1970s, fiber optic technology was available, but AT&T decided that it would delay fully converting for perhaps 30 to 40 years. It wanted to fully depreciate its old plants and equipment, and, because it enjoyed a virtual monopoly over its customers, it saw no reason to spend a lot of money on a new long distance calling system. But then an upstart company, MCI, raised a couple billion dollars through the much-maligned "junk bonds" market in order to set up its own fiber-optic network. AT&T had no choice but to keep up with its competition, and, as a result, the U.S. experienced an enormous advance in communications that has put it ahead of its foreign competitors and that has benefited hundreds of millions of consumers.

About twenty-five years ago, the federal government filed an antitrust suit against IBM because it had grown so successful that its name had become virtually synonymous with the computer industry. But the would-be trustbusters underestimated the vitality of an open marketplace. IBM's dominance of mainframe computers, microchips, and software did not prevent the rise of rival companies such as Digital Equipment, Apple Computer, Sun Microsystems, and Microsoft. Today, IBM's very existence is in jeopardy.

Around the same time, John Kenneth Galbraith wrote *The New Industrial State*, in which he argued that though the Ford Motor Company was no longer the biggest of the auto companies (GM had roughly 50 percent of all sales), Ford was so large that it did not have to pay particular attention to its shareholders or its customers. Apparently, Japanese automakers did not read John Kenneth Galbraith, or the reports of countless other "experts" who claimed that it was impossible to compete against Ford, GM, and Chrysler. They even ignored their own early failures to storm the U.S. market in the 1950s and early 1960s. Finally, after years of trying, Japanese automakers succeeded—and succeeded to an extent that no one could have predicted—in challenging the hegemony of the "giants" in Detroit.

Then there is Sears & Roebuck. What more mundane business could there be than retailing? Yet, around the turn of the century, Sears made retailing truly exciting, reaching out to millions of people with new marketing methods and new products. By the end of the 1940s, it dwarfed all competitors. In the last several decades, however, the company lost its way and became a self-serving, insulated bureaucracy. Now it is closing its doors on numerous stores. Its market share has plunged—and its profits have almost disappeared.

Why, by contrast, has another retail firm, Wal-Mart, achieved its phenomenal success? Not because its founder Sam Walton used to ride around in a pickup truck visiting his stores, though that was good publicity. It was because he recognized the importance of computer technology and had systems devised that help store operators respond to inventory information on a weekly and even daily basis. Sam Walton knew that success, even once it was achieved, was something that couldn't be taken for granted.

What should be clear from each of these examples is that capitalism is not a top-down system—it cannot be mandated or centrally planned. It operates from the bottom up, through individuals—individuals who take risks, who often "don't know any better," who venture into areas where, according to conventional wisdom, they have no business going, who see vast potential where others see nothing.

Often, these individuals literally stumble across ideas that never would have occurred to them if they were forced to work in a top-down system. And they take supposedly "worthless" substances and turn them into infinitely valuable ones. Look at penicillin. Whoever thought that stale bread could be good for anything? The same goes for oil before the invention of the gasoline engine and the automobile and for sand before the invention of glass, fiber-optics, and the microchip.

There is another important thing to remember about capitalism: Failure is not a stigma or a permanent obstacle. It is a spur to learn and try again. Edison invented the light bulb on, roughly, his ten-thousandth attempt. If we had depended on central planners to direct his experiments, we would all be sitting around in the dark today.

## Open vs. Managed Competition

This leads to the next question regarding capitalism: What is the market? Central planners don't like the word; they prefer to say, "market forces," as if describing aliens from outer space. But nothing could be further from the truth. The market is *people*. All of us. We decide what to do and what not to do, where to shop and where not to shop, what to buy and what not to buy. So when central planners trash "market forces," they are really trashing us.

Unfortunately, they are the ones who seem to be calling the shots today on a number of issues that should be left up to the market, i.e., up to us. One such issue is the spiraling costs of health care. Not surprisingly, central planners advocate a top-down approach to reform. With unconscious irony, they call it "managed competition."

But we have *already* tried managed competition; in fact, it is managed competition that has caused so many problems in the health care industry in the first place. Specifically, the tax code penalizes individuals who want to buy medical insurance by making them pay for it with after-tax dollars, even if they are self-employed. Only 25 percent of their premiums are deductible. But companies may buy health insurance with pre-tax dollars. So they, instead of their employees, have become the primary purchasers of insurance. This drives a wedge between the real customers and the real providers and obscures the real costs of such features of the system as low deductibles. Imagine if every time you went to the supermarket you gave the cash register receipt to your employer, who then submitted it to the insurance company for a claim. What would happen to food prices? They would skyrocket, because you wouldn't care whether a bottle of soda cost $10, $100, or $1,000.

The problem doesn't stop there. Growth in demand and improvements in technology— key ingredients to success in any other business—have instead led to crisis in the health care industry. More people are receiving better treatment than ever before and leading longer, healthier lives, but perversely this has sent costs up rather than down and has overloaded the delivery system.

If we want genuine health care reform, we must return to open competition. The tax code must be revised so that individuals can buy health insurance with pre-tax dollars and set up medical IRAs for their families that can be used to finance routine medical expenses. There is no doubt that a majority of Americans would choose this option. They want to have control over their own health care decisions. Many would choose policies with higher deductibles. Premiums would go down and so would paperwork. Physicians and hospitals would see their patient load come under control and would be induced to offer competitive rates and services. The potential benefits are enormous.

A couple of years ago, Forbes Inc. faced yet another round of steeply rising costs for health care. We wanted to do something that enabled our employees to police those costs in a way we, the employer, were unable to do. So we gave them a stake in the process. We offered them a *bonus*: They could keep the difference between their claims and $500—and we would double the amount. Thus, if they went through a calendar year without filing any health claims on the insurance company, we would pay them as much as $1000, tax free.

What happened? Suddenly, every employee became cost-conscious. On major medical and dental expenses, claims went down 30 percent. These savings financed the bonuses and our total health care costs went up *zero percent* last year. This was not because we compelled millions of people to participate in some "managed competition" scheme, but because we let a few hundred individuals make their own health care decisions.

## Letting Individuals Make Their Own Decisions

Letting individuals make their own decisions is what capitalism is all about, but virtually all central planners (now in their heyday under the Clinton administration) and a good many members of the U.S. Congress (Republicans as well as Democrats) fail to realize it. They do not, for example, realize that it is the decisions of individuals that really decide how much tax revenue the government collects and how well the economy prospers. Between 1982 and 1986, the American private sector created well over 18 million new jobs, including a record number of high-paying positions. Of these, 14 million were created by new businesses. But, in 1987, Congress raised the capital gains tax to one of the highest levels in the industrial world.

What happened? New business and job creation declined sharply. The nation was hit with a recession. And tax revenues, which were supposed to rise, went down. All this occurred because individuals made the decision *not* to invest. Today, there is almost *$7 trillion* of unrealized capital gains that is going begging because of high taxes. If Congress lowered the capital gains rate, it would mean *more* not *less* tax revenues. It also would overwhelm any stimulus package Washington could concoct for revitalizing the economy.

Central planners also tend to be big fans of "industrial planning," whereby government picks the "winners" in the marketplace through subsidization of select companies and technologies. They ignore the fact that this will obliterate incentives for companies to remain competitive, breed corruption and special interests, and penalize the small businesses that are the backbone of the economy.

And they want to micromanage the monetary system, knocking down the value of the dollar against the yen or raising it against some other currency in closed-door meetings with bureaucrats from other industrialized nations. They do not realize that one of the most important functions of money is to serve as a constant, reliable measure. A ruler is supposed to be 12 inches long, but they want to change it to 11 or 13 inches whenever it suits their political strategy. You and I might call this a swindle, but in Washington it is called sophisticated economic management.

Even such a simple word as "change" takes on a whole new definition in Washington, meaning change directed from above by well-intended central planners and politicians who think that they "know better" than most people when it comes to making decisions. But, in truth, the most revolutionary sweeping agent of change is capitalism. Look at what has happened in Eastern Europe, the Soviet Union, Latin America, and Asia. When people are free to make their own decisions, they have a stake in the economy, and when they have a stake in the economy, they have a stake in serving others, and when they have a stake in serving others, they have a stake in fighting for freedom.

Capitalism is the real enemy of tyranny. It stands not for accumulated wealth or greed but for human innovation, imagination, and risk-taking. It cannot be measured in mathematical models or quantified in statistical terms, which is why central planners and politicians always underestimate it. As I noted at the outset, it is up to us, then, to give three cheers for capitalism. Who knows? If we cheer loud enough, perhaps even they will listen.

# The Entrepreneur As American Hero
## Walter E. Williams (2005)

*Walter Williams is the John M. Olin Distinguished Professor of Economics at George Mason University in Virginia. He holds the Ph.D. in economics from UCLA. Dr. Williams has written six books and dozens of articles. He appears often on radio and television discussing economic issues. In this speech, Dr. Williams discusses the importance of the free market for a healthy economy.*

March 2005 *Imprimis*

Let's start off talking about the entrepreneur with a brief discussion of the sources of income. Some of the rhetoric one hears gives the impression that income is somehow distributed—that there's a dealer of dollars. Thus, one might think that the reason some Americans have more income than others is that the dollar dealer is a racist, a sexist or a multi-nationalist who deals out dollars unfairly. Alternatively, some suggest that the reason that some Americans are richer than others is because they got to the pile of money first and took an unfair share. In either case, justice requires that government take the ill-gotten gains of the few and restore them to their rightful owners—in other words, redistribute income. While no one actually describes the sources of income this way, the logic of their arguments for redistribution implies such a vision.

In truth, in a free society, income is earned through pleasing and serving one's fellow man. I mow your lawn, repair your roof or teach your kid economics. In turn you give me dollars. We can think of dollars as certificates of performance. With these certificates of performance in hand, I go to my grocer and ask him to give me a pound of steak . . . that my fellow man produced. In effect the grocer says, "You're making a claim on something your fellow man produced. You're asking him to serve you—but did you serve him?" I say, "Yes I did." The grocer responds, "Prove it!" That's when I show him my certificates of performance—namely, the money my fellow man paid me to mow his lawn.

Contrast the morality of having to serve one's fellow man as a condition of being served by him with the alternative. Government can say to me, "Williams, you don't have to serve your fellow man in order to have a claim on what he produces. As long as you're loyal to us, we will take what your fellow man produces and give it to you."

Obviously, some people are more effective at serving and pleasing their fellow man than others. They earn a greater number of certificates of performance (i.e., higher income) and hence have greater claims on what their fellow man produces. Take Luciano Pavarotti. Why is his income much higher than mine? It's because of discriminating people like you. You will plunk down $75 to hear him sing an aria from La Boheme; but how much would you be willing to pay to hear me do the same? Those who would call Pavarotti's income unfair and would have government take part of it to give to others are essentially saying, "We disagree with the decisions of millions upon millions of people acting voluntarily that resulted in Pavarotti's higher income. We are going to use the coercive powers of government to cancel out the full effect of those decisions through income redistribution." I might add that income redistribution is simply a legal version of what a thief does—namely, take the rightful property of one person for the benefit of another. The primary distinction between his behavior and that of Congress is legality.

For the most part, in a free society, people who are wealthy have become so through effectively serving their fellow man. Cyrus McCormick and his reaping machine, Thomas Watson Sr., the founder of IBM, and Lloyd Conover, who created the antibiotic tetracycline in the employ of Pfizer Company are just a few of the exceptional contributors. And while these people and their companies became extremely wealthy, society benefited far more than they did in terms of the value of healthier lives and the millions and possibly billions of lives saved.

## Capitalism Raises All Boats

Propaganda and stubborn ignorance has it that the advances of capitalism benefit only the rich. The evidence, as I've already pointed out, refutes that. Let's look at more: The rich have always been able to afford entertainment, but it was the development and marketing of radio and television that made entertainment accessible to the common man. The rich have never had the drudgery of washing and ironing clothing, beating out carpets or waxing floors. It was the development and mass production of washing machines, wash and wear clothing, vacuum cleaners and no-wax floors that spared the common man of this drudgery. At one time, only the rich could afford automobiles, telephones and computers. Now all but a tiny percentage of Americans enjoy these goods.

Today, as it has always been, the direct impetus for technological innovation and progress has been the entrepreneurial search for profits and the competitive economy. As Stephen Moore and Julian L. Simon point out in their 1999 article, "The Greatest Century That Ever Was," over the course of the 20th century life expectancy rose from 47 to 77 years of age; deaths from infectious disease fell from 700 to 50 per 100,000 of the population; agricultural workers fell from 35 to 2.5 percent of the workforce; auto ownership rose from one to 91 percent of the population; and patents granted rose from 25,000 to 150,000 a year. Controlling for inflation, household assets rose from $6 trillion to $41 trillion between 1945 and 1998.

Let's consider another factor that is nearly completely ignored. The output and wealth generated through free enterprise contributes to a more civilized society. For most of mankind's existence, he has had to spend most of his time simply eking out a living. In pre-industrial society and in many places in the world still today, the most optimistic scenario for the ordinary citizen was to be able to eke out enough to meet his physical needs for another day. But with the rise of capitalism and the concomitant rise in human productivity that yielded seemingly ceaseless economic progress, it was no longer necessary for mankind to spend his entire day simply providing for minimum physical needs. People were able to satisfy their physical needs with less and less time. This made it possible for them to have the time and resources to develop spiritually and culturally.

In other words, the rise of capitalism enabled the gradual extension of civilization to greater and greater numbers of people. More of them have time available to read, become educated in the liberal arts and gain more knowledge about the world around them. Greater wealth permits them to attend the arts, afford recreation, contemplate more fulfilling and interesting life activities and enjoy other culturally enriching activities that were formerly within the purview of only the rich. How was all this achieved? In a market system, enterprise profits are performance-related; they come about through a process of finding out what human wants are not being met and finding ways to meet them.

In reference to the motivations of the entrepreneur, Adam Smith says this: "By directing that industry in such a manner as its produce may be of the greatest value, he intends only his own gain, and he is in this, as in many other cases, led by an invisible hand to promote an end which was no part of his intention." That might very well describe an entrepreneur like Thomas Watson Sr., founder of IBM. Such previously unimaginable progress as we have seen in recent decades is the direct result of having methods of handling large amounts of data accurately and rapidly. From the 1930s onward, IBM was at the forefront in the development of the machinery to do this. The huge benefits we enjoy as a result of IBM's pioneering work was no part of the intention of Thomas Watson or his successors. They were in it for profits.

## In Defense of Profit

Profit has almost become a dirty word, so let me spend a few minutes talking about the magnitude of profits and the role that they play in a free market economy. Regarding their magnitude, only roughly six cents of each dollar companies take in represent after-tax profits. By far, wages are the largest part of that dollar, representing about 60 cents. As percentages of 2002 national income, after-tax profits represented about five percent and wages about 71 percent.

I'll discuss first what might be called normal profit and later turn to the more emotional topic of "windfall profits"—what some have labeled "obscene profits." Normal profit is the opportunity cost of using entrepreneurial abilities in the production of a good. It's what the entrepreneur could have earned in his next best alternative—say, another business venture. Just as wages, rent and interest must be paid in order to employ the services of labor, land and capital, normal profits must be paid to employ entrepreneurial services—the decisions, innovations and risks that drive economic progress.

Whether an entrepreneur makes a profit depends essentially on two things. The first is whether he is producing a good that consumers value and are willing to pay for; the second is whether he's using the scarce resources of society in the most efficient manner to produce the good.

Let's look at an example of the role of profits in providing incentives to produce what the consumer wants. Remember when Coca Cola introduced the "new" Coke in 1985? Pepsi Cola president Roger Enrico called it "the Edsel of the '80s," representing one of that decade's greatest marketing debacles. Who made the Coca Cola Company bring back the old Coke? Was it Congress, the courts, the president or other government officials acting in the interests of soda-drinking Americans? No, it was the specter of negative profits (i.e., losses) that convinced Coca Cola to bring back the old Coke. Thus, one role of profits is to discover what consumers want and to correct producers who make mistakes.

Profits also force producers to employ resources wisely. If producers waste inputs, their production costs will be higher. In order to cover their costs, they must charge prices higher than what consumers are willing to pay. After a while the company will incur unsustainable losses and go out of business. As a result, the company's resources will become available to someone else who'll put them to wiser use. This process is short-circuited if government offers bailouts in the forms of guaranteed loans, subsidies or restrictions such as tariffs and import quotas on competitive products from abroad. Government "help" enables failing companies to continue squandering resources. In this context it is important to remember that a business going bankrupt doesn't meant that its productive resources will vanish into thin air. It means someone else will own them.

So-called windfall profits are profits above and beyond those needed to keep an entrepreneur producing a good or service. But they serve a vital social function. They serve as a signal that there are unmet human wants. One of the best examples of the role of windfall profits are those that arise in the wake of a disaster and are often condemned as price gouging. In the wake of a disaster, such as a hurricane, there is an immediate change in scarcity conditions that's reflected in higher prices for goods and services. Assume, for example, that a family of four sees their home damaged or destroyed. At before-disaster prices, they might decide to rent two adjoining hotel rooms. However, when they arrive at the hotel and see that room prices have doubled, they might easily decide to tough it out in a single room. Doing so makes a room available for someone else whose home was damaged and who needs a place to spend the night. Thus, higher prices give people an incentive to economize on scarce resources.

In the wake of Florida's Hurricane Andrew, windfall profits played a vital though unappreciated role. Plywood destined to be shipped to the Midwest, West and Northeast suddenly was rerouted to South Florida. Lumber mills increased production. Truckers and other workers worked overtime in order to increase the availability of plywood and other construction materials to Floridians. Rising plywood prices meant something else as well. All that plywood heading south meant plywood prices rose in other locations, discouraging "lower valued" uses of plywood such as home improvement projects. After all, rebuilding and repairing destroyed homes is a "higher valued" use of plywood.

What caused these market participants to do what was in the social interest, namely, sacrifice or postpone alternative uses for plywood? The answer reveals perhaps the most wonderful feature of this process. Rising prices and opportunities for higher profits encouraged people to do voluntarily what was in the social interest: help their fellow man recover from a disaster.

## Williams' Law

At this juncture let me say a few words about the modern push for corporate social responsibility. Do corporations have a social responsibility? Yes, and Nobel Laureate Professor Milton Friedman put it best in 1970 when he said that in a free society "there is one and only one social responsibility of business—to use its resources and engage in activities designed to increase its profits so long as it stays within the rules of the game, which is to say, engages in open and free competition without deception or fraud."

It is only people, not businesses, who have responsibilities. A CEO is an employee, an employee of shareholders and customers. The failure of the corporate executive community to recognize this, and its willingness to engage in activities unrelated to the pursuit of profits, means national wealth will be lower, product prices will be higher and the return on investment lower.

If we care about people's wants, rather than beating up on profit-making enterprises, we should pay more attention to government-owned non-profit organizations. A good example are government schools. Many squander resources and produce a shoddy product while administrators, teachers and staff earn higher pay and perks, and customers (taxpayers) are increasingly burdened. Unlike other producers, educationists don't face the rigors of the profit discipline, and hence they're not as accountable. Ditto the U.S. Postal Service. It often provides shoddy and surly services, but its managers and workers receive increasingly higher wages while customers pay higher and higher prices. Again, wishes of customers can be safely ignored because there's no bottom line discipline of profits.

Here's Williams' law: Whenever the profit incentive is missing, the probability that people's wants can be safely ignored is the greatest. If a poll were taken asking people which services they are most satisfied with and which they are most dissatisfied with, for-profit organizations (supermarkets, computer companies and video stores) would dominate the first list while non-profit organizations (schools, offices of motor vehicle registration) would dominate the latter. In a free economy, the pursuit of profits and serving people are one and the same. No one argues that the free enterprise system is perfect, but it's the closest we'll come here on Earth.

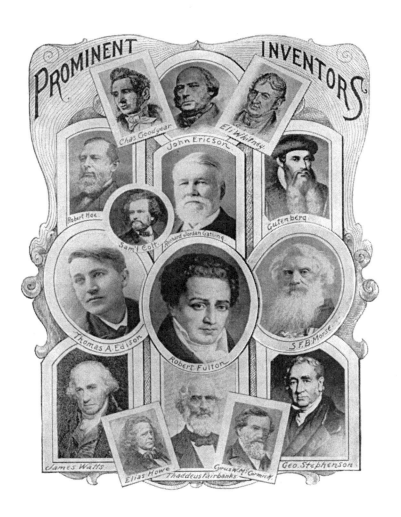

# The Market and Human Values
## John Davenport (1975)

---

*John Davenport graduated from Yale in 1926. He was a writer and economic journalist who worked at* Barron's Weekly *and* Fortune *magazines and wrote for many other publications. He wrote* The U.S. Economy *in 1964. Davenport died in 1987 at the age of 82. Here Mr. Davenport reminds us that the successful working of the free market, as he puts it, "requires a framework of law, order, and ethical consensus that involves fundamentally an affirmation of certain human values."*

May 1975 *Imprimis*

. . . I am . . . honored to be included in what has become known as the Ludwig von Mises Lecture Series, though this strikes me as inviting a boy (if an old boy) to do a man's work. After all, I am only a working journalist, whereas it is not too much to say that von Mises was a foremost economist of our times, though his role as such was never publicly acknowledged by what we may call The Establishment. He was the leading champion of the free market economy in this century. He was a devastating critic not only of Marxian socialism but of that "soft socialism" which infects so much of our thinking today. He was finally a scholar and a gentleman—a scholar ever ready to bring a vast store of learning to the principles he believed in, and a gentleman in the sense that while he did not suffer fools gladly, he never lost an Old World courtesy and graciousness which he displayed toward friends and foes alike.

I trust this spirit of tolerance is brooding over this meeting tonight as I examine two different aspects of von Mises' thought. The first part of my task is relatively easy. It is to run over rapidly the chief arguments for the market type of economy and to dispose of some of the chief criticisms that are made of it. But the second and main part of my assignment is more difficult and controversial. It is to explore the underpinnings which seem to me necessary to maintain this kind of economy in a hostile world. And here my thesis will be that while the market is self-sustaining in an economic sense, it is not necessarily self-sustaining in a moral sense. It requires a framework of law, order, and ethical consensus that involves fundamentally an affirmation of certain human values. The market is not an end in itself, but the means to higher ends. Definition of these ends leads us inevitably into the domain of philosophy and metaphysics.

## Two and One-Half Cheers for the Market

This may appear a brash statement in a so-called scientific age, but the importance of values is really implicit in the arguments which protagonists of the market make for this form of social organization. Let us briefly run over the position. It should not have taken the Arab sheiks to remind us that by definition all economic goods are scarce, whereas the hunger of man for those goods is well-nigh infinite. In this situation some means must be found for allocating scarce resources—be they work, materials or capital—to human wants. There are basically two ways in which this may be done. In the first place, we might conceive of some all-wise government which would plan out in advance what goods would be produced each year according to some master chart or plan. This is the road taken by Marxian socialism, and to my horror I see it is still being taken seriously by various intellectuals who want to set up a master-planning agency in Washington.

The trouble with such a system, of course, is that government officials are not all-wise when it comes to knowing what people want, and furthermore that the only way by which government can enforce its plans is by using some form of coercion. Economic planning in this sense cannot be squared with human freedom. It cannot even be squared, as von Mises has brilliantly shown, with rational choice and decision. It is easy for governments to decide that their people will probably want some bread to eat. They will also want shoes to put on their feet. But how much bread? How many shoes? These are the questions which officials cannot really answer.

By contrast, a market economy solves the problem of allocation smoothly and efficiently. Assuming that there is a given income distribution, consumers bid for what they want via the price mechanism. This gives them a vote in the economic arena which may be just as important as, and perhaps more important than, their vote at the ballot box. The price system is really a sophisticated signalling system which indicates what should be produced, and in what quantities. The wage system is likewise a signalling device which indicates where labor is most productive. Were labor "taken out of the market," as organized labor has declared it ought to be, we would be left without guide or rudder to determine how the world's work should be accomplished. Finally, profits—the difference between final prices and costs—are the evanescent margin of return that goes to producers and entrepreneurs for bringing labor, materials and capital together before goods can be sold. In a growing economy someone must undertake this risk, and it is far better that it be diffused among

*Tony Bruno, Shoemaker, 1925*
*Bruno made shoes for many Presidents and Cabinet members.*

individual entrepreneurs and corporations than concentrated in the hands of bureaucrats, whose mistakes in judging human needs are apt to be monumental.

It may come as a surprise to you that even the late John Maynard Keynes had no quarrel with this proposition and concluded his famous *General Theory of Employment, Interest and Money* with a ringing apologia for the market's virtues. Where Keynes broke with the classical tradition was on the question of whether the market is economically self-sustaining. Following Jean Baptiste Say, most economists before Keynes' time had assumed that production in the market creates its own demand: it is the shoes which the shoemaker makes that constitute his real purchasing power for food produced by the farmer. The heart of the General Theory is its attack on Say's law of markets and on the grounds that in a capitalist society, people will attempt to save more than they invest. From this it followed that governments must step in to fill the gap by spending and extending easy credit, if we would maintain full use of our resources.

This was, to say the least, music to the ears of politicians who for thirty-odd years have been presenting us with ever-rising government expenditures and budget deficits. With what results? With the result that inflation has predictably grown apace, while unemployment is still very much with us. . . . The truth seems to be that debasement of the currency and government efforts to pump up so-called "aggregate demand" are a self-defeating process. They may sometimes restore prosperity for a while, but in the end we suffer the worst of both worlds—namely stagflation. It is a tribute to von Mises that he never accepted the Keynesian analysis and hence never accepted its conclusions. He held that society needs a stable currency and that government may have a part in creating it. But given this framework, his position was that unemployed resources are not the result of market forces but rather the result of blockage by powerful labor unions, minimum wage laws, and other forms of government interference. Were he alive today, I suspect that his prescription would be far different from and far simpler than the ideas currently circulating in Congress and in the White House. He would propose elimination of monopoly practices in both industry and labor, combined with a cut in, or elimination of, that most foolish of all taxes—namely the corporate profit tax.

## The Limits of Neutrality

I trust that by now I have convinced you that I am a good free marketeer in the Misesian sense of the word. . . . I would like now to advance up more slippery slopes. Granted that the free market is a buttress of liberty, a coordinator of free and spontaneous collaboration, and that given proper adjustment of prices, costs and profits, it has no inherent tendency to run down—granted all this, is it a self-sustaining mechanism in a deeper sense? Can we safely argue for the virtues of the market without paying some attention to virtue itself in the ethical meaning of that word? Can the market succeed without the commitment of society and a nation to certain fundamental values that lie beyond the margin of supply and demand and so-called "indifference curves"?

And here we come to a paradox that involves the very nature of economics and the task of the economist. Von Mises and the Austrian school of economics which he represented freed us from viewing economics as some kind of spurious physical science. Economics, as von Mises made plain in his great book, *Human Action,* is not the study of physical wealth, as some earlier economists had believed. It is fundamentally the study of human choice and preferences in the face of scarce resources; and such choice is obviously psychological in nature. Human behavior is purposive in character, and purposes involving judgment of the future, as well as of the past, cannot be reduced to outward events which can be studied under the microscope. Purposes, it would seem evident, involve ends and values. And yet it was a prime tenet of von Mises' teaching, and certainly is a prime tenet of most modern economists, that economics is value free. Economics studies human choice, but when it comes to human choices it does not pass judgment. To put it bluntly, if men choose to buy cocaine instead of Coca-Cola, that is to be lamented from a social point of view. But the economist qua economist is supposed to keep his mouth shut.

Now I find that this doctrine of ethical neutrality in modern economics has something to be said for it. Economists are busy enough nowadays explaining the intricacies of supply and demand (of oil, for instance) and further explaining the intricacies of the modern money system without getting themselves involved in moral judgments. They perform a highly useful function in explaining that if a man or a nation follows course A, the consequence B is apt to follow. All of us, including government officials, do need to know the probable consequences of alternative lines of action, whether these relate to our personal lives or to social issues, such as rent control, environmental protection, or the inflation of the currency. Yet I also find this doctrine of ethical neutrality on the part of economists a puzzling and at times highly dangerous one. For one thing, few economists, and least of all my libertarian friends, are really able to stick to it. They are, in fact, constantly telling us what we ought to do rather than what we do. Indeed, the whole case for free enterprise and the market economy rests on moral evaluations—that freedom and collaboration are good, and that coercion, in general, is bad.

Moreover, I would remind you that even the most devoted of free marketeers, who are against most interferences by government in the price-profit system, still assume that some governmental framework is necessary if the market is to perform its functions. The market requires the enforcement of property rights and of contract. It assumes a framework of law which has its foundation deep within a moral public consensus. It requires a viable monetary system through which all prices, wages, and profits are registered. Government is involved here whether it adopts some form of gold standard or whether, following the advice of the Chicago school of thought, it adopts some fixed rule for enlarging the money supply, defined in terms of currency and checking accounts. Even if we assume that gold coins will circulate again, still the king's head or the American eagle will presumably be stamped on the coins.

## The Market Depends on Order

In short, the market system is dependent upon a right and just political order, and such an order, as Aristotle saw long ago, depends on our making up our minds as to what constitutes justice and other forms of the Good. I conclude that while economists may abstain, if they like, from passing judgment on individual acts of human choice, they cannot possibly remain neutral when it comes to defining the kind of economic and political order which makes freedom of individual choice possible. Perhaps we should allow them the privilege of wearing two hats, so to speak, donning one when they play the role of the economist, but putting on the other when they speak as concerned citizens. But I confess I am not too fond of hat tricks, especially when the same bald or bushy head is discovered beneath the felt!

More seriously, I wish that economists would abstain from making highly dangerous philosophic statements in their efforts to defend their alleged scientific neutrality. If you ask many of them today (not necessarily the followers of von Mises) why they are ethically neutral, their answer all too often will be that ethical judgments are, by their nature, "subjective" whereas economic judgments are "objective." Now this is a very dangerous statement. If all that is meant by it is that ethical judgments are psychological and non-physical facts, well and good. But if what is meant is that ethical judgments are *ipso facto* capricious and not subject to general moral laws, then we are in very serious trouble indeed. For in this case, we would be left with no common standards and criteria for evaluating human actions. We would be left in a world where all that could guide us would be the attitude, "You do your thing, and I'll do mine."

But I submit that this business of "you do your thing and I'll do mine" is really an invitation to anarchy or worse, if there be anything worse. It is first cousin to that Relativism and Logical Positivism (i.e., only the measurable is real) which afflict the modern world and which have undermined the very intellectual foundations of what Walter Lippmann once called the Good Society. In the Good Society it must be assumed that there are enduring standards for judging the good, the beautiful, and the true. Indeed, without belief in truth, science itself becomes impossible. In this matter it seems to me that some thinkers of the Middle Ages were far ahead of our latter-day philosophers and economists. For they posited a "natural order" which included not only the so-called facts of nature, as we observe them, but also certain moral laws that were just as real as the facts of nature, even though they could not be observed by the human eye (or the modern microscope). It is my contention that if we are to have the kind of economy free marketeers say they want, and the kind of limited government which most of us want, then some such comprehensive Natural Order must be assumed. In short, we must reconnect economics with philosophy in both branches of the latter subject—with metaphysics, the study of the Real; and with ethics, the study of the Good.

## "Get You Wisdom"

Now all this is pretty deep stuff, and I must apologize for having led you into it. Yet my remarks have been dictated by the very nature of the topic assigned. The assignment was not just to defend the market system of economy. It was to try to indicate that we cannot get very far in that defense without considering human values, and that once that Pandora's box is opened we are up against questions as old as Plato and Aristotle.

I would commend both men to your attention, especially Aristotle, who after all wrote the first short treatise on economics as part of a much broader synthesis. For Aristotle economics was part of politics, and politics in its turn flowed out of ethics. And that, when you come to think about it, is more or less how the Founding Fathers of this country proceeded. Madison, Jefferson and Hamilton did not begin by defining a full-blown economic system. On the contrary, they began with certain assumptions about the nature of man, that in the language of the Declaration, "all men are endowed by their Creator with certain inalienable rights." From that assumption flowed their concept of limited rather than unlimited government. And from that assumption flowed an economic system which, while dependent on government for its basic framework, nevertheless took from government the decisions of how the world's work should be performed and how resources—human, material, and capital—should be allocated.

Today this order of priorities has been strangely reversed. We have a vast body of so-called economic knowledge and statistics which is kept in one compartment of our thinking. Then we have our so-called "political scientists" who argue to and fro about the nature of government. Finally, we still do have our philosophers, though . . . their discussion is too often clouded by exercises in symbolic logic or arid studies of semantics and linguistics. Never mind. I hold that there still is a great philosophic tradition, and that some acquaintance with Greek and medieval philosophy will serve you well in your comprehension of modern economics.

I would add furthermore that you will not understand our civilization without exploring that other great tradition which has shaped it—namely Christianity. As Edmund Opitz has argued in his brilliant book, *Religion and Capitalism: Allies, Not Enemies*, there should be no quarrel between the deepest insights of religion and the kind of free economy we wish to preserve against the inroads of the all-powerful state. On the contrary, it is where secularism and materialism have taken deepest hold, as in Communist Russia, that the free economy has been all but eliminated. Religion, Marx held, was the "opium of the people." What force is to reinforce the Good? And what force is to stand up against the princes, principalities and dictators of this our modern secular world? . . .

# High Technology and Judeo-Christian Values: Mind, Not Money, Drives the Economy
## Warren T. Brookes (1984)

*Warren Brookes (1929-1991) was a 1952 honors graduate in economics from Harvard. He worked in industry for many years before becoming a syndicated columnist in 1975. In this speech Mr. Brookes accurately outlined the transformation of the American economy from emphasizing manufacturing to focusing on information. He makes a parallel between this emphasis on information—the mind—and Jesus' teaching that the kingdom is within a person.*

April 1984 *Imprimis*

Christ was confronted, early in the second year of his teaching, by angry members of the "establishment church," the Pharisees who wanted to know when and where "the kingdom of God should come," and what it might look like.

It was a natural question for an entrenched bureaucracy to ask. It came out of the increasingly material political perspective of a religious establishment that had long since lost sight of its spiritual mission and was much more concerned with getting along with Caesar than with knowing God.

Jesus, always the spiritual radical, quickly rejected this political and material utopianism. "The kingdom of God cometh not with observation," he said (it is not a material state to be described for the eye). "Neither shall ye say lo here! or lo there! for, behold, the kingdom of God is within you."

Not only was this a profound statement of the mental and spiritual nature of reality, but it was an affirmation that, at its roots, salvation . . . was not collective, it was individual; not the result of the equitable distribution of physical assets by a benevolent state or king, but the *individual* apprehension and application of infinite spiritual laws and principles.

This was also a presentation of ideal government as the *self-government* of each individual. . . . And, lest the simple people who followed him might think this was too abstract to be humanly practical, Christ had already laid out the applicable metaphysical principles of this ideal in the Sermon on the Mount where he promised that if we would seek first the [kingdom of God], all of the material things we needed, food, clothing, shelter, comfort, would be added unto us.

Jesus was simply restating the underlying premise of Solomon's prayer to God, not for riches, but for "a wise and an understanding heart," which, in turn, would ensure his wealth and sovereignty. Or as the Proverb urges, "Wisdom is the principal thing; therefore get wisdom; and with all thy getting get understanding."

Like it or not, these basic principles have permeated and dominated Western culture and political and economic thought ever since. They have been especially important in America, where a De Tocqueville could quickly observe that the strength and greatness of America were in her "goodness," and that these flowed more out of her churches than from her undeniably vast material resources.

From our earliest settlers, most Americans have believed that wealth and prosperity were more a function of our spiritual values than our material good fortune—that mental attitudes and qualities (or lack of them) were the precursors of material progress, or the predictors of misfortune.

## Principles Forsaken

It is really only in the last decade or so that these metaphysical principles have been scornfully lumped together as "middle-class morality" or the "Puritan ethic," and severely challenged by an increasingly materialistic and secular "new class." America became a society whose academic and technological sophistication was growing by geometric leaps while its spiritual leadership was in rank decay and full retreat before the aggressive hedonism of the "Me generation" and the righteousness of the radical left.

In this media-hype milieu of pseudo-intellectualism, it was not hard for a nation nourished on the ofttimes harsh disciplines of Adam Smith's individual-centered micro-economics of the marketplace with its Spencerian emphasis on the survival of the economically fit, to reach out hungrily for the easy promises and seemingly compassionate claims of Keynesian macro-economics and the welfare state with its promise of collective economic comfort by centralized fine tuning.

Joseph Schumpeter's clear-eyed vision of the "creative destruction" process typical of a dynamically innovative democratic capitalism, where the production of wealth, not its redistribution, was paramount, was happily traded in for the more utopian visions of "demand management" and the pursuit of an ecologically "safe" environment. Dynamism and uncertainty were traded in for the vain pursuit of cycle-free equilibrium and social security (with small s's).

Keynes, the father of macro-economics, regarded technological advancement and innovation as largely "exogenous" shocks to be absorbed and dealt with by the macro-economic machine much in the way we might survive drought or natural disasters. This was compatible with the growing share of the intellectual and spiritual leadership of our country who had begun to regard technology itself through increasingly Luddite lenses. Though this new economic and political environmentalism is profoundly materialistic and humanistic in its precepts of "limits to growth" and "collective security," it unfortunately attracted important leaders within the American religious establishment (Council of Churches, Catholic bishops) who began to equate technology with rampant materialism.

## Metaphysical Resources

Yet, as we shall see, nothing could be further from the truth. In fact, it is precisely the extraordinary onslaught of what has come to be called "high technology" that seems to me to be moving us toward the ultimate realization of Judeo-Christian principles—namely that wealth is not physical, but metaphysical; that it is to be found not in matter, but in mind; and that being in mind, it is at once *individually* liberating and expansive, *universally* available and unifying.

John Naisbitt in *Megatrends* cites as his first and paramount trend the transformation of our industrial society into an information society. "It makes no sense," Naisbitt argues, "to reindustrialize an economy that is not based on industry, but on the production and distribution of information." In 1950, less than 17 percent of American workers were in "information jobs." Now more than 60 percent of us are, and by the year 2000 it is likely to be almost 80 percent of us.

We have already moved into what I call an economy in mind, and out of an economy premised solely on material or physical resources. We are going to have to reorient totally our thinking about the true nature of wealth. This floppy disc in my word processor is made up of about ten cents worth of plastic and paper. But the program it contains is worth over $300 on the market, and the work it can do in terms of informational output displaces thousands of hours of manual clerical labor. Because it translates that physical energy into informational bits, it expands our wealth, while taking nothing from our resources.

In this sense, high technology is demonstrating what Buckminster Fuller describes as the virtually unlimited "metaphysical component of wealth" which is continually enabling us to do more with less, and which, in Fuller's words "over the last 80 years has enabled us to go from less than 1 percent of the world's people living in any reasonable level of comfort to more than half of them living at a standard virtually unimagined at the turn of the twentieth century—and all this despite the apparent decline in so-called physical resources."

Increasingly, our wealth is coming not from stockpiles of material commodities, but from tape and floppy-disc files of information programs and knowledge. As David Birch of MIT has put it, "we are working our way out of the manufacturing business into the thinking business." Birch points out that almost 90 percent of the 21 million jobs that have been created in the U.S. since 1970 have come, not in goods-producing industries, but in the broad, non-manufacturing service sector which comprises this "thinking business."

In the last dozen years of transition into this "economy in mind," the U.S. by itself has created over four times as many jobs as did all the rest of the Western democratic nations of the Common Market and Japan put together. And we did all this, *mirabile dictu*, without the industrial planning help of Robert Reich, Gary Hart, or Walter Mondale.

## Bay State Miracle

As one who has watched the transformation of Massachusetts over the past decade from a stagnant industrial state to the flagship of the high technology armada, I am more convinced than ever that the "information society" is going to expand our economic horizons far beyond our wildest imagination.

Not only is Massachusetts now employing nearly 64 percent of its adult population (the highest of any state or nation in the world), but its unemployment rate today is 5.8 percent—and in most of the so-called "high tech" beltway, the rate is between 2 and 4 percent, too tight for comfort. Our state's personal income after stagnating down to 47th slowest growing in the country in 1978 is now among the top 10. And significantly, our greatest economic and employment growth is not in industrial production, or even in the hardware side of the computer business, but in the software or information-service side.

What is important about the Massachusetts experience, of course, is that it is the result not of raw material or physical resources of which we have pathetically little, but wholly a function of our knowledge industry, our universities and research centers.

Massachusetts, like Japan, is demonstrating that the further we move into high technology and the information economy, the less physical limits there are on our wealth creation potential. Indeed, Japan, with 0.3 percent of the world's land mass, now produces nearly 10 percent of the world's GNP, a ratio of 32.7 to 1. Even the U.S. has a ratio of only 3.6 to 1. By contrast, both Russia and China have negative ratios!

There is really nothing new about all of this. The Industrial Revolution itself was nothing more than the application of ideas and the energy of thought to replace human energy, material drudgery, and brute force. The effect of this transformation was, of course, to give vast new value to previously valueless resources.

## No Limits to Growth

We are learning that all economic activity is, as Schumpeter correctly defined it, the practice of technology, the use of our unfolding knowledge and intelligence to convert seemingly useless matter into increasingly useful and valuable products, to generate wealth where none existed before. True economics, like true metaphysics, is anti-entropy, the constant imposition of the order, utility, and organization on an otherwise chaotic and seemingly depleting material world.

It is this development of the metaphysical or "know-how" component of our wealth, which has both mystified and escaped what I call the "entropicists," those who are constantly citing the Second Law of Thermodynamics as an excuse to impose "limits to growth," and to put dampers on both technology and the growth of wealth itself.

Their premise is a purely engineering and materialistic view of the world which attempts to inventory our physical resources and set a time frame within which we will "run out," using this as a pretext on the one hand for rationing our utilization of these "finite" resources, and on the other for redistributing them "fairly" around the world. Yet because they take no account of the unlimited metaphysical component of our wealth, these inventories have again and again been completely confounded by actual experience.

Julian Simon's brilliant book, *The Ultimate Resource*, documents with endless statistics the fact that our natural resources are not running out; and indeed, that the history of mankind shows, instead, a constantly expanding resource base. "Because we find new lodes, invent better production methods, and discover new substitutes," Simon writes, "the ultimate constraint upon our capacity to enjoy unlimited raw materials at acceptable prices is knowledge . . . and the source of knowledge is the human mind."

Jesus put it more simply, "It is the spirit that quickeneth; the flesh profiteth nothing." This was not merely a religious truth, but a practical statement of an infinite spiritual reality that we are only now beginning to understand, namely that it is in the ideas and concepts of mind that we find real wealth, not in depletable material resources.

## More Wealth, More Fairly Distributed

Carrying it a step further, I would suggest that the Christ-message which Jesus brought was not that maudlin sentimentalization of poverty and false humility which is sometimes idealized by the church, but rather a message of the glories of spiritual (thus real) abundance in the realm of mind: "I am come that they might have life, and that they might have it more abundantly."

It must be clear that the very thing that concerns many churchly leaders and liberal politicians, namely the seeming injustice of the maldistribution of the world's goods, was the direct result of our universal perception of the physical scarcity of those goods, a perception which led in turn to what Bucky Fuller has called "the pirate mentality" of both capitalism and socialism, the constant battle to control physical resources.

The solution to that cruel economics of scarcity may well be developing before our eyes, as we move from an economy of material limits to an economy of unlimited mind. Not only will this make wealth more infinitely available, it should make it more accessible to everyone. On the one hand, this new information economy will vastly extend the creative wealth potential of the individual human being. On the other, its universal availability will break down the corporate and nationalistic barriers and structures that now divide us. It will both liberate us—and unify us.

Recently we were treated to the spectacle of some Milwaukee teenagers using their wits and their personal computers to access some of the nation's most sophisticated and secure computer data banks from New York to California.

While the press and the politicians focused on the need for new forms of security and defense against such easy access, the incident demonstrated a simple fact: Once we translate wealth from guardable physical assets to the total fungibility of mental and intellectual concepts, or information, we will have destroyed forever the notion that wealth can be monopolized, partitioned—or even redistributed, for that matter.

In the future, our individual and collective access to the world's expanding informational wealth will be more a function of our educational systems than of our relative position and power. Distribution of the world's wealth will inevitably be broadened and shared more equally in direct proportion to the availability of literacy, knowledge, and understanding.

Which is to say that we are rapidly moving back to the Judeo-Christian concept of individual as sovereign and of wealth as the result of mental and spiritual search. In a funny sort of way, the computer is showing us that the "kingdom" is within our individual consciousness, and that its horizons are limited only by the development of one's mental and spiritual capacity.

## Market Dynamism Accelerating

Small wonder the pharisees and bureaucrats who now dominate our institutions, from government to church to multinational corporations, are so worried. In the economy of mind, we are now seeing what John Naisbitt describes, on the one hand, as the rapid shift from a national to a global market economy, united by satellites and the universal communications network, and on the other hand the trend within nations from centralization to decentralization.

The more cumbersome and gargantuan conglomerates are already starting to come apart at the seams. De-centralization and spin-offs are the new hallmark of our surprisingly entrepreneurial times. The "creative destruction" of Joseph Schumpeter's thesis is being accelerated by the information revolution, and it applies not only to products and industries, but to all institutional structures.

Is it really any wonder that in the last two years alone, this nation has witnessed the formation, in the middle of a deep recession, of more than 1.1 million new businesses, an all-time record? It may come as a shock that even though business failures reached a record high of 23,000 last year, the positive ratio of formations to failures in the last two years was a stunning 28 to one. With failures at 3.5 percent of total starts, 1981 and 1982 were our two strongest "new business years" in history.

In the economy of mind, everything is going micro, not macro; individual, not collective; toward dynamism, not equilibrium. The revival of classical supply-side economics, with its emphasis on the micro-incentives and rational responses of the individual in the marketplace, its drive for reduction of centralized bureaucratic interference in this marketplace, is thus a logical result of our times and our technology—not merely an economic fad of electoral politics.

Adam Smith is becoming more, not less relevant. The markets are becoming more efficient with each passing year and each new generation of informational technology—and infinitely more difficult either to manipulate or to regulate.

Over the last four years we have watched the Federal Reserve, for example, try valiantly to "fine tune" the growth of the money supply. Yet each day it becomes more difficult to know what that money supply looks like, or how it can be defined, let alone controlled. A deregulated financial system, coupled with an increasingly sophisticated communications network, has begun to impose its own discipline upon both the Federal Reserve and the federal government.

We have been forced, in a very curious kind of way, back on to a worldwide proxy gold and commodity standard, in which investors now freely move in and out of one paper currency or another, or back into metals, depending on their rational expectations of its future value, and our central banks have been forced to deal with these flows in much the same way the discipline of the gold or silver standards used to operate.

This, in turn, is imposing the discipline of the market upon both the profligacy of politicians, and the failures of corporate management. Through the universal democracy of the marketplace the individual investor (and there are now more than 40 million of them in America alone) has reasserted his political and economic sovereignty. His money market fund has become his political instrument, his vote of confidence-or-not, in the government system. While electoral politics may be suffering from apathy, the market is feverishly democratic!

## Higher Integrity from High-Tech

And, most important of all, the informational economy in mind is inevitably enforcing a new level of integrity in the affairs of mankind—although I admit this is contrary to the current

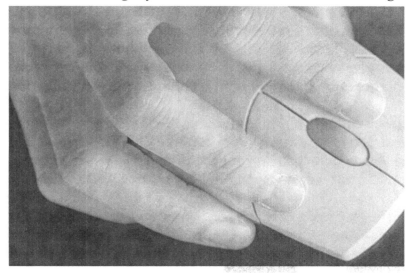

perceptions and appearances of moral degradation. "High technology" may be just that, the thrust of the human spirit into the infinite realm of pure intellect, where the premium for performance has always been integrity, honesty, discipline, logic, and excellence.

Just as Adam Smith's Invisible Hand (the capitalization, significantly, is Smith's own) makes the marketplace a cruel taskmaster for the greedy, the inefficient, the manipulative, and the cheat, so the new realm of the informational economy in mind will exact its toll on those who attempt to violate its systematic integrity or treat it with ignorance or venality.

This may be why so many young people are now taking to computers with such alacrity. They are discovering in them something that may have been missing in their homes and schools—the delight of order, of harmony, of logic, and the comforting security of discipline, along with an ability to open for them the infinite horizons of thought. Their parents may have given them uncertain guidance in right and wrong, but the ethical trumpet of the computer is never muffled or unclear.

All of which points to a fundamental fact: the only government really possible in this new worldwide, free-wheeling, freely accessible information society is individual self-government, and such self-government will be imposed to a considerable degree by the technology itself. Increasingly, all other forms of government will remain viable only so far as they do not interfere with the unregulatable and illimitable systems of mind.

The only thing that interferes with this Invisible Hand of the self-disciplining marketplace is government's clumsy attempts to insulate us from it or to meddle in it. Black markets and their ancillary forms exist only because government tries to regulate prices or supplies. Bribery and extortion are the direct result of regulation, taxes, and licensure. Most white-collar crime depends on government regulation to support it and/or tax policies to make it profitable. It is excessive government by men instead of by laws that breeds lawlessness and venality.

## How Paternalism Cheats Minorities

Yet nothing in the area of individual crimes can begin to match the systematic degradation, dehumanization, and cultural genocide that have been wreaked on black Americans, who must now face the prospect of the emerging economy in mind with more apprehension than any other group in our society—because the government in recent decades, with the best of intentions, has seduced blacks out of the rigors of the marketplace and into the stifling womb of the welfare state.

In 1962 only one black family in 20 was on welfare. Only one black child in 6 was born to a fatherless home. Black youth employment was at an even higher ratio than that of whites, and youth unemployment for that group was at 10-12 percent, roughly the same as whites.

Today, one black family in 5 is on welfare, and 55 percent of all black children were born to unwed mothers last year. Black youth unemployment is 40 percent, nearly triple that of whites, while black employment ratios have actually declined, even as white ratios have soared.

The Census Bureau freely admits that the greatest cause of rising poverty today, particularly among blacks, is the soaring incidence of female-headed households and the tragic destruction of the black American family, a tragedy which has no parallel among blacks in the rest of the world.

For more than half of all young black Americans, there is now the danger that the economy in mind with its new demands for literacy, education, and self-discipline will represent a far greater natural barrier to economic survival than the most virulent forms of racial segregation and injustice.

The National Bureau of Economic Research in mid-1983 completed an enormous study of employment, education, and income potential of inner-city minority youths. The picture it painted was that of a whole ethnic culture destroyed by the government-imposed market disincentives to work, and by the impact of those disincentives on criminal behavior, family breakup, weak education, and poor job-experience.

Curiously enough, the NBER found that the only significant thing that changed the otherwise predictable career outcome of inner-city youth, the only clearly causative determinant of those who escape, was regular church-going, which the NBER study showed cut illegal activities by 20 percent, drug use by 23 percent, and increased income potential by a whopping 47 percent.

Main Street values still live, but they do so in spite of the modern pseudo-moralists of both church and state who have left vast numbers of American youth ill-equipped to deal with the evolving information society with its growing demands for self-discipline and integrity of thought and action, and who now tell them that their only salvation lies in still greater dependence on the "kingdom without."

## Values Underlie Value

The tragedy of the black experience in the last two decades makes it abundantly clear that without the renewal of individual values, without standards and discipline, without the spiritual as well as moral education of the individual soul, indeed without a genuine revival of the search for the kingdom within, the nations of the West will no longer be able to lead. They could self-destruct. Wisdom and science are implacably ethical and demanding. In an information age, the quality of our thinking will directly affect the wealth of our nation, even more than it always has.

Jefferson warned that "if a nation expects to be ignorant and free, in a state of civilization, it expects what never was, and never will be." He understood better than most that even in the vast untapped material resources of the New World, true wealth was always more a function of what you know, than what you have.

Charles Steinmetz, the visionary electrical engineer, said in 1930, of all things:

> I think the greatest discovery will be made along spiritual lines. Here is a force which history clearly teaches has been the greatest power in the development of men and history. Yet we have merely been playing with it and have never seriously studied it as we have the physical forces. Some day people will learn that material things do not bring happiness, and are of little use in making men and women creative and powerful. Then the scientists of the world will turn their laboratories over to the study of God and prayer, and the spiritual forces that have hardly been scratched. . . .

# Free to Choose:
# A Conversation with Milton Friedman
## (2006)

*Milton Friedman (1912-2006) received a doctorate from Columbia University in 1946. He taught at the University of Chicago and later worked with the Hoover Institution at Stanford University. Friedman received the Nobel Prize in Economics in 1976. Dr. Friedman and his wife, Rose (also an economist), published* Free to Choose, *a defense and explanation of free-market ideas, in 1980. A ten-part PBS series by the same title featuring the Friedmans also aired that year. One of his main areas of study was the influence of monetary policy on the economy. He discussed this and other issues in this interview with Hillsdale College president Larry Arnn a few months before Friedman's death.*

**LARRY ARNN**: In *Free to Choose,* in the chapter on "The Tyranny of Controls," you argue that protectionism and government intervention in general breed conflict and that free markets breed cooperation. How do you reconcile this statement with the fact that we think of free markets as being competitive?

**MILTON FRIEDMAN**: They are competitive, but they are competitive over a broad range. The question is, how do you make money in a free market? You only make money if you can provide someone with something he or she is willing to pay for. You can't make money any other way. Therefore, in order to make money, you have to promote cooperation. You have to do something that your customer wants you to do. You don't do it because he orders you to. You don't do it because he threatens to hit you over the head if you don't. You do it because you offer him a better deal than he can get anywhere else. Now that's promoting cooperation. But there are other people who are trying to sell to him, too. They're your competitors. So there is competition among sellers, but cooperation between sellers and buyers.

**LA**: In the chapter on "The Tyranny of Controls," you seem gloomy about the prospects for India. Why?

**MF**: I was in India in 1955 on behalf of the American government to serve as an economic adviser to the minister of finance. I concluded then that India had tremendous potential, but none of it was being achieved. That fact underlies

*Milton and Rose Friedman,*

the passage you are referring to in *Free to Choose.* Remember, *Free to Choose* aired in January 1980, and as of that time there had been no progress in India. The population had grown, but the standard of living was as low as it had been in 1955. Now, in the past ten or fifteen years, there has been movement in India, and maybe those hidden potentials I saw in 1955 will finally be achieved. But, there is still great uncertainty there.

**LA**: In that same chapter, you wrote the following about China: "Letting the genie of . . . initiative out of the bottle even to this limited extent will give rise to political problems that, sooner or later, are likely to produce a reaction toward greater authoritarianism. The opposite outcome, the collapse of communism and its replacement by a market system, seems far less likely." What do you think about that statement today?

**MF:** I'm much more optimistic about China today than I was then. China has made great progress since that time. It certainly has not achieved complete political freedom, but it has come closer. It certainly has a great deal more economic freedom. I visited China for the first time in 1980 right after the publication of *Free to Choose*. I had been invited by the government to lecture on how to stop inflation, among other things. China at that time was in a pretty poor state. The hotel we stayed in showed every sign of being run by a communist regime. We returned to China twice, and each time, the changes were tremendous. In 1980, everybody was wearing the dull and drab Mao costume; there were bicycles all over the place and very few cars. Eight years later, we started to see some color in the clothes, there were things available for sale that hadn't been available before, and free markets were breaking out all over the place. China has continued to grow at a dramatic rate. But in the section of *Free to Choose* you refer to, I talked about the political conflict that was coming—and that broke out in Tiananmen Square. The final outcome in China will not be decided until there is a showdown between the political tyranny on the one hand and economic freedom on the other—they cannot coexist.

**LA:** Let me ask you about demographic trends. Columnist Mark Steyn writes that in ten years, 40 percent of young men in the world are going to be living in oppressed Muslim countries. What do you think the effect of that is going to be?

**MF:** What happens will depend on whether we succeed in bringing some element of greater economic freedom to those Muslim countries. Just as India in 1955 had great but unrealized potential, I think the Middle East is in a similar situation today. In part this is because of the curse of oil. Oil has been a blessing from one point of view, but a curse from another. Almost every country in the Middle East that is rich in oil is a despotism.

**LA:** Why do you think that is so?

**MF:** One reason, and one reason only—the oil is owned by the governments in question. If that oil were privately owned and thus someone's private property, the political outcome would be freedom rather than tyranny. This is why I believe the first step following the 2003 invasion of Iraq should have been the privatization of the oil fields. If the government had given every individual over 21 years of age equal shares in a corporation that had the right and responsibility to make appropriate arrangements with foreign oil companies for the purpose of discovering and developing Iraq's oil reserves, the oil income would have flowed in the form of dividends to the people—the shareholders—rather than into government coffers. This would have provided an income to the whole people of Iraq and thereby prevented the current disputes over oil between the Sunnis, Shiites and Kurds, because oil income would have been distributed on an individual rather than a group basis.

**LA:** Many Middle Eastern societies have a kind of tribal or theocratic basis and long-held habits of despotic rule that make it difficult to establish a system of contract between strangers. Is it your view that the introduction of free markets in such places could overcome those obstacles?

**MF:** Eventually, yes. I think that nothing is so important for freedom as recognizing in the law each individual's natural right to property, and giving individuals a sense that they own something that they're responsible for, that they have control over, and that they can dispose of.

**LA:** Is there an area here in the United States in which we have not been as aggressive as we should in promoting property rights and free markets?

**MF**: Yes, in the field of medical care. We have a socialist-communist system of distributing medical care. Instead of letting people hire their own physicians and pay them, no one pays his or her own medical bills. Instead, there's a third party payment system. It is a communist system and it has a communist result. Despite this, we've had numerous miracles in medical science. From the discovery of penicillin, to new surgical techniques, to MRIs and CAT scans, the last 30 or 40 years have been a period of miraculous change in medical science. On the other hand, we've seen costs skyrocket. Nobody is happy: physicians don't like it, patients don't like it. Why? Because none of them are responsible for themselves. You no longer have a situation in which a patient chooses a physician, receives a service, gets charged, and pays for it. There is no direct relation between the patient and the physician. The physician is an employee of an insurance company or an employee of the government. Today, a third party pays the bills. As a result, no one who visits the doctor asks what the charge is going to be—somebody else is going to take care of that. The end result is third party payment and, worst of all, third party treatment.

**LA**: Following the recent expansion in prescription drug benefits and Medicare, what hope is there for a return to the free market in medical care?

**MF**: It does seem that markets are on the defensive, but there is hope. The expansion of drug benefits was accompanied by the introduction of health savings accounts—HSAs. That's the one hopeful sign in the medical area, because it's a step in the direction of making people responsible for themselves and for their own care. No one spends somebody else's money as carefully as he spends his own.

**LA**: On the subject of Social Security, let me read to you a passage from *Free to Choose*: "As we have gone through the literature on Social Security, we have been shocked at the arguments that have been used to defend the program. Individuals who would not lie to their children, their friends, their colleagues, whom all of us would trust implicitly in the most important personal dealings, have propagated a false view of Social Security. Their intelligence and exposure to contrary views make it hard to believe that they have done so unintentionally and innocently. Apparently they have regarded themselves as an elite group within society that knows what is good for other people better than those people do for themselves." What do you think of these words today?

**MF**: I stick by every word there. But there has been progress since then. Let me explain: *Free to Choose* was produced and shown on television for the first time in January 1980. President Reagan was elected in November 1980. To get a clear picture of what has happened since the publication of *Free to Choose*, we really need to look at what happened before and after the election of Ronald Reagan. Before Reagan, non-defense government spending—on the federal, state and local levels—as a percentage of national income was rising rapidly. Between the early 1950s and 1980, we were in a period of what I would call galloping socialism that showed no signs of slowing. Following the election of Ronald Reagan, there was an abrupt and immediate halt to this expansion of government. But even under Reagan, government spending as a percentage of national income didn't come down: It has held constant from that time to now. Although the early years of the current Bush presidency did see spending increases, national income has risen, too. We have achieved some success at our first task: stopping the growth of government. The second task is to shrink government spending and make government smaller. We haven't done that yet, but we are making some progress. I should also mention as a cautionary tale that, prior to Reagan, the number of pages in the Federal Register was on the rise, but Reagan succeeded in reducing this number substantially. However, once Reagan was out of office, the number of pages in the Register began to rise even more quickly. We have not really succeeded in that area.

There have been real changes in our society since *Free to Choose* was published. I'm not attributing them to *Free to Choose*—I'm not saying that's the reason—but in general, there has been a complete change in public opinion. This change is probably due as much to the collapse of the Soviet Union as it is to what Friedrich Hayek or Milton Friedman or somebody else wrote. Socialism used to mean the ownership and operation of the means of production, but nobody gives it that meaning today. There is no country in the world attempting to be socialist in that sense except North Korea. And perhaps Russia is moving in that direction. Conversely, opinion has not shifted far enough in terms of the dangers of big government and the deleterious effects it can have, and that's where we're facing future problems. This clarifies the task facing institutions such as Hillsdale College: We must make clear that the only reason we have our freedom is because government is so inefficient. If the government were efficient in spending the approximately 40 percent of our income that it currently manages, we would enjoy less freedom than we do today.

**LA**: In *Free to Choose* you discuss Abraham Lincoln's "House Divided" speech, which you relate to the great task that the American people face. Like Lincoln, you argue that a house divided against itself cannot stand: America is going to be a government intervention country or it's going to be a free market country, but it cannot continue indefinitely as a mixture of both. Do you still believe that?

**MF**: Yes, I very much believe that, and I believe that we've been making some headway since *Free to Choose* appeared. However, even though it is real headway compared to what was happening before, we are mostly holding ground.

**LA**: What do you think are the major factors behind the economic growth we have experienced since the publication of *Free to Choose*?

**MF**: Economic growth since that time has been phenomenal, which has very little to do with most of what we've been talking about in terms of the conflict between government and private enterprise. It has much more to do with the technical problem of establishing sound monetary policy. The economic situation during the past 20 years has been unprecedented in the history of the world. You will find no other 20-year period in which prices have been as stable—relatively speaking—in which there has been as little variability in price levels, in which inflation has been so well-controlled, and in which output has gone up as regularly. You hear all this talk about economic difficulties, when the fact is we are at the absolute peak of prosperity in the history of the world. Never before have so many people had as much as they do today. I believe a large part of that is to be attributed to better monetary policy. The improved policy is a result of the acceptance of the view that inflation is a monetary phenomenon, not a real phenomenon. We have accepted the view that central banks are primarily responsible for maintaining stable prices and nothing else.

**LA**: Do you think the Great Depression was triggered by bad monetary policy at a crucial moment?

**MF**: Absolutely. Unfortunately, it is still the case that if you ask people what caused the Great Depression, nine out of ten will probably tell you it was a failure of business. But it's absolutely clear that the Depression was a failure of government and not a failure of business.

**LA**: You don't think the Smoot-Hawley tariff caused the Depression?

**MF**: No. I think the Smoot-Hawley tariff was a bad law. I think it did harm. But the Smoot-Hawley tariff by itself would not have made one quarter of the labor force unemployed. However, reducing the quantity of money by one third did make a quarter of the labor force unemployed. When I graduated from undergraduate college in 1932, I was baffled by the fact that there were idle machines and idle men and you couldn't get them together. Those men wanted to cooperate; they wanted to work; they wanted to produce what they wore; and they wanted to produce the food they ate. Yet something had gone wrong: The government was mismanaging the money supply.

**LA**: Do you think our government has learned its lesson about how to manage the money supply?

**MF**: I think that the lesson has been learned, but I don't think it will last forever. Sooner or later, government will want to raise funds without imposing taxes. It will want to spend money it does not have. So I hesitate to join those who are predicting two percent inflation for the next 20 years. The temptation for government to lay its hands on that money is going to be very hard to resist. The fundamental problem is that you shouldn't have an institution such as the Federal Reserve, which depends for its success on the abilities of its chairman. My first preference would be to abolish the Federal Reserve, but that's not going to happen.

**LA**: I want to talk now about education and especially about vouchers, because I know they are dear to your heart. Why do you think teachers unions oppose vouchers?

**MF**: The president of the National Education Association was once asked when his union was going to do something about students. He replied that when the students became members of the union, the union would take care of them. And that was a correct answer. Why? His responsibility as president of the NEA was to serve the members of his union, not to serve public purposes. I give him credit: The trade union has been very effective in serving its members. However, in the process, they've destroyed American education. But you see, education isn't the union's function. It's our fault for allowing the union to pursue its agenda. Consider this fact: There are two areas in the United States that suffer from the same disease—education is one and health care is the other. They both suffer from the disease that takes a system that should be bottom-up and converts it into a system that is top-down. Education is a simple case. It isn't the public purpose to build brick schools and have students taught there. The public purpose is to provide education. Think of it this way: If you want to subsidize the production of a product, there are two ways you can do it. You can subsidize the producer or you can subsidize the consumer. In education, we subsidize the producer— the school. If you subsidize the student instead—the consumer—you will have competition. The student could choose the school he attends and that would force schools to improve and to meet the demands of their students.

**LA**: Although you discuss many policy issues in *Free to Choose*, you have turned much of your attention to education, and to vouchers as a method of education reform. Why is that your focus?

**MF**: I don't see how we can maintain a decent society if we have a world split into haves and have-nots, with the haves subsidizing the have-nots. In our current educational system, close to 30 percent of the youngsters who start high school never finish. They are condemned to low-income jobs. They are condemned to a situation in which they are going to be at the bottom. That leads in turn to a divisive society; it leads to a stratified society rather than one of general cooperation and general understanding. The effective literacy rate in the United States today is almost surely less than it was 100 years ago. Before government had any involvement in education, the majority of youngsters were schooled, literate, and able to learn. It is a disgrace that in a country like the United States, 30 percent of youngsters never graduate from high school. And I haven't even mentioned those who drop out in elementary school. It's a disgrace that there are so many people who can't read and write. It's hard for me to see how we can continue to maintain a decent and free society if a large subsection of that society is condemned to poverty and to handouts.

**LA**: Do you think the voucher campaign is going well?

**MF:** No. I think it's going much too slowly. What success we have had is almost entirely in the area of income-limited vouchers. There are two kinds of vouchers: One is a charity voucher that is limited to people below a certain income level. The other is an education voucher, which, if you think of vouchers as a way of transforming the educational industry, is available to everybody. How can we make vouchers available to everybody? First, education ought to be a state and local matter, not a federal matter. The 1994 Contract with America called for the elimination of the Department of Education. Since then, the budget for the Department of Education has tripled. This trend must be reversed. Next, education ought to be a parental matter. The responsibility for educating children is with parents. But in order to make it a parental matter, we must have a situation in which parents are free to choose the schools their children attend. They aren't free to do that now. Today the schools pick the children. Children are assigned to schools by geography—by where they live. By contrast, I would argue that if the government is going to spend money on education, the money ought to travel with the children. The objective of such an expenditure ought to be educated children, not beautiful buildings. The way to accomplish this is to have a universal voucher. As I said in 1955, we should take the amount of money that we're now spending on education, divide it by the number of children, and give that amount of money to each parent. After all, that's what we're spending now, so we might as well let parents spend it in the form of vouchers.

**LA:** I have one more question for you. You describe a society in which people look after themselves because they know the most about themselves, and they will flourish if you let them. You, however, are a crusader for the rights of others. For example, you say in *Free to Choose*—and it's a very powerful statement—a tiny minority is what matters. So is it one of the weaknesses of the free market that it requires certain extremely talented and disinterested people who can defend it?

**MF:** No, that's not right. The self-interest of the kind of people you just described is promoting public policy. That's what they're interested in doing. For example, what was my self-interest in economics? My self-interest to begin with was to understand the real mystery and puzzle that was the Great Depression. My self-interest was to try to understand why that happened, and that's what I enjoyed doing—that was my self-interest. Out of that I grew to learn some things—to have some knowledge. Following that, my self-interest was to see that other people understood the same things and took appropriate action.

**LA:** Do you define self-interest as what the individual wants?

**MF:** Yes, self-interest is what the individual wants. Mother Teresa, to take one example, operated on a completely self-interested basis. Self-interest does not mean narrow self-interest. Self-interest does not mean monetary self-interest. Self-interest means pursuing those things that are valuable to you but which you can also persuade others to value. Such things very often go beyond immediate material interest.

**LA:** Does that mean self-interest is a synonym for self-sacrifice?

**MF:** If you want to see how pervasive this sort of self-interest is that I'm describing, look at the enormous amount of money contributed after Hurricane Katrina. That was a tremendous display of self-interest: The self-interest of people in that case was to help others. Self-interest, rightly understood, works for the benefit of society as a whole.

# American Free Trade Policy: Rhetoric or Reality?
## Shavano Seminar on Free Trade
## (1989)

*This discussion of free trade is a summary of a conference sponsored by Hillsdale College in 1988. No author was identified.*

August 1989 *Imprimis*

The long and often bitter controversy surrounding last spring's passage of the Omnibus Trade and Competitiveness Act of 1988 underscored the importance of international trade in America's economic life. While there is broad agreement that we should do everything we can to increase U.S. exports, there is heated debate over what to do about sales of foreign goods inside the United States, as well as about how to respond when other countries impede the flow of American products into their markets.

The two main sides of this debate were represented at Hillsdale's Shavano Institute for National Leadership conference on international trade, held August 30-31, 1989 in Louisville, Kentucky. Some speakers championed the free trade philosophy of minimum government interference, while fair trade advocates called for aggressive government moves to boost exports and counter penetration of the U.S. market.

Marshall Loeb, managing editor of *Fortune* magazine, decried what he said were three "myths" which have dominated the discussion of trade and influenced the trade bill: (1) that U.S. industry is becoming less competitive, (2) that the manufacturing portion of America's gross national product is decreasing, and (3) that restricting imports creates jobs and protects the U.S. economy.

"American business is now going through a crash diet of cutbacks, spin-offs and restructuring that is permanently changing the structure of the economy," he said. "After years of stagnation, U.S. manufacturing productivity is rising sharply. In 1987 it went up about 3.5 percent, more than double the rate of the mid to late 1970s and faster than Japan's or Germany's."

Moreover, Loeb pointed out that manufacturing currently accounts for about 20 percent of GNP, "almost exactly the figure that existed 10 or 15 years ago." And he maintained that when import restrictions are applied, "we do preserve a number of jobs, but basically, those jobs are in outmoded, declining industries."

Several speakers insisted that too much emphasis is placed on the fact that the U.S. imports more than it exports. Rather, they insisted that concern about the "trade deficit" overlooks America's real economic strength.

Economist and author George Gilder saw strongly positive implications in the imports vs. exports statistics. "What happened in the early 1980s is that the United States began growing much faster than it had in the '70s, and much faster, in fact, than its trading partners were growing," he said. "If you're an exporter from the United States, and you're exporting to a stagnant global market, clearly you won't be able to expand your exports as fast as an exporter from a country that faces a booming American market."

Gilder suggested that the trade deficit, rather than being a threat to America's economy, is actually beneficial, because much of the money earned by foreign exporters is reinvested in the U.S.

"The other side of a trade gap is necessarily a capital surplus," he said. "That's what it means when they say the United States is becoming a net debtor. People want to lend us money. And during this period when our debts were increasing, our assets were increasing much more rapidly." Gilder explained that the value of assets owned by American companies increased from 180 percent of gross national product in 1980 to 240 percent currently.

Anthony Harrigan, president of the U.S. Business and Industrial Council, disagreed sharply with the explanations of the trade situation offered by Loeb and Gilder. He voiced the view, heard frequently during the debate on the trade bill, that American companies are being overwhelmed by foreign competition, and American jobs are being lost to overseas workers.

Expressing the U.S.B.I.C.'s position on trade, Harrigan said, "The U.S. should curb the movement of American jobs offshore. This is a disaster for employees, suppliers and affected communities. It's a design for the collapse of the U.S. as a producer nation." And he took no comfort in Gilder's figures about manufacturing's GNP share. "The U.S. has the lowest share of GNP engaged in manufacturing of any industrial nation," he said.

Harrigan's view of foreign capital was no more positive. "We find absurd the argument that we are exchanging pieces of paper—dollars—for real goods," he said. "We don't believe our trading partners are fools. They are using these pieces of paper to buy corporate assets in the United States."

Raymond Waldmann, former assistant secretary of commerce for international economic policy, suggested that free trade is an ideal no longer attainable. "Traders, businessmen and investors should be able to make decisions based on market signals, with little or no interference from governments," he said. But he pointed out that about one third of foreign markets for U.S. goods are covered by import restrictions, and he insisted, "All governments, even those with highly capitalistic systems, intervene in international economic matters in a wide and bewildering variety of ways. A large proportion of trade is managed by governments, and the proportion is increasing."

Waldmann suggested that the U.S. is hobbled by its idealism. "We urge free trade for all countries, because it has worked for us," he said. "In a sense, our insistence has provided a 'free trade umbrella.' We have allowed other countries to have it both ways: free access to the United States, the largest market in the world, while they manage their own trade."

Edward Hudgins, a policy analyst for the Washington-based Heritage Foundation, took issue with Waldmann's assertion that the U.S. market has been open while other countries have restricted U.S.-made goods. "Over the last six years the United States has enacted more new trade barriers than any country in the industrialized world," he said. "We have created a cartel in steel, in computer chips with the Japanese. We have quotas against Japanese automobiles. Sugar imports have gone down, because of our quota system. We've tightened the textile trade and numerous others."

Harrigan was outspoken in urging the extension of U.S. trade barriers. He stated flatly, "We don't regard protectionism as a dirty word." The key economic force in the world today, he said, is nationalism, and "only the United States fails to assert its national interest."

Loeb pointed out that protectionism has its price, and it can be expensive. He cited the costs in higher prices to American consumers of protecting jobs in various domestic industries, such as $5.8 billion spent to protect 55,000 jobs in the U.S. auto industry (or $105,000 per job), and $6.8 billion to protect 9,000 jobs in the carbon steel industry (or $750,000 per job).

Louis Dehmlow, former chairman of the National Association of Wholesaler-Distributors, suggested that barriers protect manufacturing jobs, but invite reprisals that cause other hardships.

"Unfair trade is presumed to be something the other fellows are doing to us," he said. "Not so—it's what we do to ourselves, because we don't apply the basics of the marketplace. Instead of building protectionism to destroy world trade, we should do what is necessary in the entrepreneurial sense: be customer-oriented, and push our products with marketing and innovation."

U.S. Rep. Philip Crane, Republican congressman from Illinois and a Hillsdale alumnus, provided historical background on U.S. trade, and cautioned against being too aggressive in imposing protective measures. "You don't go to a people as proud as the Japanese, put their backs against the wall, and say. 'You've got a timetable, and you'd better observe it, or we're going to bash you,'" he said.

He insisted that the way to eliminate barriers was by positive example, such as the U.S.-Canada trade agreement, which was then before the Canadian parliament, and would eliminate virtually every restriction on products moving between Canada and the U.S.

Yoshiji Nogami, economic counselor to the Embassy of Japan, offered a Japanese perspective on U.S. trade policy. "People [in the U.S.] tend to say that whatever is different from the American system is unfair. When American agriculture is subsidized, it's called export enhancement. But when the European Economic Community subsidizes agricultural products, it's unfair. Japanese beef can't be exported to the U.S., and that is not unfair. On the other hand, we buy 30 percent of our total [beef] consumption from the United States, and that's fair. This fairness/unfairness concept is very whimsical."

Nogami said that the Japanese government is prepared to go to the World Court to fight any U.S. measure which Japan considers unacceptable under the new bill.

The discussion of trade in Louisville was wide ranging, touching even on the moral aspects of international commerce. Hudgins, especially, saw a moral dimension in the trade issue. "The fundamental principle which I believe the free market is based upon is the idea of individual choice," he said. "Protectionism is an attempt to gain a value from somebody through force, by prohibiting them from buying from some other group and forcing them to buy from you. Protectionism is a form of extortion."

*Packing Oranges for Export
Near the Mediterranean Sea, Early 1900s*

Margaret Maxey, professor from the University of Texas at Austin, saw a moral responsibility to extend trade in order to help developing countries. She suggested that the major trading nations must become less concerned with protecting "little fiefdoms of privilege," and think more about how trade can "take people in Third World nations, and give them the incentive of enterprise and entrepreneurship. If we want to drive a nail into the coffin of war," she said, "we must turn have-not nations into prosperous states."

## How Nations Manage Trade

Governments use several techniques to boost exports of their own industries and to try to protect domestic manufacturers and domestic jobs from the competition of imported products. . . .

## Quotas

The most direct method is the imposition of outright quotas, or numerical limits, on quantities of certain types of products imported from specific countries or from all overseas sources. This method is usually employed to protect domestic industries (or their unions) that are especially hard hit by imports, that are generally on shaky economic ground, or that have special political clout.

## Tariffs

Imposing a tariff, or import duty, has an effect similar to a direct quota (and is done for the same reasons), but relies more on the market as the mechanism to control the flow of imports. Demand for a foreign good decreases, because the duty makes its price uncompetitive with equivalent domestic products. Import duties also provide revenue for the government, an advantage of the tariff system not lost on lawmakers.

## Non-Tariff Barriers

A more subtle method for suppressing imports is by imposing regulations or requirements that make it costly and troublesome for overseas manufacturers to invade the domestic market. Such measures include product standards, labeling requirements, health and safety inspections, or special insurance imposed on imports but not on domestic products. Governments, which are major consumers of all kinds of items themselves, can also restrict their own procurement to domestic products. Non-tariff barriers (or "NTBs") can be highly effective in discouraging foreign competition, when the more direct methods of tariffs and quotas are unfeasible or politically inconvenient.

## Export Subsidies

Rather than block foreign competition (or often in addition to raising barriers), governments try to give their domestic manufacturers a leg up by subsidizing exports. Low-interest loans, grants, tax incentives and other mechanisms are used widely, generally in the name of "economic development."

## Countertrade

An increasing number of countries are attempting to balance imports with their own exports by insisting that foreign sellers must take domestic products, instead of money, in payment for their goods. Bartering now accounts for 25 to 30 percent of all world trade.

## Special Agreements

A government can negotiate an arrangement with another country to mutually limit exports, and attempt to stabilize both markets. Or special trading preferences can be arranged that shut out third parties or establish special trade areas, such as the European Common Market. Also, cartels can be created by groups of countries wishing to promote key industries they have in common, such as the OPEC oil cartel.

## Embargoes

The most drastic method used to control trade is imposing a complete embargo on certain types of products or on the goods of a particular nation. Prohibiting imports or exports is done mainly in wartime to deny commerce with an enemy. But it can also be used to enforce some critical national policy (such as President Jimmy Carter's embargo on grain sales to the Soviets after their invasion of Afghanistan), or to punish a trading partner for breaking an agreement or trading in bad faith.

*Poster for the New York City Department of Docks, c. 1938*

# Free Trade Under Attack:
# What Americans Can Do
## Murray L. Weidenbaum (1984)

*After serving as chairman of the Economics Department at Washington University in St. Louis, Murray Weidenbaum was named the university's Mallinckrodt Distinguished Professor of Economics. In 1981-1982, he served as the first chairman of the Council of Economic Advisors under President Ronald Reagan. Dr. Weidenbaum received his doctorate from Princeton University. He has written seven books and hundreds of articles. In this lecture, Dr. Weidenbaum discusses issues related to free trade versus trade restrictions. Some of the specific circumstances he mentions have changed since 1984, but the principles involved remain relevant to economic issues today.*

July 1984 *Imprimis*

For a conservative economist, it is a great pleasure to present the Ludwig von Mises Lecture. I will try to do him appropriate honor by dealing with the current and pressing problem of maintaining free markets at a time of rising protectionist pressures.

The sad fact is that the open trading system of the free world is under attack at home and abroad. It is especially important, therefore, that we reinforce our intellectual defense of the free market, especially its international dimensions.

The case for free trade is rooted in a basic economic law: the principle of comparative advantage, which holds that total economic welfare will be enhanced if each nation specializes in the production of items that it can produce, in relative terms, most efficiently. This, of course, is an important case of Adam Smith's more general point concerning the advantages of the specialization of labor.

Through most of the twentieth century, the United States has played a strong leadership role in developing the world trading system. During the 1930s, however, the United States and many other countries followed "beggar-thy-neighbor" trade policies which contributed substantially to the worldwide depression.

After World War II, this country embarked on a program of reciprocal trade agreements. Initially arranged bilaterally, they evolved into the effective multilateral trading system of the postwar years. This approach broke down many of the historical barriers to world trade. An especially fine example occurred in the 1960s. The acceleration in world trade and economic growth in that decade followed a sharp and mutual reduction in tariff barriers which contributed to lower prices for consumers. We continue today to reap benefits from the policies initiated in those years.

## U.S. Began as a Trader

We can turn to our own economic history for earlier examples of the benefits of an open economy. This country began as a trading nation. If the concept of "Gross National Product" had existed in the eighteenth and nineteenth centuries, people would have pointed to the United States as one of the more open economies in the world, as measured by the share of GNP involved in foreign trade. I say that even though tariff debates were common throughout the nineteenth century.

Around the turn of the century the dynamics of the American economy shifted. Exports and imports became smaller shares of GNP and remained rather stable. U.S. investment abroad increased, gradually transforming us from an international debtor into a world creditor. Increasingly, we became a self-sufficient economy. Only in the last 20 years has the international sector once again begun to increase its relative importance in our economy.

Foreign trade is now an important element in U.S. business and employment. Exports and imports of goods and services each now represent over 12 percent of our Gross National Product. Twenty years ago, exports were less than 6 percent of GNP; imports, less than 5 percent.

Much of this shift has occurred in the past decade, when imports and exports as a share of GNP have doubled and a positive export balance has been maintained.

In passing, we should note that there is a close, but not generally appreciated, connection between imports and exports. A strong trade position requires both a high volume of imports and a high volume of exports. In fact, the only way, in the long run, to increase a country's exports is to increase its imports. U.S. exporters need to find foreign buyers with the dollars necessary to buy their goods and services. In general, these dollars are obtained when Americans import and pay for foreign goods and services.

In the short run, it is true that we can and do lend foreigners the dollars with which to buy our exports. When such loans are made at market rates of interest, trade is properly advanced. But when government-subsidized credit is provided, such funds are denied to other, more productive uses in the domestic economy.

## Two-Way Street

Imports put dollars in the hands of foreigners—dollars which can then be used to buy our exports. It follows that restrictions in imports will result in fewer dollars in the hands of those in other countries who might want to buy our wheat, aircraft, chemicals or machinery—unless, of course, we make up the difference by loans or transfer payments to foreigners.

In some cases, the connection between imports and exports is even more direct. Import restraints can reduce employment and profits in our more productive export industries, in many cases in the same region of the country. For example, in the non-rubber footwear industry, U.S. exports of hides to foreign shoe producers suffered as a result of our restraints on the import of foreign shoes.

Let us generalize from historical experience. The benefits of free trade are numerous. Open trade contributes to lowering inflationary pressures by increasing the supply of goods and services competing for the consumer's dollar. Thus, the question of free trade is basically a consumer issue, and an extremely important one. Open trade minimizes the role of government in influencing private-sector decisions. This allows individuals and business firms to respond to the needs and pressures of the international marketplace. Viewed in this light, free trade is key to promoting economic freedom and the private-enterprise system. Open trade improves the efficiency with which our own resources are allocated. Thus, we can see that free trade yields more growth, higher levels of employment, and an improved living standard here at home.

Aside from the direct and measurable aspects, trade stimulates competition, stirs creative energies, rewards individual initiative, and increases national productivity. Among nations, it speeds the exchange of new ideas and advanced technology. In the long run, international trade means the creation of new jobs and the reduction of inflation.

In this time of great interest in benefit/cost analysis, we may inquire as to what are the costs of free trade as well as the benefits. The obvious costs are those borne by the workers who become unemployed as a result of imports—assuming that imports are the cause.

## Forced Transfers, Made in Washington

What is less apparent, however, is that any form of trade restraint to help a specific industry affected by imports really is an internal transfer of income and wealth to that industry from U.S. consumers. That transfer takes the form of shifts of income and wealth away from American workers and owners of our export industries, who bear the brunt of retaliatory trade restrictions in the form of lower wages and lower profits.

Moreover, many of the benefits of protectionist measures, even to the group advocating them, turn out to be very temporary. For example, quotas on shoe imports resulted in an upgrading in the quality of imports. Thus, American producers found themselves threatened in that part of the market in which, prior to the protectionist action, they firmly dominated. The same process is taking place in the current case of "voluntary" restraints of Japanese auto imports.

One of the great difficulties in public policy discussions involving protectionist measures is that the beneficiaries are usually few in number. Yet each has a large individual stake in the outcome. Moreover, those who benefit from protectionism have little concern about the likelihood of retaliation by foreign governments on other American industries. Thus, the incentive is strong for vigorous and concentrated political activity designed to erect special-interest trade barriers.

In addition, pleas for protectionism reflect the ability of relatively small but influential groups to convince legislatures to adopt policies that benefit them, albeit at the expense of citizens at large. The balance of power is extremely uneven, given the limited knowledge that consumers currently have about these matters.

Those who benefit from exports and from the greater supply of goods and services are generally not even aware of the process by which they benefit. Although the benefits of open trade may far exceed the costs, those benefits—such as lower prices to consumers—are widely diffused among 50 states and 225 million residents. Any single consumer's stake in the outcome is quite small. The individual consumer almost surely is not aware of why the price of a given item is going down—or not rising. Consequently, resistance at the grassroots level to protectionist measures often is considerably less than pressures for their adoption. Nevertheless, the consumer savings from freer trade exceed any sensible adjustment programs instituted for those who are initially hurt by the change.

Scholarly studies typically show that the total benefits of freer trade far exceed the costs. These gains from trade include savings to consumers, gains from moving resources out of inefficient sectors, stimulus to investment, and increased economies of scale. One study concluded that the benefits of tariff reductions are approximately 80 times as large as the costs of labor adjustments. Those costs are primarily the unemployment resulting from increased imports.

High ratios of economic benefits of trade liberalization to labor adjustment costs have also been estimated for other nations, ranging from 49 to 1 in Japan to 96 to 1 in the European

Economic Community. Both aggregate and specific comparisons show that the benefits of protectionist measures are far less than the total costs imposed on society.

## Resenting Their Barriers, Excusing Ours

Despite the lip service that is paid so often to the virtues of free trade, there is great danger that the United States may be taking the lead in the current rush toward protectionism. Public policy debates are increasingly dominated by one-sided, self-serving views of international trade. Everyone wants open markets and free trade overseas. We all know how urgent it is to eliminate their barriers to our exports. But our barriers in the United States to their exports do not generate much interest over here.

The problem can be explained with a simple example—Country A and Country B. Country B has a large export surplus with Country A. Country A has great difficulty getting its exports into Country B. Sounds familiar? Of course, Country B (large trade surplus) is Japan and Country A (large trade deficit) is the United States.

But that is not the end of the story. When we take another look, we find that Country B (large trade surplus) is also the United States and Country A (large trade deficit), Western Europe. After all, we have enjoyed a trade surplus with the Common Market over the last decade, about as large as Japan's surplus with us. It would help to clear the air in international trade discussions if the United States were to acknowledge that we do not have clean hands.

Let us remind ourselves of our many departures from free trade. For example, "Buy American" statutes give preference to domestic producers in government procurement. As much as a 50 percent differential is paid for military goods produced at home. In addition, the Surface Transportation Assistance Act requires that, for most purchases over $500,000, American materials and products be used. Also, American flag vessels must be used to transport at least 50 percent of the gross tonnage of all commodities financed with U.S. foreign aid funds.

And then there are the Buy American laws of the various states. New York requires state agencies to buy American steel. New Jersey requires that all state cars must be domestically produced. In addition, numerous states and municipal authorities require use of American materials in utilities, whether privately owned or publicly owned.

## Block That Mushroom

Let us not forget the Jones Act. That piece of special-interest legislation prohibits foreign ships from engaging in commerce between American ports. This law, of course, effectively bars all competition in U.S. domestic marine transport. The perverse effects of such cabotage laws are greater than might be expected. For example, at times Canadian lumber transported in Japanese flag vessels has undersold domestic timber from Oregon in the lucrative Southern California markets. In such cases, both the American merchant marine and the American timber industry suffer damage.

Many other statutes limit imports of products such as sugar, beef, dairy produce, and mandarin oranges. Under the Meat Import Act, the President has authority to impose import quotas on beef if imports reach a certain trigger level. In practice, the U.S. has "encouraged" foreign exporters to restrain their sales "voluntarily" to avoid the imposition of formal quotas.

Although our average tariff rates are low, high tariffs are levied on selective items. Tariffs on textiles average 20 percent. Duties on fruit juices are over 27 percent, and the rate on ceramic products is over 14 percent. All this is in addition to numerous nontariff barriers, often of a regulatory nature and imposed by federal, state, county, and municipal governments.

Despite this nation's overall free-trade posture, protection against imports into the United States now covers such basic industries as automobiles, steel, and textiles. Pleas for further trade restrictions extend to such esoteric sectors as mushrooms, ceramic tableware, and mechanics' shop towels. It is not a question of merely accepting the existing array of protection. The challenge is to deal with the rising pressures for further restriction of world trade.

Protectionist measures are a two-edged sword. They may reduce imports from abroad. The United States was "successful" in getting the Common Market to restrict its exports of steel to this country. But let us examine the results. First of all, the domestic automobile industry, a major purchaser of steel, bears the burden of higher costs, which in turn make it less competitive. In addition, lower imports mean fewer dollars abroad to buy American exports. All this generates pressures for more protection.

Furthermore, protection often generates retaliatory measures, which hit the unprotected sectors of the economy. For example, in January 1983, the U.S. government imposed import quotas on textiles and apparel from China. It is interesting to note that this action followed the breakdown of negotiations for the extension of a "voluntary" quota that expired at the end of 1982. The Chinese government retaliated by canceling new contracts for the importation of U.S. cotton, synthetic fiber, and soybeans. China's retaliation to our trade restrictions hit a very different sector of the economy and had a much broader regional effect than the beneficiaries of the protectionist action.

## How We Impede Exports

Moreover, we must acknowledge that in the United States many laws and regulations limit our exports. In many ways—and often without considering the effects—we have enacted laws and promulgated regulations that prohibit U.S. exports or make it more difficult for American companies to export.

For example, the Trans-Alaskan Pipeline Authorization Act prohibits the export of oil from North Slope fields.

A provision added to an appropriations act for the Interior Department bans timber exports from federal lands west of the 100th meridian.

The Export Administration Act provides for controls on exports of goods and technology to protect national security. That sounds fine. But, in practice, the law mandates controls over a great variety of products, including domestically produced crude oil, refined petroleum products, unprocessed red cedar and, my favorite, horses exported by sea.

In 1980 the act was employed to embargo grain exports to the Soviet Union. It was invoked again in 1982 to carry out the ban against U.S. firms participating in the construction of the natural-gas pipeline between the U.S.S.R. and Western Europe.

Studies of how export controls actually work conclude that the more sensitive applications for approval under the Export Administration Act get tied up in a bureaucratic morass. There is a good deal of evidence that the licensing system has been a powerful disincentive to exporting.

Exports controls do more than limit U.S. international trade for the time they are imposed. Such restrictions call into question the long-term reliability of the United States as a future supplier of products to other countries. Those nations are likely to develop alternative sources.

A clear example is soybeans—hardly a product that could be considered a strategic item. The main effect of the U.S. embargo of soybean exports in 1974 was to induce Japan to turn to other producing countries, particularly Brazil. Japan proceeded to invest huge amounts in that country to develop alternatives to U.S. production, thus effectively and permanently reducing our share of the world soybean market.

The United States also conducts a great variety of domestic regulatory activities that impose costly burdens on American manufacturers. In many cases, foreign producers are not subject to similar burdens. In addition, the federal government has imposed special burdens on companies involved in foreign trade. The Foreign Corrupt Practices Act requires strict recordkeeping standards to monitor the anti-bribery sections of the statute. It is difficult to discuss that law without being criticized for callousness on ethical matters. However, the sad fact is that this international trade statute has established a regulatory regime that displays the same cavalier attitude toward the burdens it imposes on American business as do so many domestic-oriented regulations.

A former Chairman of the Securities and Exchange Commission, the agency administering the act, has stated, "The anxieties created by the Foreign Corrupt Practices Act—among men and women of

*Freighter Loaded with Sea Containers*

utmost good faith—have been, in my experience, without equal." The language of the act is so sweeping and ambiguous that American firms turn down foreign business when they merely suspect that they could be charged with actions that technically might be classified as bribery, although in practice these payments may be closer to paying protection money to the Mafia. The General Accounting Office found, in a survey of 250 American companies, that 30 percent of the respondents engaged in foreign trade had lost business as a result of the Foreign Corrupt Practices Act.

In addition to the effects of trade policies themselves, the strong foreign exchange value of the dollar makes it difficult for American companies to compete in world markets. Many factors influence the strength of a nation's currency. But our extraordinarily high real interest rates are very important. In turn, the large budget deficits are a key influence on those high rates—and we cannot blame the deficits on "foreign devils." They have a made-in-America label.

## Foreign Threats to International Trade

By no means is the United States the only nation with trade barriers. Every nation has them. The European Community levies duties on wheat, barley, oats, sorghum, rye and rice. Italy bans foreign-produced television commercials. Japan finds all sorts of reasons for keeping out baseball bats.

Japan commands our attention in this regard, and some special consideration of this important trading nation is appropriate. Viewed from a broad, historical perspective, Japan, of all the major developed nations, has most recently made the transition from a developing country to a mature, industrialized economy. However, it has only begun to change its policies and customs to reflect that fundamental shift. Yet, looking at the decade of the 1980s, it is clear that Japan now has a key stake in the health of the world trading system. It has benefited most substantially from the greater openness of the economies of the rest of the world. Without that liberal environment, I doubt that its export-led growth would have occurred. Surely, steps to open its markets more widely to foreign trade and investment are long overdue.

The sooner that Japan succeeds in adjusting its trade posture to current economic realities worldwide, the sooner will its trade relations with more open economies move to a more amicable basis. Under the circumstances, I am pleased to note the recent steps that the Government of Japan has taken to reduce its tariffs and to soften administrative barriers to imports. As Foreign Minister Abe (the former head of MITI) has said, "I myself do not feel that the requests from America regarding market liberalization are pressures. These are things that Japan should be doing anyway." No doubt, from the viewpoint of Japan, the recent moves to liberalize trade came very rapidly. To outside observers, however, it is more a matter of making up for a very late start.

Threats to free trade are multiplying, with a growing array of industrial sectors obtaining "protection." The concerns of these producers and the public will be better served by responding to the underlying problems that generate pressures for protectionism. This leads me to the policy implications of these remarks.

## Four Positive Strategies

As I see it, the United States should simultaneously pursue four positive and mutually supportive approaches in combating protectionism and promoting free trade. First and most fundamental is carrying out domestic economic policies that expand production and incomes while holding down inflation. This, of course, is a plea for tax cuts, reduction in government spending, and regulatory relief. A healthy economy nips the protectionist bud at its source.

The second approach to promoting free trade is to achieve greater stability and balance in macroeconomic policies. The shift in 1981 to tight monetary policy and expansive fiscal policy in the United States contributed substantially to high interest rates and a rise in the value of the dollar coupled with recession. If we are not careful, we will now see an easy-money policy—coupled with out-sized budget deficits—lead to another inflationary spiral. That would further reduce the competitiveness of U.S. products in world markets.

The third approach to promoting free trade is to limit any governmental "trade adjustment assistance"—which seems to be a politically necessary part of any comprehensive trade policy—to temporary aid in shifting labor and capital from industries hard hit by imports to more competitive activities. All too often, the government aid merely maintains an inefficient and uncompetitive industrial structure. That, in turn, adversely affects our competitiveness in world markets and, predictably, generates further pressure for additional protectionist measures. The result is to lower domestic employment, which, in turn, generates additional pressures for government interference. That is an example of a more general principle: government intervention begets more government intervention.

In a healthy and dynamic economy we must expect that some industries and regions will grow more rapidly than others and that some sectors will experience difficulty in maintaining their position and may even decline. We must rely primarily on market forces, and not on government bailouts, to make the appropriate adjustments.

In a related aspect, the developing nations need adequate access to the markets of the more developed countries if they are going to be able to service the massive indebtedness that they have incurred. However painful, the developed nations must adjust their economic structures to this reality.

The fourth approach to promoting free trade is to acknowledge the positive role of multinational corporations in the world economy. Multinationals adapt to change more readily and are less likely to plead for protection than other companies. They also are the private-sector alternative to foreign aid and other types of government intervention. This, of course, explains why so-called transnational enterprises are not universally popular, especially among the bureaucracies of international governmental organizations.

## Ending the Monday-Wednesday Charade

The serious question facing us is how to encourage our trading partners to open their markets without using mechanisms that harm the international trading system or start a spiral of retaliation. The current interest in what is now called "reciprocity" raises such dangers. Yet, until markets are open more fully, these pressures will continue.

But the current economic problems that face most countries will not be solved by responding to the parochial concerns of steel producers, citrus growers, and automobile makers. Nor should international economic relations be dominated by short-term protectionist pressures from the producers of edible seaweeds, casein, and manhole covers, to name some recent candidates for protection.

The question is frequently asked, "Other nations do not have a policy of freer trade, so why should we?" But rather than talking in absolutes, the more appropriate question to ask is, "Are the trade policies of other nations more open today than they would be without the continued pressure of agreed international 'rules of the game'—rules developed under the persistent and patient influence of the United States?"

The answer is a resounding "yes." Trade policy, here and elsewhere, is far more open today as a result of our efforts and of our example of an open domestic market. Our federal system, after all, was the original common market.

Is the U.S. better off with lower trade barriers? Again, the response is positive. The goods we import are cheaper than domestic substitutes. Our 225 million consumers have more choice. The markets for our exports are less restricted than they otherwise would be. Thus, despite the numerous real obstacles, many American companies have experienced significant success in penetrating foreign markets. Coca Cola is the largest-selling soft drink in Japan, Schick is number one in their razor market, and Nestle commands 70 percent of Japan's instant coffee market.

The credibility of this country's commitment to open and freer trade is not enhanced by companies sending their lawyers to Washington on Monday to seek the removal of import barriers overseas; and then turning around on Wednesday to send the same attorneys back to Washington to advocate import restrictions on the products of their foreign competitors.

International trade policy will not remain static. The choice is between a further drift to protectionism and a joint effort to remove trade barriers. The longer we wait to move decisively to freer world trade, the more obstacles will be in place and the more difficult it will be to remove them. The best time to move to free trade is now.

# Market Entrepreneurs: Building Empires of Service
## Burton W. Folsom Jr. (1997)

*Burton Folsom is a professor of history at Hillsdale College. He received a doctorate in history from the University of Pittsburgh. Dr. Folsom has written extensively on the economic history of America. Here he highlights some successful businessmen in Michigan's history in material adapted from his book,* Empire Builders: How Michigan Entrepreneurs Helped Make America Great.

December 1997 *Imprimis*

We can pinpoint a time—the late 1800s and early 1900s—when America rose to world dominance. And we can pinpoint a group of entrepreneurs who built economic empires that caused the balance of power in the world to shift from the Old World to the New World. Finally, we can pinpoint a strong Judaeo-Christian culture that values limited government and individual liberty. This convergence of a time period, a group of heroes, and a spirit of the age is a story worth telling.

## Empire Builders in Michigan History

One of the most exciting ways to tell this story starts with Michigan—an underdog state long dismissed as a frozen wasteland. From the time Michigan entered the union in 1837, the governor and the legislators wanted to make the state an economic powerhouse. Their first effort was to enlist massive government aid in building railroads and canals throughout Michigan.

When this experiment with state control failed, they tried free enterprise and individual liberty. They sold the railroads to private owners and, when that succeeded, they wrote a new constitution that opened Michigan to entrepreneurs and barred the state from intruding on private enterprise. Michigan's future was to be left in the hands of its entrepreneurs.

How well did this experiment work? Let's look at some examples. In 1883, a young physician named William was troubled by problems he had with pills that would not dissolve in the stomachs of his patients. William set aside his mornings—prime earning hours for physicians—to conduct experiment after experiment in the small attic of his house in Hastings, Michigan. He rejected the standard method of making pills from paste; instead he created them from "starter particles." He added powdered drugs and moistening agents while he rotated the particles in a revolving pan. The result was a pill that held its contents, but was soft enough to dissolve easily when swallowed.

In 1885, William—Dr. William E. Upjohn—patented his "friable pill" and started the Upjohn Pill and Granule Company in a small brick building in nearby Kalamazoo. His first price list included 186 formulas for everything from quinine pills to iron pills. In the next six years, Upjohn sold millions of pills and generated the capital needed to enter the pharmaceutical market. In the next forty years, he marketed a superior product that sold widely throughout the United States and even the world. His business did not rely on any natural resources found in his state. He could have done his work anywhere. He stayed in Michigan because its economic system triggered his entrepreneurial energy and allowed him to keep the profits he made.

Let's look at another example that parallels the Upjohn story. One Sunday evening in 1927 in the town of Fremont, a young man named Dan waited impatiently for his wife Dorothy to feed their daughter, who was seven months old. They had a social engagement that evening, and Dan was ready to go. He paced back and forth, looking at his watch and waiting. Dorothy, meanwhile, was tediously straining vegetables into a bowl, piece by piece. Soon her fidgety husband stomped into the kitchen, pleading with his wife to hurry up. That's when Dorothy decided to teach him a lesson. "To press the point," Dorothy later recalled, "I dumped a whole container of peas into a strainer and bowl, placed them in Dan's lap, and asked him to see how he'd like to do that three times a day, seven days a week."

Dan got the message. The next day, when he went to work in his family-owned cannery, he had an idea for something new to put in the cans: strained baby food. During the next year, Dan Gerber would establish the baby food market and then dominate it for decades. He test-marketed strained carrots, peas, prunes, and spinach on babies in Fremont. Then he persuaded grocery stores around the country to carry his product. Thousands of mothers chose to pay to save time and energy; they bought 590,000 cans of Gerber's baby food at 15 cents per can in the first year.

Gerber, like Upjohn, did not need his state's resources to flourish. But he needed Michigan's entrepreneurial spirit and freedom from heavy taxation and stifling regulation. In the late 1800s and early 1900s, of course, the whole United States had a small federal government, no income tax, and strong constitutional support for free enterprise. But Michigan, through its liberating state constitution, went out of the way to limit government and stake the state's future on what its entrepreneurs could accomplish.

Business was booming. Even blacks, who were subject to much discrimination, had opportunities in Michigan. A good example is the great inventor Elijah McCoy. McCoy was born in 1843 in Canada, where his parents had fled from Kentucky to escape slavery. After the Civil War ended and blacks were legally free, McCoy settled in Ypsilanti, where he began work for the Michigan Central Railroad as a locomotive fireman.

He immediately applied his skills to a major problem: the dangerous overheating of locomotives. Trains had to stop regularly to oil engine parts to reduce friction. If they stopped infrequently, the overheating could damage parts or start fires. If they stopped too often, freight and passengers would be delayed. McCoy invented a lubricating cup that oiled engine parts as the train was moving. He secured a patent in 1872 and steadily improved the device.

Others tried to imitate his invention, but he kept ahead of them with superior engineering skills. The standard of quality was so high that to distinguish his product from cheaper imitations people began calling it "the real McCoy."

McCoy showed remarkable creative energy during the next half-century. He received 51 more patents for inventions ranging from a forerunner of the ironing board to a special cup for administering medicine. Not even old age dimmed his creative light. When he was 77, he patented an improved air brake lubricator; when he was 80, he patented a vehicle tire.

McCoy was not an isolated example of black entrepreneurship. In 1887, Fred Pelham was president of his class at the University of Michigan. From there he became assistant civil engineer with the Michigan Central Railroad. His innovations in structure and design included the "skew arch" bridge. Some of the twenty bridges he built still stand in Michigan today.

Why, then, did so much of the building of the American empire take place in Michigan? To find out, we need to see why Michigan chose free enterprise over government direction. Then we need to study what some of the state's early residents accomplished. In a recent book on this subject, I examined seven of them:

> John Jacob Astor, who began fur trading in the Michigan Territory in the early 1800s; Stevens T. Mason, a politician whose state-financed railroad scheme backfired, leading him to belatedly champion free enterprise; Henry Crapo, who helped Michigan become the top lumber-producing state in the union; Henry Ford and William Durant, who made the state the world center for automobile manufacturing, one of the greatest industries of the 20th century; Herbert Dow, who helped break forever European monopolies in chemicals; and Will Kellogg, who introduced flaked cereal, thus changing breakfast habits throughout the Western world.

## Succeeding Through Serving Others

These men, with the exception of Mason, were indeed empire builders. The word *empire* comes from the Latin *imperium*, or dominion, and *imperare*, which means to command. The best entrepreneurs fulfill these terms. They dominate their industries and extend their command into new territories around the world. From a central location or capital, they expand their markets and control their industries—not by force but by service: selling products that customers want at competitive prices.

Several points are striking about Michigan's most successful entrepreneurs. First, they built their empires locally—in places like Flint, Midland, Battle Creek, and Dearborn—but expanded them to locations around the nation and then around the world. Many middle class families, whether in New York, Paris, or Buenos Aires, ate Cornflakes for breakfast, drove Chevys to work, used Dow's bleach on their clothes and his bromine for sedatives. Kellogg, Durant, Dow, and Ford, like Astor in an earlier generation, built empires that shaped the world long after their deaths.

*Rubber Tires in a Factory Stock Room, c. 1917*

Second, they were highly inventive and highly creative. They not only took risks and carved out markets but also introduced many of the key products needed to establish their empires of service. Dow heads the list with his 107 patents, but Kellogg and Ford were in some ways even more impressive. Kellogg, with help from his brother, practically invented the whole flaked-cereal industry. His example inspired others, and, from Rice Krispies to All-Bran, Kellogg cereals set the standard. Henry Ford, among other things, invented the V-8 engine and assembled the team that made plate glass from a continuous ribbon with no hand work. More than this, his whole company was for years an experiment in creativity—from the assembly line to raising wages to cutting work hours.

A third point to remember about Michigan's entrepreneurs is that they wanted to build empires more than they wanted to make money. Of course, the two usually go together. But making such a distinction is critical to understanding the mind of Michigan's early entrepreneurs. Money, or capital, is valued not as an end but as a means to create an economic empire. In the same way, weapons are valued by an army not as an end but as a means to conquer people and territory. Capital is a tool for the entrepreneur in the same way that weapons are tools for the soldier. The big difference here is that an army creates and expands its empire by force; entrepreneurs create and expand their empires by service to others. A soldier controls by using weapons to threaten violence; an entrepreneur persuades by using capital to offer better products at lower prices.

The challenge to entrepreneurs in an undeveloped area like Michigan was raising capital. John Jacob Astor made his money in New York and plowed it into Michigan. Henry Crapo forged a complex network for wheedling capital from his cautious friends in New Bedford and Boston. Herbert Dow lobbied established businessmen in Cleveland. Will Kellogg sought help from a large investor in St. Louis. By the early 1900s, some Michigan cities were rich enough to support their own entrepreneurs. Henry Ford, with mixed success, solicited a variety of investors in Detroit. William Durant tapped the bankers of Flint—first to build carriages and later, Chevrolets.

With capital in hand, the next step was mobilizing workers behind tough and compelling goals. For Ford, the task was building a reliable car so cheaply that middle class Americans could afford it. For Dow, the issue was survival—how to make bleach, bromine, and dyes cheap enough to compete with European cartels. Kellogg and Durant started with high quality products, so the challenge was in marketing: how to get every American to eat a bowl of Cornflakes and to ride in a blue ribbon carriage.

Workers, like soldiers, will usually follow if the leader knows how to lead. The prevailing theory of management said that employees must be controlled, directed, and closely supervised. Michigan's entrepreneurs, by contrast, tended to give their workers freedom to create, personal responsibility for hard tasks, and rewards and bonuses for jobs well done. Henry Ford wanted the best workers in Michigan, and he launched the "five dollar day" to get them. Will Kellogg liked to reward worthy employees with a handshake that contained a $20 bill. Herbert Dow might argue loudly with his chemists, but he trusted their abilities, paid them well, and turned them loose to invent and create.

Fourth, Michigan's empire builders all followed biblical principles, even though not all of them were practicing Christians. As George Gilder has observed, they truly believed in the commandments, "Do unto others as you would have them do unto you" and "Give and you will be given unto." He also notes that they suppressed their own desires to serve the desires of others, and they committed their work and wealth to bring to the world new goods that they knew might well be rejected.

The faith of these empire builders was continually tested. They all either went bankrupt or verged on it at some critical point in their lives. They did not experience the steady growth and predictable success that one might have expected from talented men with good and popular products to sell. They took leaps of faith, fell flat on their faces, then desperately changed their tactics and tried to raise new capital to stay afloat.

Herbert Dow, for example, failed in his first business venture; in his second, he was ousted from control. On his third try, he went into the bleach business, and he calculated his costs of production very carefully. Then came the unexpected. He was immediately challenged by a British cartel, which cut its price for bleach in half. Dow had to find ways to slash costs even more or he would fail a third time. When Will Kellogg finally broke loose from his old menial job, he calculated the cost of making Cornflakes. What he didn't count on was having his factory burn down and his main competitor buy up all the new equipment for making cereal. Henry Crapo floundered in the lumber business until he doubled his risks, bought some sawmills, and began to process and market his own timber. Only after years of cutting costs, improving products, and removing bottlenecks did these men make breakthroughs. Henry Ford refused to listen to the experts, who claimed that steam and electricity were the only practical options for automobiles; instead he developed the internal combustion engine. When Ford was losing sales to competitors, he was forced to adopt drastic measures, slashing the price of the Model T by 20 percent. Sales doubled, but who could have known his gamble would pay off? Only hindsight makes such accomplishments seem easy and inevitable.

The fifth trait of Michigan's empire builders was their fierce independence and their aversion to monopoly and to government solutions to problems. Even before statehood, John Jacob Astor displayed this independence with his American Fur Company when he challenged the government fur factories. The next two generations of Michigan entrepreneurs were among the most independent our nation has ever produced. When Henry Crapo served as governor, his defense of the Constitution of 1850 was intense. He sacrificed popularity, party loyalty, and even his health so that he could veto bill after bill that allowed Michigan cities to subsidize local railroads. Crapo was an expert in attracting outside capital, and he knew the dangers that subsidizing railroads posed to individual liberty and to the integrity and credit rating of his adopted state.

In 1919, fifty years after Crapo's death, his grandson, William Durant, was president of General Motors. In a speech that year, Durant sounded just like his grandfather:

> Competition is the life of trade. I stand for competition. I am opposed to monopoly or control on the principle that it destroys initiative, curtails freedom of action, and frequently leads to abuse of power.

Durant's chief competitor, Henry Ford, could not have agreed more. Ford, in fact, was one of the main reasons the auto industry was so free of monopoly and government control. The resulting pressure of competition improved the quality of cars dramatically—automatic starters, hydraulic brakes, and gas gauges became standard by 1930. With Ford and General Motors locked in combat, the American consumer was the winner. Vehicle sales soared from 181,000 in 1910 to over 5,000,000 in 1929. Trucks for moving freight were part of this rise because the railroad industry, with its price fixing and government controls, was too expensive and too cumbersome.

In the 1930s, Ford led the opposition to President Roosevelt's National Recovery Administration (NRA). Auto companies were pressured to join together to regulate wages, prices, and hours of work. Ford refused to join. Durant was out at General Motors, so he stood virtually alone. When the federal bureaucrats refused to accept his low bids on government contracts, Ford ignored them and survived on private sector business. The irony here is that Ford already led American industry in paying high wages. Why should a government agency set minimum wages, Ford wondered, when he set the standard long before the 1930s? Referring to the NRA auto code, he said, "If we tried to live up to it, we would have to live down to it." Before the government could coerce him into joining the NRA's auto cartel, however, the Supreme Court stepped in and declared the NRA unconstitutional.

If possible, Herbert Dow opposed government activism even more strongly than Ford (except for protective tariffs). Dow actually built his chemical empire by challenging government-supported monopolies. In the 1890s, when Dow entered the chemical business, the British and the Germans had long dominated the chemical industry—and their governments encouraged them to form cartels and to control prices and production. American chemical companies not only lagged far behind Europe, they often faced predatory price cutting whenever they sold abroad. Some American companies, like DuPont, carved niches in special markets, such as gunpowder. But Dow was the first American to openly challenge the Europeans where they were already established—in areas like bleach, bromides, and indigo.

In doing so, Dow gave the world a model demonstration in how to defeat predatory price cutting. Before Dow, many people could argue against monopolies and oligopolies this way: "If a corporation is big enough, it can cut prices below cost, drive out its small competitors, and then raise prices to whatever it wants to charge. Therefore, we need government regulation, antitrust laws perhaps, to control large greedy corporations." Dow showed how a small company could beat large firms. In the bromide industry, the Germans cut prices below cost with the specific intent of destroying Dow. In response, Dow secretly bought the cheap German bromides, repackaged them, and sold them at a profit in markets around the world! It was a brilliant strategy. During the early 1900s, Dow regularly expanded his chemical empire when the Germans tried to reap large profits from their cartels in indigo, magnesium, and other products.

## New Empires

The 1920s was the last decade when an empire could be built without major interference from the federal government. With the Great Depression came the rapid expansion of federal powers. The Smoot-Hawley Tariff, passed in 1930, was the most restrictive tariff in U.S. history. The Reconstruction Finance Corporation had the government financing banks, railroads, and other industries. The Agricultural Adjustment Act regulated farm production; the National Industrial Recovery Act regulated most corporations—except for the Ford Motor Company. And later the Wagner Act shifted the balance of power from the entrepreneurs to the labor union bosses.

The tax revenues needed to pay for these and other new programs were astonishing. The top federal income tax rate in 1930 was 24 percent. In 1932, under President Hoover, the rate was hiked to 63 percent. Under President Roosevelt the rate was first raised to 79 percent and later jumped to over 90 percent. Large inheritance taxes scooped up what the income tax missed. During the 1930s, the empire builders were, in effect, asked to send their empires to Washington.

Herbert Dow died in 1930, before he could denounce such a request. William Durant lost his fortune on the stock market, before Washington could confiscate it. Ford and Kellogg chose to shelter their wealth from the swirling storms. With the Ford and Kellogg foundations quickly in place they preserved their empires, but they were no longer the commanders. The era of "laissez faire" was essentially over. A new breed of businessman began to emerge: the "political entrepreneur," who sought special concessions from government and empires built on political power instead of service. The old "market entrepreneur," who found success through creating better products at a lower cost, found it harder and harder to survive. . . .

# American Small Business: The Quiet Giant
## John E. Sloan (1984)

*In this speech, John Sloan described some of the ways in which small businesses have an impact in the economy. At the time he made this presentation, Mr. Sloan was president and chief executive officer of the National Federation of Independent Business. He was a graduate of Vanderbilt University and Stonier Graduate School of Banking at Rutgers University. Mr. Sloan died in 1992.*

September 1984 *Imprimis*

The great economic attribute of small business is said to be its entrepreneurial bent. Obviously, not all small businesses are entrepreneurial—at least by most definitions of "entrepreneur"—and not all the activity of larger firms is non-entrepreneurial. Bell Labs and its development of the transistor is an example of the latter. But I intend to approach the discussion from the perspective that small firms tend to be entrepreneurial and large firms tend to be managerial—and the two are at opposite ends of a continuum.

Entrepreneurship and entrepreneurial change are often couched in terms of technological innovation. The small firm which develops and markets a new widget is considered to be "entrepreneurial." The precise contribution of small business and independent inventors to technological change defies an answer. From the quantitative standpoint, however, a variety of studies indicate that small firms and individual inventors produced anywhere from twenty percent to one hundred percent of the important innovations; the fifty percent range was the most common result. Typical is a study conducted in 1982 among 246 award-winning innovations in food processing and manufacturing industries which concluded that forty-five percent of these innovations could be attributed to small firms.

**From the qualitative standpoint, however, there is support for the thesis that small firms provide the truly big breakthroughs.**

The following major small-business innovations are only a small portion of a list containing some very familiar products: air-conditioning, airplane, catalytic petroleum cracking, continuous casting, gyrocompass, insulin, laser, optical scanner, pacemaker, personal computer, turbojet engine, and xerography.

Besides the frequency and importance of small-business technological innovations, small firms appear to produce them using fewer financial resources and fewer people—and bring those products to market more rapidly. A recent study conducted for the Small Business Administration found that small firms produced two and one-half times more innovations per employee than did large firms; they also brought them to market in only two-thirds the amount of time. Further, small businesses have usually done so without the benefits and/or liabilities of government financial support. Only six percent of the $16 billion spent by the federal government on R&D [research and development] in a recent year was directed to small firms. The Small Business Innovation Development Act will change that, hopefully to the benefit of small entrepreneurs and the nation as a whole.

**Innovation in organizational methods has an impact on productivity and growth just as does technological change, and here too small business is deeply involved.**

Henry Ford and Ray Kroc provide two obvious examples. And if imitation is the highest form of flattery, then it should be noted that large firms are increasingly shifting their focus to smaller, more personalized and possibly more entrepreneurial structures.

Israel Kirzner of New York University, another speaker at this same CCA Seminar, views entrepreneurial activity as fundamentally creating disequilibrium. No pun intended—entrepreneurs are, therefore, to be considered movers and shakers—non-conformists, if you will. They continually punch holes in the existing status-quo creating vacuums which must be filled. When xerography was developed, for example, large gaps were blown in the existing way of doing things. Carbon copies were out, broader dissemination of information was in. But from a slightly different vantage point, an entrepreneurial event, i.e., a more efficient use of resources, can create equilibrium through the filling of gaps or holes in the market.

Being entrepreneurial, small business fills market gaps and fills them rapidly. Small business is highly flexible and adaptive—not necessarily as individual firms, but as an aggregate entity. The gaps which are filled by small firms include the following: 1) highly specialized markets or markets with limited demand, 2) new markets which will eventually become mass markets, and 3) markets affected by new economies of scale.

The principal attribute of the large corporation is its capacity to marshal and manage resources for the purpose of mass producing for mass markets. However, there are markets too small or too specialized for large firms—markets where economies of scale reach maximum efficiency points very quickly.

Examples of such businesses are all around us. Often we think of them in terms of various service and retail industries where quality and personal relationships are integral parts of a business sale—the private physician in contrast to the HMO, the boutique in contrast to K-Mart, the French restaurant in contrast to Howard Johnson's. But that is a far too limited view. It is no coincidence, for example, that the machine tool and metalworking machinery industries possess large proportions of small firms. The same is true of the home-repair industries. Both have a limited or specialized market where few economies of scale exist.

The critical value of these small and highly specialized markets is two-fold: first, it permits the large firms to obtain their inputs in the most efficient manner possible, and second, it provides the consumer with an infinite variety of products and services. Let me illustrate both points.

*Efficiency:* Think of a giant manufacturing firm—spread across the country and probably throughout the world. The firm will have several in-house departments not inherent to its production process. For example, there may be a carpentry department, a mail room, reproduction facilities, etc. Wise management recognizes that in general these facilities should be kept at a point where they are constantly operating. You don't hire for a peak period; down time is expensive. But in-house mailing facilities get backlogged, reproduction machinery breaks down or there is an overload, and so on. It is no coincidence, therefore, the mailing, reproduction, and stenographic services industry consists almost exclusively of small businesses. Management and public relations firms, certain types of computer software, and testing laboratories have a somewhat similar size distribution in their industries. All these largely small-business functions serve to support mass producers for mass markets.

*Variety:* After test marketing, McDonald's decided not to introduce its new McRib barbeque sandwich. Apparently, it wasn't readily accepted in all sections of the country. Now, I happen to like barbeque. However, the efficiencies gained by McDonald's through a national menu would not have allowed me the choice of eating a barbeque sandwich should my choice of restaurants be limited to a national chain.

Small or specialized markets often function as the market in a geographically defined area, most notably in the rural regions. Here, small firms operate in substantially greater numbers on a per capita basis than in urban areas primarily due to the number of retailers. In the really remote areas, small business provides, in one form or another, the only goods and services that are available.

Small firms also fill gaps by initially producing products or services that after a certain point become mass products for mass markets. In one sense, this idea is an extension of the technology and technological innovation point previously noted. This is a very risky business for a small firm since it must either eventually grow and compete head-on with large firms, or perish. The personal computer business is a case in point, and the divergent fates of Apple and Osbourne battling IBM the best single example available.

**We are now witnessing a devolution of many large production units in response to new, smaller economies of scale resulting from the broad movement of our developed economy into the service industries and from inherent problems in adapting a hierarchical organization to the cultural and social values of our increasingly educated society.**

Norman Macrae, one of the few thoughtful people on the subject, attributes two fundamental difficulties to Henry Ford's hierarchical structure, the structure which has made several nations, including our own, rich. Macrae sees these difficulties as a "people problem" and an "enterprise problem." The former stems from the notion that educated people do not like to be run from the top down. Macrae argues that industrialized nations have attempted to cope with people in three ways, importing more amenable workers from poorer countries, sending multi-national factories to less developed parts of the world, and trying to persuade natives to love factories through use of worker participation groups. None have been, nor will be, truly successful for a variety of obvious reasons.

The "enterprise problem" is largely a function of automation. People are working with their muscles less and their brains more. Even within manufacturing industries, the proportion of people "on the line" vis-a-vis those in service or ancillary activities is diminishing. This is part of the entire economy's movement toward the service industries.

**We have a new ballgame in the post-industrial economy—a ballgame far more conducive to operation of smaller firms than we have seen in the past several decades.**

And should you believe this evaluation provides a one-way ticket to economic disaster, let me simply point out that during the decade of the '70s, the number of Americans working rose an astonishing 26 percent. Those nations which have not yet felt and accepted the challenge of this new entrepreneurial era waned miserably in comparison—British employment grew 2 percent in the decade, for example; Japanese 9 percent; West Germany's actually declined. Thus, social and cultural values of an educated, independent people have combined with advancing technologies to alter our headlong rush to the "new industrial state."

Professor David L. Birch of MIT, in *The Job Generation Process*, determined that over half of the net new jobs created between 1969 and 1976 were in independent businesses. He also found that 80 percent were in business locations or establishments with fewer than 100 employees, and in businesses less than five years old.

**The profile of the job generating firm according to Birch is as follows: It is small. It tends to be independent. It is volatile. This profile does not change much across industries and regions.**

Peter Drucker noted that between 1981 and 1983, the Fortune 500 lost a total of three million domestic jobs. "Entrepreneurial business," as he calls it, added approximately one million.

The Birch data really shouldn't have been as surprising as they were. If indeed the role of larger firms is to mass produce for mass markets and the role of small firms is to fill old gaps and create new ones, then almost by definition we should expect that an implicit attribute of small business will be job generation—at least relative to other economic structures. Moreover, we should expect many of these jobs to be particularly suited for certain groups of people. And they are.

**An important function of small business is to provide the bulk of jobs and hence a large share of on-the-job training for young Americans.**

This is a function largely thrust on small business due to the price-fixing activities of the government and organized labor, such as minimum wage, Davis-Bacon, etc. But it is more complicated than that. Small firms by definition have a modest hierarchy, and usually face a competitive condition which does not permit wages, particularly at the entry level, to rise far above market value. The result is a concentration of young, less experienced employees whose initial conditioning to the workplace must be accomplished by small employers.

We are only beginning to explore the role of small firms in the business cycle and their interaction with larger firms in general economic phenomena. But we know that role is a dynamic one.

For example, our own work at NFIB demonstrates that small entrepreneurs and small-business owners, in aggregate, often prove far more sensitive to approaching market developments than do all the econometricians with all their sophisticated mathematical models.

David Mills at the University of Virginia provides evidence that assigns small firms the role of industrial "shock absorbers." His argument runs: "Large firms produce more efficiently at normal levels of demand, but small firms are more flexible and produce more efficiently when demand is very high or very low. Thus, small businesses are a stabilizing factor particularly in industries experiencing significant demand fluctuations due to cyclical factors."

**Small business also enhances operation of the free market. Put another way, it doesn't have the potential to detract from operation of the free market.**

Chrysler is a case in point. Chrysler management and the United Auto Workers (UAW) leadership made a series of ghastly errors in the '60s and '70s. The penalty imposed by market discipline was bankruptcy, and Chrysler was clearly headed in that direction. Lee Iacocca came to Washington, tin cup in hand, pleading for a bailout. Despite the confusing rhetoric, Chrysler's argument was that the company was too big to fail; there were too many employees; there were too many stockholders; there were too many small-business suppliers. The Carter Administration and the Congress swallowed the argument, and the rest is history. Chrysler has survived, repaid its creditors, and helped bludgeon the Reagan Administration into another new bailout scheme—import quotas.

The point of this episode is not to chastise Chrysler or Mr. Iacocca; the point is to demonstrate that large firms have the capacity to distort and interrupt operation of free markets. In this instance, the distortion occurred due to political activity. Small businesses usually cannot follow suit, though I would concede that there are those that would do so if they believed they could. Market discipline dooms a foundering small business to failure. The broader benefit of such personally unfortunate incidents is to reduce the total cost of unsuccessful ventures.

By extracting a penalty recognizable to both the public and the business community, superfluous efforts and fly-by-night operations are winnowed. Thus, penalty is every bit as much a part of the incentive structure as is reward.

E. F. Schumacher's book *Small Is Beautiful* was a favorite in the late '70s, particularly among those who considered themselves "socially and environmentally conscious." The book's central thesis, that small-scale technologies and small economic units serve social (including quality of life) functions as well as economic purposes, was important. But unfortunately, proponents of Schumacher's thesis, led by Governor Jerry Brown of California, blindly kept the discussion in terms of "small is beautiful," instead of "small is beautiful and economically efficient." Free-market advocates responded by largely dismissing or ignoring Schumacher's thesis. So, what resulted was that two perspectives, often at odds, missed their essential compatibility when it came to small business. Yes, small business is highly efficient in various markets, as we have seen. Yes, small business provides enormous social functions, as we are about to see. And one doesn't necessarily detract from the other.

**What motivates the entrepreneur? What attracts people into small business?**

In my judgment, no one factor is the primary motivation for entrepreneurial endeavor. There are many, and often they are complexly interwoven within the same individual. Financial reward or profit is obviously one type of motivation; independence or being one's own boss is another; doing what the individual likes to do is yet a third.

The only real evidence one needs to prove that entrepreneurial endeavor fulfills some personal need is to note that an increasingly large percentage of Americans is involved—over 10 percent of adults in 1977 contrasted to only about 8 percent just 30 years earlier. These data represent an historic reversal in the fortunes of small entrepreneurs. The full effect of the Industrial Revolution, including the farm to city migration, on the proportion of entrepreneurs appears to have passed.

These data also confirm the results of numerous opinion polls which consistently conclude that self-employment or small-business ownership is a highly desirable occupation. For example, 3,300 high school seniors surveyed by the University of Michigan preferred self-employment, followed by employment in a small business. Employment in larger institutions such as big business, government, military, was well down the list. A poll conducted by *U.S. News* found that of 25 major socioeconomic entities, small business ranked third in a combination of integrity, dependability and influence. Only science and technology, and television and radio news had higher combined scores.

While there is no empirical evidence of which I am aware directly and systematically linking entrepreneurial activity to personal rises in social and economic status, it is clear various individuals and immigrant groups have used small businesses to that end. Jewish Americans, Chinese Americans, and most recently Cuban Americans are highly visible examples. Each of these immigrant groups faced language barriers which often closed doors to them. But the entrepreneurial door has always been wide open. Many have successfully passed through. However black Americans, economically the poorest major identifiable ethnic group in the United States, to this day have not. They remain grossly underrepresented in the entrepreneurial population.

**For most communities, it is the small-business population that provides a community with its identity, its hope, its goodwill, and its spiritual leadership—and often without the occasional obtrusiveness or beneficence associated with large firms.**

A few years ago, NFIB conducted a survey of its urban members. One of the questions asked was, "Overall, what do you think of your city's prospects for economic improvement in the next twenty years?" As expected, small-business owners in more affluent, rapidly growing areas evaluated their prospects more favorably than did those in non-affluent areas. The surprise was small-business owners located in some of our more distressed cities,—the Detroits, the Newarks, etc. Seventy percent of this group believed the future economic prospects of their city were average or better with more of them believing that their cities would grow at above average rates than at below average rates.

The community cannot remain strong without the confidence of its business community—and it is the small-business owner who provides that confidence where and when it is needed most. Most small entrepreneurs are indigenous; their businesses are located where they live and usually have lived for several years prior to business entry. There is a personal commitment of the small-business owner to the community which extends beyond the interests of his business—a commitment that can be found over and over again, in small business after small business, in city after city across the country.

**Finally, small business disperses economic decision-making within our society.**

Please note I used the term "economic decision-making" rather than "ownership." The fact that more than 30 million Americans own stock directly and, with some overlapping, another 30 million indirectly through vested pension rights is to be applauded. However, dispersal of ownership is not tantamount to dispersal of decision-making, and broad decision-making, at least in a democratic society, is important, if not more so than broad ownership.

The owner of a small business has some economic decision-making power. He can set prices, make or not make investments, move or retain his location, hire or lay-off employees, and so on. . . . But he does exercise some influence which in concert with the influence exercised by others effectively defines operation of a market. In contrast, the individual possessing stock ownership in a large firm usually has absolutely no decision-making power. The best he can hope to do under normal circumstances is harass management once a year at the annual shareholder's meeting.

In 1976, it was estimated by the Federal Trade Commission (FTC) that the manufacturing and retail sectors held over $1 trillion in assets. More than half of those assets were held by about 200 firms with over $1 billion in assets each. Those relatively few large firms were owned by a hefty percentage of the nation's 30 million direct stockholders. Yet, how many stockholders had any say over any decision made by the corporation? Very few. Contrast that with the decision-making capacity of the small-business owner. His share of assets was individually minimal, but he determines their entire disposition. In such a manner, small business serves to disperse the nation's economic decision-making power.

**Does small business play a significant role in our economy and our society?**

Without hesitation, I will tell you that it does. I will also tell you I believe small business will continue to play a significant role in our economy and in our society. But not only do I believe it, the evidence supports it.

In 1840, Alexis de Tocqueville provided one of the more interesting observations ever made about the American economy. He wrote:

> [W]hat most astonished me in the United States was not so much the grandeur of some undertakings as the innumerable multitude of small ones.

I think that should an equally observant Frenchman visit this land in the year 2040, he would make a similar observation.

# Socialism, Free Enterprise, and the Common Good
## Robert A. Sirico (2007)

---

*Robert Sirico is co-founder and president of the Acton Institute for the Study of Religion and Liberty (www.acton.org). A Roman Catholic priest with a special interest in economic issues, Sirico received his Master of Divinity degree from the Catholic University of America, following undergraduate study at the University of Southern California and the University of London. He has written for numerous publications. He is also currently pastor of St. Mary Catholic Church in Kalamazoo, Michigan. This essay compares the real effects of capitalism and socialism on the well-being of people.*

May 2007 *Imprimis*

In chapter 21 of St. Matthew's Gospel, Jesus proposes a moral dilemma in the form of a parable: A man asks his two sons to go to work for him in his vineyard. The first son declines, but later ends up going. The second son tells his father he will go, but never does. "Who," Jesus asks, "did the will of his father?" Although I am loath to argue that Jesus's point in this parable was an economic one, we may nonetheless derive from it a moral lesson with which to evaluate economic systems in terms of achieving the common good.

Modern history presents us with two divergent models of economic arrangement: socialism and capitalism. One of these appears preoccupied with the common good and social betterment, the other with profits and production. But let us keep the parable in mind as we take a brief tour of economic history.

The idea of socialism, of course, dates back to the ancient world, but here I will focus on its modern incarnation. And if we look to socialism's modern beginnings, we find it optimistic and well-intentioned. In contrast to contemporary varieties that tend to bemoan prosperity, romanticize poverty, and promote the idea that civil rights are of secondary concern, at least some of the early socialists sought the fullest possible flourishing of humanity—which is to say, the common good.

A half-century before Karl Marx published the *Communist Manifesto*, there was Gracchus Babeuf's *Plebeian Manifesto* (later revised by Sylvain Marechal and renamed the *Manifesto of the Equals*). Babeuf was an early communist who lived from 1760 to 1797 and wrote during the revolutionary period in France. Although he was jailed and eventually executed, his ideas would later have an enormous impact. And his explicit political goal had nothing to do with impeding prosperity. To the contrary, he wrote:

> The French Revolution was nothing but a precursor of another revolution, one that will be bigger, more solemn, and which will be the last. . . . We reach for something more sublime and more just: the common good or the community of goods! No more individual property in land: the land belongs to no one. We demand, we want, the common enjoyment of the fruits of the land: the fruits belong to all.

110

We see in Babeuf's writings two themes that would remain dominant in socialist theory until the twentieth century: an aspiration to prosperity through ownership by all and an equation of the common good with the commonality of goods. Indeed, Marx took more from Babeuf than Marx himself would ever acknowledge.

In our own time, we think of socialists as opposing capitalist excess, disparaging the mass availability of goods and services, and seeking to restrict the freedom to produce and enjoy wealth. Consider, for instance, the wrath that modern socialists feel towards fast food, large discount stores, and specialty financial services for the poor. They accuse the mass consumer market of institutionalizing false needs, commodifying the commons, glorifying the banal, homogenizing culture—all at the expense of the environment and of equality of condition, the highest socialist goal. Improving the standard of living in society is far down the list of modern socialist priorities.

But to repeat, it was not always so. Early socialists believed that socialism would bring about an advance of civilization and an increase in wealth. Babeuf, for example, predicted that socialism would "[have] us eat four good meals a day, [dress] us most elegantly, and also [provide] those of us who are fathers of families with charming houses worth a thousand louis each." In short, socialism would distribute prosperity across the entire population. A particularly poetic rendering of this vision was offered by none other than Oscar Wilde:

> Under Socialism . . . there will be no people living in fetid dens and fetid rags, and bringing up unhealthy, hunger-pinched children in the midst of impossible and absolutely repulsive surroundings. . . . Each member of the society will share in the general prosperity and happiness of the society, and if a frost comes no one will practically be anything the worse. . . .

The core of the old socialist hope was a mass prosperity that would free all people from the burden of laboring for others and place them in a position to pursue higher ends, such as art and philosophy, in a conflict-free society. But there was a practical problem: The Marxist prediction of a revolution that would bring about this good society rested on the assumption that the condition of the working classes would grow ever worse under capitalism. But by the early twentieth century it was clear that this assumption was completely wrong. Indeed, the reverse was occurring: As wealth grew through capitalist means, the standard of living of all was improving.

## Lifting All Boats

Historians now realize that even in the early years of the Industrial Revolution, workers were becoming better off. Prices were falling, incomes rising, health and sanitation improving, diets becoming more varied, and working conditions constantly improving. The new wealth generated by capitalism dramatically lengthened life spans and decreased child mortality rates. The new jobs being created in industry paid more than most people could make in agriculture. Housing conditions improved. The new heroes of society came from the middle class as business owners and industrialists displaced the nobility and gentry in the cultural hierarchy.

Much has been made about the rise of child labor and too little about the fact that, for the first time, there was remunerative work available for people of all ages. As economist W. H. Hutt has shown, work in the factories for young people was far less grueling than it had been on the farm, which is one reason parents favored the factory. As for working hours, it

*Workers at a Cigar Factory in Rhode Island, 1912*

is documented that when factories would reduce hours, the employees would leave to go to work for factories that made it possible for them to work longer hours and earn additional wages. The main effect of legislation that limited working hours for minors was to drive employment to smaller workshops that could more easily evade the law.

In the midst of all this change, many people seemed only to observe an increase in the number of the poor. In a paradoxical way, this too was a sign of social progress, since so many of these unfortunate people might have been dead in past ages. But the deaths of the past were unseen and forgotten, whereas current poverty was omnipresent. Meanwhile, as economic development expanded in the nineteenth century, there was a dramatic growth of a middle class that now had access to consumer goods once available only to kings—not to mention plenty of new goods being created by the engine of capitalism.

These economic advances continued throughout the period of the rise of socialist ideology. The poor didn't get poorer because the rich were getting richer (a familiar socialist refrain even today) as the socialists had predicted. Instead, the underlying reality was that capitalism had created the first societies in history in which living standards were rising in all sectors of society. In a sense, free market capitalism was coming closest to realizing what Marx himself had imagined: "the all round development of individuals" in which "the productive forces will also have increased" and "the springs of social wealth will flow more freely."

There was one Marxist in England who seemed to understand what was happening. Eduard Bernstein, who lived from 1850 to 1932, is hardly known today. His writings are not studied, except by specialists. But he was the leading Marxist after Marx and Engels. Engels considered him their successor, and even asked him to finish editing Marx's fourth volume of *Capital*.

In the 1890s, Bernstein began to observe the positive effects of capitalism on living standards. "What characterizes the modern mode of production above all," he wrote, "is the great increase in the productive power of labour. The result is a no less increase of production—the production of masses of commodities." This empirical fact struck at the very heart of the Marxist case. Bernstein also observed that the numbers of businesses and of people who were well-off were rising along with incomes. As he put it, "The increase of social wealth is not accompanied by a diminishing number of capitalist magnates, but by an increasing number of capitalists of all degrees." In fact, in the 50 years after the publication of the Communist Manifesto, incomes in England and Germany doubled—precisely the opposite of what Marx had predicted. To quote Bernstein again, from 1899:

> If the collapse of modern society depends on the disappearance of the middle ranks between the apex and the base of the social pyramid, if it is dependent upon the absorption of these middle classes by the extremes above and below them, then its realisation is no nearer in England, France, and Germany today than at any earlier time in the nineteenth century.

The basis of Marxist doctrine had been the idea that society under capitalism consisted of two classes—one small and rich, the other vast and increasingly impoverished. The reality, however, was that the numbers of the rich were growing more rapidly than those of the poor, while the vast majority was falling into a category that socialism didn't anticipate: the middle class. Doctrinaire Marxists were of course furious with Bernstein for noticing these developments. Rosa Luxemburg, for one, wrote a famous essay in 1890 attacking him.

One might assume, then, that Bernstein changed sides—abandoning socialism upon seeing its false premises—and took up instead the classical liberal cause of free enterprise. I'm sorry to report that this is not the case. What Bernstein changed instead were his tactics. He still favored the expropriation of the English capitalists, but now through a different method—not through revolution, but through the use of political mechanisms. And indeed, the political success of socialism during the twentieth century would bring England to the brink of catastrophe more than once.

## Ideology vs. Reality

If one becomes aware that the older moral argument for socialism is wrong—that capitalism is actually benefiting people and serving the common good—why would one hold on to the ideology rather than abandon it? Clearly, it is difficult to abandon a lifelong ideology, especially if one considers the only available alternative to be tainted with evil. Thus socialism was, for Bernstein's generation of socialists and for many that followed, simply an entrenched dogma. It was possible for them to argue the finer points, but not to abandon it.

However understandable this might be, it is not praiseworthy. To hold on to a doctrine that is demonstrably false is to abandon all pretense of objectivity. If someone could demonstrate to me that free markets and private property rights lead to impoverishment, dictatorship, and the violation of human rights on a mass scale, I would like to think that I would have the sense and ability to concede the point and move on. In any case, socialists like Bernstein lacked any such intellectual humility. They clung to their faith—their false religion—as if their lives were at stake. Many continue to do so today.

Most intellectuals in the world are aware of what socialism did to Russia. And yet many still cling to the socialist ideal. The truth about Mao's reign of terror is no longer a secret. And yet it remains intellectually fashionable to regret the advance of capitalism in China, even as the increasing freedom of the Chinese people to engage in commerce has enhanced their lives. Many Europeans are fully aware of how damaging democratic socialism has been in Germany, France, and Spain. And yet they continue to oppose the liberalization of these economies. Here in the United States, we've seen the failure of mass programs of redistribution and the fiscal crises to which they give rise. And yet many continue to defend and promote them.

There have long been cases where grotesque examples of the failure of socialism exist alongside glowing examples of capitalist success, and yet many people will use every excuse to avoid attributing the differences to their economic systems. Even a superficial comparison of North and South Korea, East and West Germany before the Berlin Wall fell, Hong Kong and mainland China before reforms, or Cuba and other countries of Latin America, demonstrates that free economies are superior at promoting the common good. And yet the truth has not sunk in.

The older socialists dreamed of a world in which all classes the world over would share in the fruits of production. Today, we see something like this as Wal-Marts—to cite only the most conspicuous example—spring up daily in town after town worldwide. Within each of these stores is a veritable cornucopia of goods designed to improve human well-being, at prices that make them affordable for all. Here is a company that has created many millions of jobs and brought prosperity to places where it was sorely needed. And who owns Wal-Mart? Shareholders, people of mostly moderate incomes who have invested their savings. We might call them worker-capitalists. Such an institution was beyond the imaginings of the socialists of old.

Although the free enterprise system obviously does not incorporate the old socialists' idea of a commonality of goods, it does seem to achieve the common good as they conceived it. What then can we say of those who today remain attached to socialism as a political goal? We can say that they do not know or have not understood the economic history of the last 300 years. Or perhaps we can say that they are more attached to socialism as an ideology than they are to the professed goals of its founders. I'm particularly struck by the neo-socialist concern for the well-being of plants, animals, lakes and rivers, rain forests and deserts—particularly when the concern for the environment appears far more intense than the concern for the human family.

## The Good of Freedom

When we speak of the common good, we need also to be clear-minded about the political and juridical institutions that are most likely to bring it about. These happen to be the very institutions that socialists have worked so hard to discredit. Let me list them: private property in the means of production; stable money to serve as a means of exchange; the freedom of enterprise that allows people to start businesses; the free association of workers that permits people to choose where they would like to work and under what conditions; the enforcement of contracts that provides institutional support for the idea that people should keep their promises; and a vibrant trade within and among nations to permit the fullest possible flowering of the division of labor. These institutions must be supported by a cultural infrastructure that respects private property, regards the human person as possessing an inherent dignity, and confers its first loyalty to transcendent authority over civil authority. This is the basis of freedom, without which the common good is unreachable. Thus Pope John Paul II wrote of economic initiative:

> It is a right which is important not only for the individual but also for the common good. Experience shows us that the denial of this right, or its limitation in the name of an alleged "equality" of everyone in society, diminishes, or in practice absolutely destroys, the spirit of initiative, that is to say the creative subjectivity of the citizen.

To summarize: We are all entitled to call ourselves socialist, if by the term we mean that we are devoted to the early socialist goal of the well-being of all members of society. Reason and experience make clear that the means to achieve this is not through central planning by the state, but through political and economic freedom. Thomas Aquinas had an axiom: *bonum est diffusivum sui.* "The good pours itself out." The good of freedom has indeed poured itself out to the benefit of humanity.

In conclusion, I ask you, "Who did the will of the Father?"

# Labor Unions in a Free Market
## Ernest van den Haag (1979)

*Dr. Ernest van den Haag (1914-2002) was a writer, a professor, and a psychoanalyst. An immigrant to the United States, he received his Ph.D. from New York University. In this presentation he dealt with important issues related to labor unions. The footnotes are part of the original text.*

March 1979 *Imprimis*

I shall try to deal with four topics: I. Why do labor unions exist? What do they do? II. What are the effects of their activities? III. Strikes and restrictive practices. IV. How could the law control labor unions and their activities in the public interest?

## I. Why do labor unions exist? What do they do?

G. F. W. Hegel once said, "Everything that is, is rational." Surely that is not true if rational means "desirable." But it is true, if rational means explainable as the effect of causes. For, actions are undertaken, and associations continue, only as long as they foster the interests—material or psychological—of at least some persons. That goes for the Mafia, and for the police department, for Hillsdale College—and for labor unions.

Unions yield power, prestige, and income to their officers; but they would not be supported by the members if their interests were not served too. They are: unions often succeed in raising wages and other benefits. Because they can obtain these advantages, unions are supported by many employees. In the U.S. one-fourth of the labor force is unionized; in other countries the proportion is even higher.

Unions also give workers a feeling, so often lacking in our life, of participation, of solidarity with fellow employees and of community. This feeling is not generated by simply working with others. It is created when unions succeed in providing fringe benefits (e.g., health services, or pensions, or life insurance) tied to the job and common leisure activities (outings, vacations, etc.) for their members. These things could be provided by employers, too (they are in Japan) regardless of unions. But in the U.S. employers have acted in this area only for executives. This failure has helped unions to give workers a proprietary stake in their jobs while fostering solidarity among members and antagonism to employers. Unions have been able to create solidarity among members by helping them to perceive one another as brothers standing together against a hostile and exploitative father figure on whom they depend: the boss. Few things strengthen solidarity more than a common enemy. To be sure, economic life actually rests on cooperation. Without employers there can be no employees. Yet there is ambivalence and occasional conflict about how the products of the common work of employees and management, of labor and capital, are to be shared, and about who is to make decisions. Unions capitalize on the feelings of members that they ought to get more power and money and promise to get both for them.

Unions do not always benefit members. Some workers feel they are better off on their own. Others resent specific union practices or policies, or the cost of membership. Wherefore quite a number of workers resist unionization; they are often pressured and sometimes legally compelled to join unions if they want to keep their jobs. Despite these practices, union members are now a smaller proportion of all employees than they were in the past. Unions retain high membership mainly where there is a strong union tradition, or where workers are compelled to join. They have gained new members chiefly among government workers: the employer—the government—has been politically unwilling or unable to resist them. Public, unlike private, employers have a nearly bottomless purse, fed by the printing press, or by taxation. Thus, New York City, as employer, hovers near bankruptcy because of too many overpaid employees. The unions prevent the necessary firings and wage and pension decreases.

## II. What are the effects of their activities?

When unions benefit their members by obtaining higher wages, the money cannot come out of the profits of employers, although members are encouraged to believe that it does. All the employer's yearly profit hardly ever suffices to pay for a single hefty pay raise. (If he were deprived of all profit, the employer would have no reason to stay in business.) On the average, employers make a profit of roughly .05 per dollar of sales. Labor costs usually make up more than half of the sales dollar. Hence an increase cannot come out of profits. Thus the money for raises must come:

1. Out of higher productivity—more value produced per unit of input. But productivity increases only 3% a year on the average (less in the last few years). Unions attempt to raise wage rates far beyond that.

2. From higher prices for whatever is produced by the workers whose wage rate has risen. But when prices rise, less is being sold than would be sold at a lower price—else sellers would have charged more to begin with. When less is sold, less is produced and fewer workers are employed in the industries that had to raise prices. Or, sometimes, prices do not rise despite higher wage costs. The market may not permit price hikes without excessive sales losses. In that case the least efficient producers lose money and drop out. Once more, less is produced and fewer workers are employed.

Either way, union members get higher wages only at the expense of workers who do not get, or do not keep, jobs because of lower sales and less production. These workers remain unemployed or have to go into lower paying non-unionized jobs. (Recently some of the losses have been shifted to taxpayers. Those who become unemployed, because of the higher wage rates union demand, receive unemployment and other benefits. As a result they may not be willing to work in low paying occupations.)

3. If real wages for all workers—their actual purchasing power—could be increased by union activity (or by government decree), Italian or English wages, or Soviet wages, would be higher than ours. They are not. Or, our government could double all wages by law and get itself reelected forever. This sort of thing often has been tried (minimum wage laws are a remnant of such attempts) but it does not work [see footnote 1]. Actually, if all wages are increased—by concerted union action or by governments—one of two things happens:

(a) If the government does not allow the volume of monetary circulation to increase, inflation is prevented: prices cannot rise as wages do. When wages increase and prices (or productivity) do not (or not as much), profits decline and become losses for some; many firms stop, or reduce production, and hardly any expand. There is unemployment, and the real income of the population as a whole is reduced, although the workers who keep their jobs do well. They are not likely to enjoy it though. They lose overtime. Also they may fear for their jobs as others are fired and production is reduced. And among the fired, they may have relatives and friends.

(b) If the government allows the volume of monetary circulation to increase as wages do, there is inflation. Prices rise, and real wages (purchasing power) do not go up. Workers get more and have to pay more. People on fixed incomes suffer, and so do creditors who get the money due them but can buy less for it. All kinds of undesirable things happen, and there either is hyperinflation—rapid devaluation of the currency (rapid price level increases) and a return to barter—or the government deflates after all, i.e., it finally reduces the volume of monetary circulation. The government can do so by reducing its own expenditure financed by creating money, by increasing interest rates, and by other means which shrink the volume of money in circulation. In a major deflation prices fall and so do profits, employment and production. This is what Chile had to do after President Allende decreed wage increases financed by inflation, and to some extent we are doing so now [in 1978 and 1979]. In a minor deflation, such as we are bringing about, prices merely stop rising, or rise at a lower rate.

That much if all wages rise. The rise does not help workers, whether they have unions or not, because the real wage level (the wages of workers as a group, as distinguished from the wages of groups of workers) does not depend on unions, or laws, but on productivity. However, as indicated, unions can benefit their members by increasing not the wage level but the wages of groups of members, or of unionized industries and firms, at the expense of causing unemployment and an oversupply of workers, or depressed wages, in non-unionized industries.

*Women's Auxiliary Typographical Union Float in a Labor Day Parade, New York City, 1909*

Thus, unions do not foster the interest of the working class as a whole—but members may find that unions can increase their own wages and benefits. Even if inflation occurs, union members usually do not understand the role of unions in causing it: greedy speculators and businessmen are blamed by union leaders. The members are led to feel that the union continues to serve their interests and to protect them from the effects of the inflation for which "speculators" or "business" are blamed.

### III. Strikes and restrictive practices.

With or without unions, wage rates are determined by the demand for, and the supply of, different kinds of labor. But with unions the market is not free. The function of unions is to attempt to monopolize and restrict the supply of labor—at least of labor in specific places and of specific kinds—and to obtain a monopoly price for it, higher than the free market price would be [see footnote 2]. This is done in two ways:

1. By restricting union membership while compelling employers to hire only union members. This is how craft unions prevent employers from availing themselves of the full labor pool. Thus, the drivers of newspaper delivery trucks in New York get high wages. They allow very few people to join the union and prevent the newspapers from hiring non-union members. They can bargain from the monopoly position they create because New York law, and the practices of the New York police department, would make it impossible for the newspapers to hire non-union drivers: they might be killed, and their trucks would be sabotaged.

2. By threatening to strike, unions may be able to compel employers to confine their hiring to union members and to pay them higher than free market wages. Even when industrial (as distinguished from craft) unions permit employers to hire non-union members, or allow anyone to join, the strike threat can be used to raise wages whenever enough employees can be persuaded or intimidated into refraining from work in a concerted effort to support union demands.

To strike is to refrain from working while keeping one's job and discouraging, or preventing, others from doing it [see footnote 3]. In economic terms, to strike is to withhold the supply of labor, to prevent its being replaced, and to attempt to compel employers to pay the price the union wishes to charge. Unless the employer can break the strike, by hiring non-strikers, or by getting strikers to return, he has to accept the union's terms. He has to pay a wage higher than the free market wage—the wage just high enough to attract the workers he needs.

Strikes—and all union-imposed monopoly prices for labor—are contrary to the public interest. If lost by the union, strikes leave the status quo ante in force—after a loss of production and income by employers and employees and, often, considerable losses to third parties. If won by the union, strikes, in addition to losses of income and production, lead to a redistribution of income from non-union to union members; this increases the inequality of incomes while not increasing the

*Cloak-Makers on Strike in New York City, 1916*

income of workers as a whole. Finally, if they lead to general wage increases, strikes generate inflation. Strikes cannot redistribute income from employers to employees.

Nonetheless, it would be a mistake to blame unions for all strikes. Strikes can happen without unions, as history shows, and against unions, as "wild cat" strikes show. Indeed, unionization may prevent strikes as well as bring them about. As much may be said about most other union activity. It is true that much union activity is harmful to the public interest. Feather-bedding is; so are work rules which require employment of unproductive workers;

and jurisdictional disputes: all of these reduce productivity. But the free market, though efficient, is also uncomfortable. Groups always have tried to protect themselves against some of the most uncomfortable effects of the free market, such as loss of jobs in any industry because of technological change, or competition. (Employment elsewhere may be available, but the transition is difficult.) Groups of employers have tried to protect themselves by tariffs, or laws, or licensing requirements. Groups of workers, too, will protect themselves spontaneously, and it is futile merely to point out that their actions are against the public interest. People tend to protect their own. At best we can minimize the harmful effects of special interest actions, including those of unions. To this I shall turn now.

## IV. How could the law control labor unions and their activities in the public interest?

In the U.S., unions and their relations with employers and with the community at large are to a great extent regulated by law. This regulation is a mixed blessing. But other countries, such as England, with much less legal regulation, are not better off. Thus the issue is how much and what kind of regulation is needed, and how it can be made effective in the public interest. In the U.S. a deliberate attempt has been made to legally protect unions against what was thought of as the overwhelming power of employers. But the power distribution has changed, partly as a result of these laws, and today employers, individuals, and the public, do need protection from unions more than unions need protection from employers. Nonetheless, present law still attempts

1. to protect and foster union activities;

2. to compel employers to bargain;

3. to compel employers not to replace strikers;

4. to give unions a monopoly in representing workers to employers, in fixing the price of labor and the conditions of employment;

5. to compel the government to pay union wages (in practice more than union wages) to all its employees and to force government contractors to do so (the Davis-Bacon Act).

6. Very little regulation restricts the power of unions to interfere with the processes of production, to determine how many people and who will do a particular job, to strike at will, and to deprive society of needed services.

As long as employers have a chance to resist strikes by replacing workers or by moving away, union demands can be restrained. But there is little chance of doing so. Usually employers have to yield or give up their businesses. The latter possibility, which would deprive union members of employment, may or may not restrain union demands. It seldom does, for union leaders depend on the votes of their members. They cannot easily moderate their demands on employers, for other more militant leaders may be elected in their stead. Hence, when unions have enough power to use the strike threat effectively, the wages of members tend to rise, making unemployment of non-members, or inflation, hard to avoid.

A union must be bargained with by law, if the majority of employees join. The union then will bargain for non-members as well—whether or not they like it; usually it can compel the minority to join as a condition of continued employment. Employers must bargain not only for wages, but also for working conditions, promotions, seniority, manning, hiring and firing, the use of technology, the amount of production per worker, and fringe benefits [see footnote 4]. Unions are allowed to picket to advertise disputes. And although pickets legally are not allowed to intimidate or to prevent workers or others who wish to work, or to enter the plant, from doing so, in practice pickets can prevent non-strikers from working. Unions also are allowed to boycott products and producers and to harass customers and third parties not involved in a labor conflict so as to get indirectly at their employers.

One peculiar result is that unions have driven the price of labor so high in some industries (e.g., maritime and housing) that government subsidies become necessary if the industry is to continue. Unions have used political means to get these subsidies. Thus, in effect, the higher wages are paid by taxpayers who pay subsidies for housing and maritime activity.

What could regulation do to protect the public interest while being fair to all parties involved? It will be convenient to deal with occupations and industries according to the degree of interest the public has in avoiding strikes.

1. Strikes should not be permitted in public service industries or by public employees— e.g., police and firemen, garbage men, teachers, hospital or nursing home personnel, and workers in major utilities, such as electricity producers or mass transportation facilities, whether publicly or privately owned.

Here strikes should be altogether prohibited because quite obviously the harm they cause to innocent bystanders—electricity consumers, hospital patients, school children—is far greater than any conceivable benefit to the parties in conflict could be. Workers volunteer to work in the public service industries. In accepting employment they should be notified that strikes are prohibited by law. Indeed there are such prohibitions in many states. But they are not enforceable because the penalties have been kept so mild as not to deter strikes. Appropriate penalties would have to include:

(a) Fines of sufficient size levied on the union: e.g., for the first day of strike (or slowdown) an amount equal to one year's dues for each member; for the second and third an amount equal to two years' dues, etc.

(b) Each striking union member would lose three years' seniority for each day of striking.

(c) Each striker would lose a part of his pension benefits for each day of striking so that on the fifth day all his pension benefits would be lost (except for any amount he himself paid in).

(d) A similar reduction in other accumulated benefits [see footnote 5].

All of the above should be mandatory: neither courts, nor employers, nor public authorities, should be allowed to reduce these penalties once the existence of an illegal strike and the participation of the union and of the individual strikers involved has been established.

It is most unlikely that under these conditions strikes would take place—they would be suicidal for the unions and for their members. This is the point. To repeat, strikes in public service industries do harm to innocent bystanders far in excess of any benefit the strikers can hope to receive.

In the absence of effective strike threats, what would prevent employers, public or private, from driving down the wages of employees? If these wages (including fringe benefits) were to fall below what employees can earn in other occupations, a shortage of labor would develop. The industry that pays low wages would be compelled to raise them to get the workers it needs. On the other hand, as long as there are more eligible people who want to be teachers, or policemen, than there are jobs for them, teachers and policemen are not underpaid. If the supply greatly exceeds the demand, they are overpaid, if we use not moral but market standards. (The medieval moral notion of a "fair wage"—*pretium justum*—ignores market forces and makes no economic sense.)

There remain a host of questions about which employees may wish to bargain through a union. They can do so without strike threats. Grievance and obligatory arbitration procedures may be set up and even binding arbitration may be required. However, wages should not be subject to arbitration—for they will be regulated satisfactorily by the market in the absence of arbitration. And arbitrators could do no more than guess what the market wage is likely to be. (Moreover they have a tendency to be generous with other people's money.)

2. What about strikes in privately owned industries less directly affecting the public interest—e.g., newspapers, steel mills, coal mines, textile firms . . . ? There are gradations. Present law gives considerable power to the President to take action to prevent or delay strikes if he finds there is a national emergency. Such strikes may be a menace even when they do not paralyze essential services. A steel strike may harm automobile workers who are not involved and even make them unemployed if it lasts long enough. However, except in time of war, such a strike need not create an emergency.

I suggest the following:

(a) Strikes should be legal only if not contrary to contracts.

(b) Union members should vote on authorizing strikes only after governmental mediation and non-binding arbitration have failed.

(c) Strikers, who, after all, voluntarily refrain from working and earning, should not be entitled to receive unemployment or welfare benefits.

(d) Nor should strikers be allowed to intimidate others or to prevent them from working.

(e) Employers should be free to keep employees hired during a strike and to fire strikers for being strikers. (Thus employers will have a chance to win as well as lose. Strikes will become more risky for unions.)

(f) While unions should be free to bargain on working conditions, wages and benefits, they should not be allowed to compel employers to hire or keep workers they feel are not needed. Featherbedding should be outlawed, and manning should not be subject to bargaining. Featherbedding increases the cost of production (which ultimately has to be paid for by the public) and keeps workers paid for something unproductive, preventing them from doing something productive. (Featherbedding has greatly contributed to ruining our railroads.)

(g) Unions should be able to bargain on pensions (and on severance pay). But, by law, pensions should never be permitted to exceed two-thirds of the pay received by employees while on the job. Else, the employer might have to pay the same whether a worker is working or not—which would lead to a reduction in social productivity. (These rules must be enforced by effective penalties. Hefty mandatory fines for violators might be enough—unions don't like to lose their treasure.)

The proposed restrictions on union activity may appear one-sided and, therefore, unfair. Actually they restore the balance that has been tilted in favor of unions by legislation. Moreover, employer-employee relations are not like a football match in which both teams should have an equal chance under fair conditions.

Strikes harm third persons, not just employers and employees. Unions and employers fight, win or lose, at the expense of the public interest. The public loses more, in all major strikes, than either party can hope to win. And if the union wins and compels the employer to pay wages in excess of those that demand and supply in a free market would have brought about, union members benefit at the expense of other workers and of the public at large. Thus the problem is not of arranging a fair fight between unions and employers, but rather of avoiding a fight altogether, and of limiting the results of union victories in the interest of other workers and of the public at large. The very existence of unions and of strikes, however unavoidable, tilts the mechanism of the free market in an unfair manner in favor of the union members and against other workers and the public. Legal restrictions on union power, far from being unfair, merely reduce the invasion of the labor market by monopoly power.

Footnotes:

[1] Minimum wage laws, where the government rather than unions raises the wage, result in high unemployment among the least productive workers—mainly black adolescents. Employers do not hire those to whom they have to pay more than the market value of their contribution to production. Many of those unemployed because of minimum wage laws turn to crime—an uncovered occupation. Hence the crime rate among black adolescents is particularly high. They have been excluded from legitimate occupations owing to the efforts, presumably on their behalf, of their liberal and union friends.

[2] Unions are legally exempted from anti-monopoly legislation.

[3] A "lock-out"—an attempt by an employer to pressure workers to accept his wages and working conditions by refusing to employ them otherwise and dismissing those who are employed—apart from occurring quite rarely, is not parallel to a strike: employers do not attempt, by pickets or otherwise, to prevent their employees from finding other jobs.

[4] To bargain is defined as yielding on some of one's initial positions.

[5] Jailing of strikers or strike leaders has been shown to be wholly ineffective. So are fines, unless massive size is mandated.

# The Legitimate Role of Government in a Free Society
## Walter E. Williams (2000)

*Walter Williams is the John M. Olin Distinguished Professor of Economics at George Mason University in Virginia. He holds the Ph.D. in economics from UCLA. Dr. Williams has written six books and dozens of articles. He appears often on radio and television discussing economic issues. In this speech Dr. Williams discusses a vital but often overlooked topic.*

August 2000 *Imprimis*

What did the founders of the United States see as the legitimate role of government? To answer that question we should turn to the rule book they gave us: the United States Constitution. Most of what they considered legitimate functions of the federal government are found in Article I, Section 8 of our Constitution, which says, in part: "The Congress shall have Power To lay and collect Taxes, Duties, Imposts and Excises, to pay the Debts and provide for the common Defense and general Welfare of the United States . . . To borrow Money on the credit of the United States . . . To regulate Commerce with foreign Nations, and among the several States, and with the Indian tribes . . . To coin money . . . To establish Post Offices and post Roads . . . To raise and support Armies." The framers granted Congress taxing and spending powers for a few other activities, but nowhere in the Constitution do we find authority for up to three-quarters of what Congress taxes and spends for today. There is no constitutional authorization for farm subsidies, bank bailouts, or food stamps—not to mention midnight basketball. We have made a significant departure from the constitutional principles of individual freedom and limited government that made us a rich nation in the first place.

These principles of freedom were embodied in our nation through the combined institutions of private ownership of property and free enterprise, both of which have suffered devastating attacks and are mere skeletons of what they were in the past.

## The Social Value of Private Property and Free Enterprise

Private property performs at least two important social functions: it encourages people to do voluntarily what is in the social interest, and it minimizes the coercive power that one man or the state can have over another. And it performs these functions without appeals to beneficence.

I do not care much about future generations. After all, what has a child born in 2050 A.D. ever done for me? My actions, however, do not reflect this personal sentiment. Several years ago I planted young trees on my property and made other improvements. I will be dead by the time the trees mature. A child born in 2050 A.D. will enjoy the fruits of my sacrifices. I could just as easily have spent the money for [things] which I would have fully enjoyed all to myself. Why did I make these improvements to my property? At least part of the reason is that I will get a higher price when I sell the property if its quality is higher and it can be expected to provide housing services for a longer period of time. By pursuing my own interest, I made it possible for future generations to have a nice house. Would I have had the same strong incentive if the government owned my house? Obviously not.

Look around the world: you will see that what receives the least care tends to be commonly owned; that which receives the best care tends to be privately owned. In free markets, one's personal wealth is held hostage to socially responsible behavior. To take another example, the citizens of New York derive their daily meals not from the benevolence of the Missouri farmer (who may in fact hate New Yorkers) but because it is in his own private self-interest to supply them. Most things get done because of self-interest and private property rights.

The Founders understood that relatively free markets are the most effective form of social organization for promoting individual freedom. Indeed, capitalism is defined as a system wherein individuals are free to pursue their own interests, make voluntary exchanges, and hold private property rights in goods and services. Much of the original intent of the United States Constitution, as seen in the document itself and in the Federalist Papers that advocated its ratification, was to bring about a climate in which this kind of social organization could occur. In a free society, most relationships should be voluntary, and involuntary exchange should be minimized.

Widespread private control and ownership of property is consistent with this objective. Despite the size and alleged power of industrial giants like IBM, AT&T, and General Motors, in a free market they cannot get a dollar from me unless I volunteer to give it to them. Widespread government ownership and/or control of property is the antithesis of voluntary exchange. Government is the major source of forced exchanges, the most prominent of which is taxation.

## A Totalitarian Future?

Anything that weakens the institution of private property interferes with the attainment of the socially desirable outcomes just described. Taxes represent government claims on private property. As taxes rise, you own less and less of what you earn. If the tax rate were ever to reach 100 percent, the government would have destroyed private property, and you would own none of what you had earned. Keep in mind that a working definition of slavery is that you work but do not have any rights to the fruit of your labor.

Taxation and regulation constitute the confiscation of some or all of the freedom to own and use property. This confiscation has reached unprecedented proportions. In 1902 expenditures at all levels of government totaled $1.7 billion, and the average taxpayer paid only $60 a year in taxes. In fact, from 1787 to 1920, federal expenditures never exceeded 4 percent of the Gross National Product (GNP), except in wartime. Today federal expenditures alone are $1.8 trillion—almost 30 percent of GNP—and state and local governments spend over a trillion more. The average taxpayer now pays more than $8,000 a year, working from January 1 to May 8 to pay federal, state, and local taxes. In addition to the out-of-pocket cost, Americans spend 5.4 billion hours each year complying with the federal tax code—roughly the equivalent of 3 million people working full time. If it were employed in productive activity, the labor now devoted to tax compliance would be worth $232 billion annually. The federal cost of hiring 93,000 IRS employees is $6 billion. If these Americans weren't fooling around with the tax code, they could produce the entire annual output of the aircraft, trucking, auto, and food-processing industries combined.

In spite of the tax burden, capitalism has been so successful in eliminating disease, pestilence, hunger, and gross poverty that other human problems now appear both unbearable and inexcusable. Free enterprise thus is threatened today not because of its failure but, somewhat ironically, because of its success. Although the rise of capitalism brought better treatment to women, racial minorities, the handicapped, criminals, and the insane, social reformers assert that "it doesn't work" and "is dehumanizing." In the name of ideals such as income equality, sex and race balance, affordable housing and medical care, orderly markets, consumer protection, and energy conservation, to name just a few, we have imposed widespread government controls that have subordinated us to a point at which considerations of personal freedom are but secondary or tertiary matters. If you take tiny steps toward a goal, one day you will get there, and the ultimate end of this process is totalitarianism, which is no more than a reduced form of servitude. As David Hume said, "It is seldom that liberty of any kind is lost all at once."

In the vanguard of this totalitarian movement are defenders of the "new human rights," the chief advocates of curtailing rights to property and profits. They are anti-competition and pro-monopoly. They support control and coercion by the state. They believe that they have more intelligence and wisdom than the masses and that they are ordained to impose that wisdom forcibly on the rest of us. They want to replace the market with economic planning, which is nothing more than the forcible superseding of other people's plans by a powerful elite. Of course they have what they call good reasons, but every tyrant has what he calls a good reason for restricting the freedom of others.

The elites' assault on the principles of freedom would have been less devastating had not Americans from all walks of life, whether they realized it or not, demonstrated a deep and abiding contempt for private property rights and economic freedom that stemmed primarily from their desire for government to do good. They decided that government should care for the poor, the disadvantaged, the elderly, failing businesses, college students, and many other "deserving" segments of our society. It's nice to do those things, but we have to recognize that government has no resources of its own. Congressmen and senators are not spending their own money for these programs.

Furthermore, there is no Tooth Fairy or Santa Claus who gives them the resources. The only way the government can give one American one dollar is to confiscate it first, under intimidation, threats, and coercion, from another American. In other words, for government to do good, it must first do evil. If a private person were to do the things that government does, he would be condemned as a common thief. The only difference is legality, and legality alone is no talisman for moral people. This reasoning explains why socialism is evil. It uses bad means (coercion) to achieve what are seen as good ends (helping people).

## From Good Intentions to Corruption

Government was not long in the business of doing good before Americans found they could use government to live at the expense of other Americans, both through the tax code and through "privilege granting," a government activity that dates back to medieval times in Europe, where guilds and mercantile associations controlled trade in their particular areas. With a payment to the king or a reigning lord they were granted monopoly privileges. In modern times, we have the equivalent; we just call them political contributions.

Almost every group in the nation has come to feel that the government owes it a special privilege or favor. Manufacturers feel that the government owes them protective tariffs. Farmers feel that the government owes them crop subsidies. Unions feel that the government should keep their jobs protected from non-union competition. Residents of coastal areas feel that the government should give them funds for rivers and harbors. Intellectuals feel that the government should give them funds for research. The unemployed and the unemployable feel that the government owes them a living. Big business feels that the government should protect them from the rigors of market competition. Members of almost every occupation, profession, or trade feel that the government should use licensing requirements and other forms of regulation to protect their incomes from competition that would be caused by others entering the trade.

Conservatives are by no means exempt from this practice. They rail against food stamps, legal aid, and Aid to Families with Dependent Children, but they come out in favor of aid to dependent farmers, aid to dependent banks, and aid to dependent motorcycle companies. They don't have a moral leg to stand on. They merely prove to the nation that it is just a matter of whose ox is being gored. Conservatives as well as liberals validate H. L. Mencken's definition of an election: "—government is a broker in pillage, and every election is a sort of advance auction sale of stolen goods." To the extent he was right, we must acknowledge that we, not the politicians, are the problem.

## The Way Back

Our government has become destructive of the ends it was created to serve. John Stuart Mill, who wrote the classic text *On Liberty*, said, in discussing the limits of government power, "[T]he only purpose for which power can be rightfully exercised over any member of a civilized society, against his will, is to prevent harm to others. His own good, either physical or moral, is not sufficient warrant." Mill added, "He cannot rightfully be compelled because it would be better for him to do so . . . because it will make him happier" or because, in the opinion of others, "to do so would be wise, or even right." Finally, Mill said, "These are good reasons for remonstrating him, or persuading him, but not for compelling him, or visiting him with an evil in the case he do otherwise."

We have gone much further than what Mill and John Locke argued are the limits to coercion in a free society. Part of the problem is that the Constitution contains little language explicitly protecting economic rights. We must find a way to set a limit on what Congress can take from us. It should take the form of a constitutional amendment limiting peacetime federal spending to a specific, lower percentage of the Gross Domestic Product. If we can't get Congress to pass such an amendment, we should reconvene the constitutional convention for the narrow purpose of a spending-limitation amendment. . . .

If the Founders were to come back to today's America, I think they would be very disappointed in our choice to accept what we see as safety in exchange for liberty. But I would also say that it is not too late for us to wake up and respond to the erosion of our liberties. Americans have never done wrong things for a long while. But we must get about the task of putting government back where our Founders intended while we have the liberty to do so.

# The Deficit and Our Obligation to Future Generations
## James M. Buchanan (1987)

*James Buchanan (born 1919) has been associated with George Mason University for many years, as professor of economics (now retired) and as director of the James Buchanan Center for Political Economy. He received his undergraduate degree from Middle Tennessee State University and his doctorate from the University of Chicago. In 1986, Dr. Buchanan received the Nobel Prize in Economics for his work in public choice economic theory, which studies how the choices of the public, politicians, and the government affect the economy in terms of the use of scarce resources. Here he challenges the practice of deficit spending by government because of its negative impact on future generations.*

January 1987 *Imprimis*

## Introduction

Philosophers and social scientists alike have seemed surprisingly reluctant to discuss the modern practice of continuous deficit financing in intergenerational terms. In part, this reluctance stems from the long-continuing confusion in economists' understanding of the elementary principles of government borrowing. Until and unless economists get their theory of public debt in order, we can scarcely criticize the philosophers for failing to examine the moral content of the behavior that debt represents. So long as economists suggest that the relevant variables are levels or rates of change in the national product, national income, consumption, saving, investment, and capital formation, they will necessarily concentrate attention on secondary rather than primary consequences of deficit financing.

Whether the borrower is an individual, a corporation, or a government, borrowing, as an institution, allows the borrower to shift patterns of outlay over time; borrowing makes spending possible now, but eventually the time comes when the incurred debt must be paid off or rolled over and upon which interest must be paid. This elementary logic holds regardless of the usage to which borrowed funds are put.

With an individual or a firm there is, however, a direct linkage between the act of borrowing and the accompanying assignment of

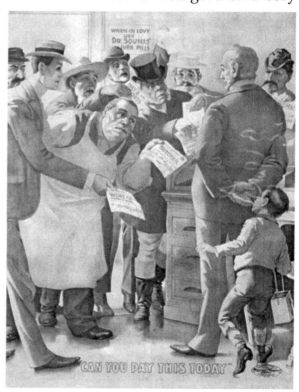

*Poster of Bill Collectors at a Doctor's Office, 1899*

liabilities, a linkage that operates to insure that the institution is not abused. The profligate individual who incurs debt to expand current consumption suffers the consequences; he alone is liable for interest-amortization charges later. This responsibility to pay the price for borrowing is recognized by both the individual and his potential creditors. And the corporation knows it must put borrowed funds to productive use in order to survive in a competitive economy.

But there is no such burden of responsibility when it comes to the national debt. A government may expand current rates of spending by borrowing the funds, but those persons who, as agents for the state, make fiscal decisions do not face obligations to repay its creditors. If the borrowed funds are used to finance current rates of public consumption (including transfers), the decision makers, personally and/or through their constituents, secure benefits without directly suffering losses.

There are two closely related reasons to suggest why the government's, i.e. our, sense of obligation is so faint. First of all, we as individuals do not live forever, and our interests in our progeny may be somewhat less than our interest in ourselves, especially when we may not have any children at all. Secondly, some of us may desire to leave negatively-valued "bequests, " even for our own progeny, a desire that the institution of public debt can satisfy. My point here can be put simply in a comparative illustration. If I borrow $1000 personally, I create a future obligation against myself or my estate in the present value of $1000. Regardless of my usage of the funds, I cannot, by the act of borrowing, impose an external cost on others. Unless I leave positively-valued assets against which my debts can be satisfied, my creditors cannot oblige my heirs to pay off their claims. By contrast, suppose I "vote for" an issue of public debt in the amount of $1000 per person. I may recognize that this debt embodies a future tax liability on some persons, but I need not reckon on the full $1000 liability being assigned to me. If I leave no positively-valued assets, the government's creditors can still enforce claims on my progeny as members of the future-period taxpaying group. Further, the membership in the taxpaying group itself shifts over time. New entrants, and not only those who descend directly from those of us who make a borrowing-spending decision, are obligated to meet debt interest and amortization charges.

In sum, the institution of public debt introduces a unique problem that is usually absent with private debt; persons who are decision makers in one period are allowed to impose possible financial losses on persons in future generations. It follows that the institution is liable to abuse this and overextend its borrowing practices. There are moral and ethical problems with government deficit financing that simply are not present with the private counterpart.

## Classical Precepts and the Keynesian Revolution

The simple logic of public debt, sketched out above, was fully recognized in classical public finance theory, and its implications were embodied in classical norms for the debt issue. These norms justified financing government outlay by borrowing only in two circumstances, (1) when the funds were devoted to capital investment projects, and (2) when there were extraordinary demands on revenues, such as war emergencies. In either of these settings, resort to public debt allows for a closer matching of the time patterns of costs and benefits than seem to be available through tax financing. In all other settings, whether through formal constitutional restriction or through voluntary adherence to rules for fiscal prudence, governments were not authorized to borrow to cover revenue needs.

The Keynesian revolution in the theory of macroeconomic policy essentially repealed these classical norms. This paper is not the place for me to detail the many intersecting confusions that this theory of macroeconomic policy reflected. Suffice it to say that, as interpreted by practicing politicians in democracy, the effects have been indeed dramatic. Since roughly the early 1960s, political decision makers have felt free to finance outlays by debt, quite independently of the classical restraints. As a result, in the 1980s much of our current public consumption is financed by debt. We are, as members of the body politic in 1986, currently enjoying the benefits of public outlays that must be paid for by those who come after us. We are imposing external costs on future generations.

## The Benefit Principle of Taxation

Here, I want to look critically and carefully at the moral dimension of the debt issue, and, specifically, at the moral and ethical foundations of the classical norms of government spending. Why should public debt be limited to the financing of either capital projects or extraordinary revenue needs? Why should not we, as citizens in the 1980s, finance current benefits by imposing taxes on those who will pay taxes in the 2000s? What theory of rights allows us to say that the classical principles are justified? Or, to repeat the title for this paper, what are our obligations to future generations in these respects?

The classical norms are based on the same ethical foundations as the benefit principle to taxation, which states that those who enjoy the benefits of public spending programs should be those who are required to pay the taxes necessary to finance them. This precept reflects a straightforward extension of the commutative justice of market exchange to the public sector, and it finds its most sophisticated exposition in the Wicksell-Lindahl model of fiscal process.

There is moral and ethical content in the quid pro quo of market dealings, and this content applies to strictly voluntary exchange of the marketplace to the implied voluntary exchange that takes place in the public sector. This conceptualization, in its turn, embodies a theory of the state itself. The state is conceived as the means or instrument through which persons cooperate to secure benefits that cannot be secured efficiently in the market sector. Conceptually at least, the individual's claims are both prior to and separate from the collectivity in which he has membership.

If this essentially Lockean theory of the state is accepted, the exchange or benefit principle for taxation seems a natural consequence, and the classical norms for public debt fall clearly into place. Indeed, these norms are simply the temporal extension of the benefit principle. Those who exist when the benefits from public spending are enjoyed should be required to pay the taxes necessary to finance such benefits. To depart from this putative exchange nexus of costs and benefits, save in the two circumstances noted, violates the founding principles and values of a society of free persons.

Or so it should seem. The analogy with the benefit principle of taxation should, however, give us pause. We must acknowledge that, in the mainstream of normal public finance over the last century, the benefit principle has not been universally applied, and perhaps has not even occupied a dominating place among alternatives for tax share allocation. The most familiar alternative has been "ability to pay." Progressive or proportional rates of taxation to finance genuinely redistributive transfers could never be derived from any simple application of the benefit principle. There is no quid pro quo. Taxes take from the rich; transfers give to the poor. Any ethical justification for this sort of fiscal action must be informed by a different argument than the benefit principle.

Can we possibly justify current debt financing of public spending on some grounds analogous to those advanced in support of the modern redistributive fiscal regime? Transfers occupy ever-increasing shares in the budgets of modern governments, and, as noted, taxes to finance such transfers could never be justified on any simple application of the benefit principle. The first point to be made here is that the debt financing of current-period consumption is a temporal tax-transfer system in many respects akin to the within-period tax-transfer system of the modern welfare state. Persons who enjoy the benefits of the spending now do so at the expense of persons who will, in subsequent time periods, be required to pay the taxes required to meet the interest and amortization charges.

## Justification of In-Period Redistributive Transfers

If, as both normative and methodological individualists, we refuse to acknowledge the existence of some organic collectivity that has purpose apart from those of its members, we must try to locate any justification of an in-period tax-transfer system in some conceptualized contractual agreement among all members of the polity. A multi-period perspective must be taken, and it is necessary to distinguish carefully between the choice of rules or institutions that remain in force over many periods and the choices made under the operation of a specific set of such rules within a single period. That is to say, we must adopt what is essentially a "constitutional" perspective.

If we do this, it does become possible to derive an ethical argument in support of fiscal redistribution, and, indirectly, of those institutions of taxes and transfers that facilitate such redistribution. The individual who chooses among basic social institutions that are expected to remain in existence for some time is necessarily operating behind a veil of uncertainty; he cannot fully identify his own position in any one future period during which the chosen institution will be operative. In this setting, which was introduced by myself along with Gordon Tullock in *The Calculus of Consent* (1962), the individual may prefer some institutional-constitutional arrangement that will involve some elements of an in-period tax-transfer system. The analogous setting for constitutional choice, in which the veil of ignorance becomes more central, was used by John Rawls in *A Theory of Justice* (1971), to derive the ethical argument for some fiscal redistribution.

The economy grows through time, and because persons in future periods will be wealthier than persons who live now, the postponement of the tax payments for currently enjoyed spending will embody a rich-to-poor redistribution that may be dictated by the same precepts applied to the in-period model.

The logic seems straightforward. Consider a highly simplified two-period model in which there is only one person alive at any period, and where persons live for only one period. Suppose that the income in Period 1 is 100 units, and that in Period 2 is 200 units. These income flows are known, but the selector among institutions remains totally ignorant as to whether he will be alive in Period 1 or Period 2. . . . [In terms of pollution,] Our record suggests an absence of concern for the well-being of future generations. Debt financing of currently enjoyed public [pollution-control] program benefits imposes charges on all future taxpayers, just as surely as pollution exacts a toll on their welfare. Why do we observe such an apparent disparity in both public attitudes and in political response? Why is there so much political support for toxic waste cleanup and so little for reforms like budget amendment?

There are at least three separate arguments that may explain the differences here. First of all, the modern concern over environmental quality is motivated, at least in part, by an anti-capitalist, or anti-market, mindset. The "evildoers" are business firms seeking profits, not the benevolent government. With deficit financing, by contrast, no fingers can be pointed directly at profit-seeking business firms, or even at persons in their private capacities. The costs that deficits impose on future generations are imposed by government, by the working of democratic political process, by duly elected political representatives of the people who are electorally responsible to us all. We should not, therefore, be much surprised that the Ralph Naders of the age should remain relatively silent.

A second, and possibly much more important reason for the relative disparity in concern lies in the wide income [differential] between periods. [Deficit spending on pollution control in Period 1 with a resulting adjustment of income in Period 2] would be preferred if institutional arrangements could be made to facilitate such adjustment. If spending in Period 1, over and beyond 100 units, could be financed by some borrowing against the income of Period 2, the individual chooser, when adopting the constitution, might well authorize such an institution.

But should this argument be taken seriously? Before we do so, it is necessary to consider the sources of economic growth and the attitudes of the individual toward such growth. Suppose we remain with the one-person-per-period, two-period model, but we postulate that economic growth is dependent upon the resourcefulness and behavior of the person alive during Period 1. Suppose, further, that this person saves one-half of his income of 100 units, invests this in productive capital, which yields a rate of return of 100 percent. The potential consumption of the person alive in Period 2 is then 200 units, as in the first model examined. But would an individual, behind the intertemporal veil, prefer an adjustment in the income levels between the two periods? Would the individual authorize an institution that facilitated borrowing against Period 2 income to finance a potential rate of consumption greater than 100 units in Period 1? If it turns out that he is alive in Period 2, then clearly the debt financing of Period 1 consumption would have undesirable consequences.

Since economic growth is dependent upon the behavior of persons in the economy, there seems to be no contractarian argument that will justify the constitutional authorization of the debt financing of current period consumption. Separated in time or by generation, individuals cannot be considered as players in the "same game." So any other arguments in favor of equal opportunity, redistribution and "fairness" lose much of their meaning as well.

## Pollution and the Fiscal Environment

I have suggested that there is no plausibly supportable ethical justification for imposing net fiscal charges on persons who pay taxes in future periods. I have not directly addressed the more difficult question concerning our positive obligations to future generations. We live in an era characterized by mounting concern over environmental quality that is presumably motivated in part by a sense that our generation should not so despoil the atmosphere as to make living less pleasant for those persons who will follow us. Note that this expression of concern implies that we have an obligation toward future generations in our capacities as citizens, as members of the body politic, and that where required, we should, and do, act collectively through our government to implement such an obligation, even if constraints are placed on our individual liberties to act.

It is surely singular, if not bizarre, that . . . confusion among economists, noted at the outset of this paper, [has occurred alongside a lack of indignation by the public over] the intergenerational effects of debt financing. A third reason prompts both the economists' confusion and the public's failure to express indignation at the gross violation of norms for intergenerational equity that the deficit regime embodies. There is no counterpart to the observable physical deterioration of the atmosphere that persons may see and that the scientists can measure. The piling up of claims against future-period incomes of taxpayers does not physically enter the consciousness of present-period persons; these claims do not float about for all to see. This difference suggests that the pollution of our fiscal environment is all the more pernicious. No present person's laundry gets dirtier, yet many persons clearly secure net benefits.

## Debt, Default, and Future Generations

Does the last reason noted give pause when we compare fiscal with atmospheric pollution? Precisely because the claims against the incomes of future taxpayers are just that—claims—has there been any actual destruction of value involved in the whole debt-deficit operation? Must the financial levels attainable for persons of future generations be lower as a result of the deficit regime than they might have been under a balanced budget? To raise this question prompts attention to possible default. What would occur if future taxpayers, or rather, if the government acting on their behalf, simply refused to pay the claims? What if the government, say in the year 2000, repudiated all of the debt claims held against it, and indirectly, against those who would be subjected to the taxes required to meet these claims?

In such a scenario, future generations of persons, as taxpayers, would, indeed, escape damage. But persons play several roles simultaneously, and those members of future generations who are bequeathed government securities (bonds, notes, bills) held against the government would find them subject to capital-value confiscation. These persons, rather than the more inclusive group of taxpayers, would be the losers in the process. These future creditors of government would be the persons on whom the final incidence of payment for the benefits of currently enjoyed spending rests. In effect, these future creditors, future taxpayers themselves, would pay in two ways for our fiscal profligacy. Default doesn't exempt them from bearing our costs.

*Poster Promoting U.S. Liberty Bonds, 1917*

## Mortgages and the Destruction of Capital

In another version of this paper, the title includes the word "mortgage." But this analogy is misleading, since by standard dictionary definition the word "mortgage" means the conveyance of a property that secures the debt, a property that presumably yields a stream of value to the user. The use of the mortgage analogy to apply to government debt would indeed be appropriate if the debt was created in the process of financing a genuine capital investment project, but no pretense is made that the outlays financed are anything other than ordinary expenses of government, expenses required to provide the goods and services and transfers for the various interest groups who are successful in getting their demands met by politicians. There is no capital value against which the debt claims are or could be offset. Nothing of lasting value emerges from the fiscal operation that will make the servicing of the debt claims easier or less onerous for those members of future generations who will be faced with the tax charges. Not only do current debt-financing schemes fail to yield capital; they destroy opportunities to create it.

## Our Obligation

I have tried, throughout this paper, to avoid the sometimes murky discourse on the general question concerning our obligations to future generations. I have restricted my remarks to the currently observed regime of debt-financed current public consumption and to the implications of this single institution to the larger and more inclusive question. I have tried to demonstrate that there is little or no ethical justification for such an institution, and that the classical principles for public debt issue carefully specify the circumstances in which governments may justifiably raise revenues by borrowing.

The basic moral dimension of fiscal policy must be elevated to center stage in public and political discussion. In no other way can we begin to determine what constitutes responsible collective behavior. The hour is late and we have already inflicted major damage on those who will come after us, damage that must be permanent. Let us not add to the damage by tolerating continued debt financing of current program benefits.

# The Greatest Story Never Told: Today's Economy in Perspective
## Patrick Toomey (2008)

*Patrick Toomey is president of the Club for Growth, a national organization that promotes conservative issues. He is a graduate of Harvard University with a degree in government, and he served as a member of the U.S. House of Representatives from Pennsylvania from 1999-2005. He has been a business owner and has worked in investment banking. This speech was given in January 2008, as the 2008 recession was just beginning but before most people believed that the country was in a recession. Toomey used a number of economic statistics to support his point.*

May 2008 *Imprimis*

There is a debate going on today over whether our economy is in recession. Polls show sagging public confidence. But some perspective is sorely needed. The fact of the matter is that we in the United States, and to a lesser degree the entire world, have just lived through—and continue to live in—the greatest period of prosperity in human history. Over the last 25 years, more wealth has been created, more people have been lifted out of poverty, standards of living have been elevated more dramatically, and the quality and length of life have improved, more than ever before in recorded history. Unfortunately, as Larry Kudlow says, this is "the greatest story never told." We need to start telling the story, and also to think about its causes.

First, let us focus on the United States (and I say this with full knowledge that the State of Michigan is a unique exception among the 50 states to America's extraordinary recent prosperity; but the causes of Michigan's peculiar problems are a topic for another day): Average economic growth in the U.S. has not only been positive for almost the entire last quarter century, but for much of this period the rate of growth has accelerated. Our nation's total economic output in 1982 was $5.1 trillion; last year it was $11.3 trillion (in real 2000 dollars). Per capita economic output in 1982 was $22,400; last year it was $37,807 (in real 2000 dollars). The average unemployment rate in the 1970s was nearly seven percent; it has been declining, on average, every decade since, and has remained below five percent since 2003. The service sector of our economy has been on fire, growing from $1 trillion in 1982 to $5.5 trillion in 2006. And do you know how far back one has to go to find the year when America's total manufacturing output peaked? All the way back to 2007! Yes, U.S. factories produced more last year than in any previous year in our history. That's the "hollowing out"—as its critics like to say—of America's economy.

This expanding economy has, of course, resulted in huge gains in wealth. The Dow Jones Industrial Average began the 1980s at 825; today, despite its recent declines, it remains above 12,000, a 1,400 percent increase. And with the democratization of the capital markets that has occurred through savings programs like IRAs and 401(k)s and investment vehicles like mutual funds, the average family's wealth has grown dramatically, too. In 1983, 19 percent of American households owned stocks; in 2005, 50 percent were investors. In 1989, the median family net worth was $69,000; in 2004, it was $93,000.

These gains in income and wealth have resulted directly in a better standard of living for virtually every segment of American society—including the poor. Among families living below the official poverty line in the early 1970s, less than 40 percent had a car, almost none had color televisions, and air conditioning was virtually unheard of; in 2004, 46 percent owned their own homes, almost 75 percent owned a car (indeed, 30 percent owned two or more cars), 97 percent had color TVs, and 67 percent had air conditioning. The poor in the U.S. have an average of 721 square feet of living space per person, as compared with 430 in Sweden and 92 in Mexico.

Similarly, technology has become accessible to all sectors of society. There were 9.8 million cable TV subscribers in 1975, and 65 million in 2006; 2.1 million personal computers in 1985, and 243 million in 2007; 340 cell phone subscribers in 1985, and 243 million in 2007.

Health indicators track similarly. Infant mortality dropped from 20 deaths per 1,000 people in 1970 to seven deaths per 1,000 people in 2002. In 1980, American life expectancy was less than 74 years. Today it is 78.

Nor is America totally unique in this regard. While we have led the world in most measures of prosperity and growth, other countries have been enjoying the broadest expansion of wealth in history as well. A recent issue of *The Economist* documents the tremendous worldwide improvement in both the social conditions in poor countries and the alleviation of poverty: Between 1999 and 2004, some 135 million people emerged from destitution, and there are now twice as many countries with fast-growing economies as there were in 1980.

## Keys to Prosperity

This long period of sustained economic growth and the huge quality-of-life improvements it made possible didn't happen by accident. They were a result of a major expansion in economic freedom, initially in the U.S., then increasingly around the world. This expansion took many forms, but three of the most important were a dramatic reduction in marginal tax rates, a series of major deregulations, and a broad expansion of trade.

After decades of top marginal tax rates in percentiles from the 70s into the 90s, President Reagan signed the Economic Recovery Tax Act of 1981. The top marginal rate was reduced from 70 to 50 percent, and by the time Reagan left office, it was down to 28 percent. During Reagan's two terms, the top corporate tax rate was reduced from 34 to 28 percent, individual tax brackets were indexed for inflation, and—although there were some tax increases—the devastatingly high top marginal tax rates that preceded Reagan were gone. Nor have they come back—at least not yet.

In subsequent years, President Bush the elder and President Clinton raised some taxes too much, but lowered others; and it didn't appear smart to anyone that we should return to the levels that had prevailed prior to Reagan. The current President Bush has lowered taxes dramatically—not so well in 2001, but then very effectively in 2003. The effect was to lower marginal tax rates, phase out the death tax, offer marriage penalty relief, and lower taxes on capital gains and dividends.

Major deregulation was another part of the expansion of economic freedom that has enabled 25 years of strong growth. Interestingly enough, this deregulation began when President Carter signed the Airline Deregulation Act of 1978, lifting price and route controls that had forced higher prices and fewer choices on consumers. Without these controls, airlines could offer deals to fill otherwise half-empty planes and choose more efficient routes. The airline industry has obviously struggled for many reasons in subsequent years, but consumers have been the big winners in terms of increased safety, more choices, and lower prices. Deregulation is responsible for ten to 18 percent lower fares, saving travelers $5-$10 billion a year.

Following this, in 1980, Carter signed the Motor Carrier Act, deregulating an industry that had been closely controlled by the government since 1935. This put a stop to regulations dictating what products truckers could transport and what routes they could travel. The kind of inefficiency that resulted from these regulations can best be understood by the following example: A motor carrier with authority to travel from Cleveland to Buffalo that purchased another carrier's right to go from Buffalo to Pittsburgh was required to ship goods from Cleveland to Pittsburgh via Buffalo, adding an unnecessary and wasteful 272 miles to the trip.

As a result of easing these regulations, prices for truckload-size shipments fell 25 percent by 1982, and efficiency gains and cost savings helped to make possible the "just-in-time" inventory system that has transformed retailing, lowered consumer costs, and, arguably, diminished the economy's susceptibility to recessions.

President Reagan accelerated the trend toward less regulation, easing or eliminating price controls on oil and natural gas, cable television, long-distance telephone service, interstate bus service, and ocean shipping. In addition, banks were allowed to invest in a broader set of assets, and the scope of antitrust laws was reduced.

More recently, economic freedom has expanded in the form of freer international trade. In 1993, NAFTA eliminated a majority of tariffs on products traded among the U.S., Canada, and Mexico, and phased out others. In 2004, CAFTA eliminated tariffs immediately on more than 80 percent of U.S. exports of consumer and industrial goods to Central America and phased out the rest over ten years. Since 1985, we've had bilateral or multilateral trade agreements with 16 countries. International trade is freer today than it has been at any time in the last 100 years.

## Why Turn Back?

This "greatest story never told" is indeed a tremendous story. It's the story of the fastest-growing period of prosperity—and the most dramatic mass elevation from poverty—in the history of the world. And it's all been possible because—bit by bit, in fits and starts, with advances and retreats—the U.S. and other countries have been moving toward greater economic freedom.

In light of this story—which, to repeat, is ongoing, so that you don't have to go back to medieval or classical times to find the evidence—it is utterly perplexing that so much of the election year rhetoric of late is aimed at reversing our economic course. For instance, it's hard to find a domestic policy that can be proven to be as successful as the Bush tax cuts—even by presumably Democratic standards. It's simply a matter of fact that these tax cuts shifted the tax burden substantially to higher income earners and took millions of lower income workers off the tax rolls altogether. The economy took off and ran for at least five years after implementation, and the federal deficit shrank dramatically after the tax cuts were enacted. Yet calls to reverse these tax cuts abound.

For the Democratic Party, of course, there are other reasons for rolling back economic freedom. One is the powerful special interest groups within its coalition—organized labor in particular—which rely on government for special treatment and benefits they could never obtain in free and fair market-based negotiations. Unfortunately, the resulting higher costs and inefficiencies can devastate industries and regions—Michigan being a prime example.

But if we can expect Democrats to resist economic freedom, how do we explain the timidity on the Republican side to defend the economic ideas that have fueled recent advances in prosperity? The answer is that most politicians are ultimately motivated by their perceptions of public opinion. And despite the evidence, the public doesn't seem to realize the period of unprecedented progress we are in.

As a side note, the increasing lack of opposition among the American people to higher income taxes should not be surprising when an increasingly progressive tax code means ever fewer Americans are paying any taxes at all: In 2005, the top one percent of earners in the U.S. paid 39 percent of all income taxes, while the bottom 50 percent of earners paid just three percent. Over time, if half of the population believes that it is entitled to have someone else pay for government, we should not be surprised if public support for economic freedom continues to erode.

As one who has done a lot of campaigning over the years, I'll admit, it can be hard to explain to some audiences why they should have to buy their own health insurance when the other side is offering to have the government give it to them for free. But that doesn't absolve politicians of the moral obligation to present the principled and true argument.

# Solving the Problem of Poverty
## Steve Mariotti (1998)

*Steve Mariotti founded the non-profit National Foundation for Teaching Entrepreneurship (www.nfte.com) in 1988. NFTE has taught more than 230,000 young people the principles of starting their own business. It has programs in 22 states and 13 countries. Mr. Mariotti received an MBA in 1977 from the University of Michigan and has pursued additional studies at Harvard, Stanford, and Brooklyn College. He has co-authored several books. In this speech he tells his own dramatic story and relates how the work of NFTE helps young people accomplish the dream expressed by one of the program's graduates: "My dream is not to die in poverty, but to have poverty die in me."*

November 1998 *Imprimis*

I know a secret which, if fully understood by our government, business, and community leaders, could have enormous positive implications for the future of our society. Simply put, the secret is this: Children born into poverty have special gifts that prepare them for business formation and wealth creation. They are mentally strong, resilient, and full of chutzpah. They are skeptical of hierarchies and the status quo. They are long-suffering in the face of adversity. They are comfortable with risk and uncertainty. They know how to deal with stress and conflict.

*A West Virginia Family in Front of Their Rented Home, 1921*

These are the attitudes and abilities that make them ideally suited for breaking out of the cycle of dependency that so often comes with poverty and for getting ahead in the marketplace. In short, poor kids are "street smart," or what we at the National Foundation for Teaching Entrepreneurship call "business smart." Precisely because of their poverty—that is, because of their experience surviving in a challenging world—they are able to perceive and pursue fleeting opportunities that others, more content with their lot in life, tend to miss.

## Destructive Welfare Programs and Tax Laws

Children born into poverty have all the characteristics of the classic entrepreneurs like Henry Ford, Andrew Carnegie, and Thomas Edison—the heroes of our capitalist system. It stands to reason, therefore, that as a society we should make special efforts to encourage the development of entrepreneurial skills among low-income youths. But we have done just the opposite, spending over $1.5 trillion since the beginning of the "War on Poverty" in the

1960s on public assistance programs that are actually designed to protect children *from* the free enterprise system.

In today's dollars, $1.5 trillion would be enough to purchase half of all the Fortune 500 companies in America. Such a colossal malinvestment has cost millions of dollars in lost revenue, and it has also discouraged millions of would-be young entrepreneurs from ever entering the marketplace.

This is a particular personal tragedy for children born into poverty, for, as the Nobel Prize winning economist F. A. Hayek once noted, the free market offers the most effective way of identifying what we are good at and how our comparative advantages can be developed. Public assistance limits and, in many cases even prevents, its recipients from engaging in this vital process of self-discovery. As a result, generation after generation of children born into poverty are settling for the security of welfare while missing out on the thrills and challenges of competition. Properly developed, their skills might be highly valued in the marketplace—but they will never find out.

Even more misguided than our national welfare strategy is our 7.5-million-word tax code. Even the most respected tax experts can't claim to understand fully this maze of vague and often contradictory rules that runs no less than 38,000 pages. How can we expect young people who have never even seen a W-2 form to make sense out of the thousands of tax regulations that apply to starting and running a business? The U. S. tax code has been a terrible burden for the business community, but for low-income youths it has been absolutely devastating.

Besides the length of the tax code, there is something even more insidious: The code itself changes all the time. There is no constant body of information that can be regarded as definite and enduring. For this reason, studying the current tax laws is like studying alchemy and finding that there are no basic principles!

To summarize, the financial loss represented by the $1.5 trillion I mentioned earlier has been minimal in comparison with the psychological damage to millions of people who have been told, in effect, by welfare and tax bureaucrats that they are "worthless goods" in the marketplace and that they will be rewarded for unproductive behavior.

## Founding NFTE

I founded the National Foundation for Teaching Entrepreneurship on the premise, which is still a secret to most, that children born into poverty have enormous potential in business. Let me share with you some of the history of NFTE.

After receiving an MBA from the University of Michigan, I won a Liberty Fund fellowship to study Austrian economics at the Institute for Humane Studies (IHS) with F. A. Hayek, who had just won the Nobel Prize in Economics. Although I was well versed in free market principles because of my contacts at places such as Hillsdale College, this fellowship enabled me to increase my knowledge of Austrian trade cycle theory and international finance.

After leaving IHS, I spent the next 30 months at Ford Motor Company as the South African and Latin American treasury analyst. Then I pulled up stakes and moved to New York to open an import-export firm specializing in African small businesses. This was great fun, and my business was profitable. But, as it happened, in 1981, I was robbed and beaten by a group of young men.

As a way of working through this traumatic event, I began a career as a special education teacher in New York's most difficult impoverished neighborhoods. My first year was almost as traumatic as the mugging. I was assigned remedial students. In each of my classes, there was a group of six or seven students whose behavior was so disruptive that I had to stop the class every five minutes to get them to quiet down. On one occasion, in my third-period class, I was forced to throw out all the boys.

Ironically, it was these "troublemakers" who provided me with the valuable insight that set me on the road to teaching entrepreneurship. I took them out to dinner one evening and asked them why they had acted so badly in class. They said my class was boring and that I had nothing to teach them. [This account is adapted from *The Young Entrepreneur's Guide to Starting and Running a Business*, co-authored by Steve Mariotti.] I asked if anything I taught in class interested them. One fellow responded that I had caught his attention when I had discussed my import-export business. He rattled off various figures I had mentioned in class, calculated my profit margin, and concluded that my business was doing well.

I was dazzled to find such business smarts in a student whom the public schools had labeled "borderline retarded." This was my first inkling that something was wrong not only with my teaching but also with the standard remedial education curriculum.

Meanwhile, the situation at school worsened. I began to lose control of my classroom, almost on a daily basis. One student set fire to the back of another student's coat—the student with the coat was as astonished as I was. In a rage, I ordered the arsonist out of class, and he was expelled the same day. Days later, I was locked out of my eighth-period class. The students wouldn't open the door. Finally, just as I was going to admit defeat and find a security guard, one of the girls took pity on me and opened it.

I didn't know how to deal with this kind of nightmarish situation. I wanted to walk out of school and call it quits. After a minute or two, I realized that I couldn't do that. I stepped into the hallway to regain my composure. I thought about my dinner with the young men from my third-period class. They had said I was boring—except when I talked about business and about making money. I walked back into the classroom and, without any introductory comments, launched a mock sales pitch, selling my own watch to the class. I enumerated the benefits of the watch. I explained why the students should purchase it from me at the low price of only six dollars. The students quieted down and became interested in hearing what I had to say. I didn't know it at the time, but this incident, born of desperation, was pointing me toward my real vocation—teaching entrepreneurship to low-income youths.

After I had gained the students' attention, I moved from the sales talk into a conventional arithmetic lesson: If you buy a watch at three dollars and sell it for six dollars, your profit is three dollars, or 100 percent. Without realizing it, I was touching on the business fundamental concept of "buy low/sell high," and on the more advanced concept of "return on investment."

Before long, I began offering a special class, "How to Start, Finance, and Manage a Small Business—A Guide for the Urban Entrepreneur." During the next seven years, this course became so successful that even the most challenging and disruptive students settled down and learned a great deal. In my last teaching assignment in the Fort Apache area of the South Bronx, 100 percent of my students started small businesses and reported that they experienced major positive changes in their lives. The difference teaching entrepreneurship seemed to be making in regard to student behavior was incredible; I noticed among my students that chronic problems such as absenteeism, dropping out, pregnancy, drug use, drug dealing, and violent behavior seemed to be significantly alleviated.

The overwhelming success of this class gave me the confidence to launch the National Foundation for Teaching Entrepreneurship in 1988. NFTE's mission is to teach low-income youths the basics of starting their own businesses by creating a curriculum, training teachers, and providing graduate services. . . .

## Testing NFTE's Impact

In 1993, in conjunction with the Heller School at Brandeis University, we completed a study which found that NFTE program graduates were far more likely than their peers to start a business. Here are some specifics: 32 times more NFTE graduates than non-graduates were running a business, and a post-program survey found that 33 percent of those graduates were still running a business. And in 1998, the David H. Koch Charitable Foundation sponsored one of the most comprehensive examinations of entrepreneurship training ever conducted. An organization known as Research & Evaluation for Philanthropy tracked two different randomly selected groups: one comprised of 120 low-income Washington, D.C. residents between the ages of 18 and 30 who had completed the NFTE program and one comprised of 152 of their peers who had received no training. Here are some of the highlights of the Koch study:

> 91 percent of the NFTE alumni stated that they wanted to start their own business, compared with 75 percent of the comparison group and 50 percent of the U. S. public. NFTE alumni were two times more likely to be current business owners (12 percent in the NFTE group vs. 5 percent in the comparison group). In fact, the rate of business formation was substantially higher than the 1-3 percent rate for minority adults nationwide. NFTE participation increased the likelihood of starting a business four-fold. NFTE increased high school students' exposure to business and entrepreneurship training fourteen-fold. 88 percent of NFTE alumni stated that they gave serious consideration to going into business after completing the program. 99 percent of NFTE alumni indicated that the program gave them a more positive view of business, and they were two times more likely to predict that they would own a business in five years. 68 percent of NFTE alumni were the first in their families to start a business. 97 percent of NFTE alumni reported improved business skills and knowledge. 100 percent said they would recommend the program to others. NFTE alumni were two times less likely to prefer government employment over business ownership and corporate management.

## Going to Scale

This study demonstrates that teaching about the free enterprise system and encouraging children to start businesses and create wealth are powerful tools that promote independence and self-sufficiency. Today, we at NFTE are confident that our program is adding significant value to thousands of young people's lives. We plan to "go to scale" and create a national movement in which every low-income child is taught entrepreneurial skills and elementary business principles.

Our plan is two-fold. First, we intend to recruit the best business and academic minds to help us in our efforts. NFTE's board and sponsors now include some of America's leading businessmen and philanthropists.

Second, we intend to use high technology in all of NFTE's teaching models. This will help our students to compete in the 21st century. Through an exciting partnership with Microsoft, NFTE has developed BizTech, a state-of-the-art learning site that offers an on-line curriculum. BizTech lets students anywhere in the world access information on entrepreneurship 24 hours a day, seven days a week. Under the direction of NFTE's CEO, Michael J. Caslin III, BizTech will also enable them to begin trading on-line.

BizTech is currently operating as a pilot program in dozens of schools, and it has generated a huge positive response. Fortunately, we are now able to deliver much of our program at a fraction of the initial cost. And a great selling point for the program is the fact that the administrative record-keeping function is on-line, which liberates the teacher from cumbersome paperwork and allows him to become a true guide and coach. Perhaps most

exciting is the news that NFTE, in cooperation with some of the country's leading educators, is developing state-of-the-art lesson plans that fully integrate information technology into a classroom environment.

At NFTE, the future is bright for low-income youths. By combining the most recent technology with the time-tested principles of capitalism, we are developing solutions for one of the most serious threats to our society: poverty. Sure, we are small, but we are growing like a mustard seed. One of our greatest strengths is the unquenchable optimism of the young men and women we serve. As one of NFTE's graduates put it so aptly, "My dream is not to die in poverty, but to have poverty die in me."

# A Prescription for American Health Care
## John C. Goodman (2009)

*John C. Goodman is the president, CEO, and Kellye Wright Fellow at the National Center for Policy Analysis, which has offices in Dallas, Texas and Washington, D.C. He received his Ph.D. in economics from Columbia University, and has taught and done research at Columbia University, Stanford University, Dartmouth College, Southern Methodist University, and the University of Dallas. He writes regularly for several newspapers and is the author of nine books.*

March 2009 *Imprimis*

I'll start with the bad news: When we get through the economic time that we're in right now, we're going to be confronted with an even bigger problem. The first of the Baby Boomers started signing up for early retirement under Social Security last year. Two years from now they will start signing up for Medicare. All told, 78 million people are going to stop working, stop paying taxes, stop paying into retirement programs, and start drawing benefits. The problem is, neither Social Security nor Medicare is ready for them. The federal government has made explicit and implicit promises to millions of people, but has put no money aside in order to keep those promises. Some of you may wonder where Bernie Madoff got the idea for his Ponzi scheme. Clearly he was studying federal entitlement policy.

Meanwhile, in the private sector, many employer-sponsored pension plans are not fully funded. Nor is the federal government insurance scheme behind those plans. We have a potential taxpayer liability of between 500 billion and one trillion dollars for those private pension plans, depending on the markets. And on top of that, roughly one-third of all Baby Boomers work for an employer who has promised post-retirement health care. As with the auto companies, almost none of that is funded either. Nor are most state and local post-retirement health benefit plans. Some California localities have already declared bankruptcy because of their employee retirement plans and the first of the Baby Boomers is still only 63 years old.

What all this means is that we're looking at a huge gap between what an entire generation thinks is going to happen during its retirement years and the funds that are there—or, more accurately, are not there—to make good on all those promises. Somebody is going to be really disappointed. Either the Baby Boomers are not going to have the retirement life that they expect or taxpayers are going to be hit with a tremendously huge bill. Or both.

## The Mess We're In

How did this crisis come about? After all, the need to deal with risk is not a new human problem. From the beginning of time, people have faced the risks of growing old and outliving their assets, dying young without having provided for their dependents, becoming disabled and not being able to support themselves and their families, becoming ill and needing health care and not being able to afford it, or discovering that their skills are no longer needed in the job market. These risks are not new. What is new is how we deal with them.

143

Prior to the 20th century, we handled risks with the help of family and extended family. In the 19th century, by the time a child was nine years old, he was usually paying his own way in the household. In effect, children were their parents' retirement plan. But during the 20th century, families became smaller and more dispersed—thus less useful as insurance against risk. So people turned to government for help. In fact, the main reason why governments throughout the developed world have undergone such tremendous growth has been to insure middle class families against risks that they could not easily insure against on their own. This is why our government today is a major player in retirement, health care, disability and unemployment.

*Ten-Year-Old Boy Working in a Berry Field, 1910*

Government, however, has performed abysmally. It has spent money it doesn't have and made promises it can't keep, all on the backs of future taxpayers. The Trustees of Social Security estimate a current unfunded liability in excess of $100 trillion in 2009 dollars. This means that the federal government has promised more than $100 trillion over and above any taxes or premiums it expects to receive. In other words, for Social Security to be financially sound, the federal government should have $100 trillion—a sum of money six-and-a-half times the size of our entire economy—in the bank and earning interest right now. But it doesn't. And while many believe that Social Security represents our greatest entitlement problem, Medicare is six times larger in terms of unfunded obligations. These numbers are admittedly based on future projections. But consider the situation in this light: What if we asked the federal government to account for its obligations the same way the private sector is forced to account for its pensions? In other words, if the federal government suddenly closed down Social Security and Medicare, how much would be owed in terms of benefits already earned? The answer is $52 trillion, an amount several times the size of the U.S. economy.

What does this mean for the future? We know that Social Security and Medicare have been spending more than they are taking in for quite some time. As the Baby Boomers start retiring, this deficit is going to grow dramatically. In 2012, only three years from now, Social Security and Medicare will need one out of every ten general income tax dollars to make up for their combined deficits. By 2020—just eleven years down the road—the federal government will need one out of every four income tax dollars to pay for these programs. By 2030, the midpoint of the Baby Boomer retirement years, it will require one of every two income tax dollars. So it is clear that the federal government will be forced either to scale back everything else it's doing in a drastic way or raise taxes dramatically.

I have not even mentioned Medicaid, but it is almost as large a problem in this regard as Medicare. A recent forecast by the Congressional Budget Office—an economic forecasting agency that is controlled by the Democrats in Congress, not by some conservative private sector outfit—shows that Medicare and Medicaid alone are going to crowd out everything else the federal government is doing by mid-century. And that means everything—national defense, energy, education, the whole works. We'll only have health care. If, on the other hand, the government continues with everything else it is doing today and raises taxes to pay for Medicare and Medicaid, the Congressional Budget Office estimates that, by mid-century, a middle-income family will have to pay two-thirds of its income in taxes!

## Cleaning Up the Mess

The only sensible alternative to relying on a welfare state to solve our health care needs is a renewed reliance on private sector institutions that utilize individual choice and free markets to insure against unforeseen contingencies. In the case of Medicare, our single largest health care problem, such a solution would need to do three things: liberate the patients, liberate the doctors, and pre-fund the system as we move through time.

By liberating the patients I mean giving them more control over their money—at a minimum, one-third of their Medicare dollars. Designate what the patient is able to pay for with this money, and then give him control over it. Based on our experience with health savings accounts, people who are managing their own money make radically different choices. They find ways to be far more prudent and economical in their consumption.

As for doctors, most people don't realize that they are trapped in a system where they have virtually no ability to re-price or re-package their services the way every other professional does. Medicare dictates what it will pay for, what it won't pay for, and the final price. One example of the many harmful effects of this system is the absence of telephone consultations. Almost no one talks to his or her doctor on the phone. Why? Because Medicare doesn't pay a doctor to talk to you on the phone. And private insurers, who tend to follow Medicare's lead, don't pay for phone consultations either. The same goes for e-mail: Only about two percent of patients and doctors e-mail each other—something that is normal in every other profession.

What about digitizing medical records? Doctors typically do not do this, which means that they can't make use of software that allows electronic prescriptions and makes it easier to detect dangerous drug interactions or mistaken dosages. Again, this is something that Medicare doesn't pay for. Likewise patient education: A great deal of medical care can be handled in the home without ever seeing a doctor or a nurse—e.g., the treatment of diabetes. But someone has to give patients the initial instruction, and Medicare doesn't pay for that.

If we want to move medicine into the 21st century, we have to give doctors and hospitals the freedom to re-price and re-package their services in ways that neither increase the cost to government nor decrease the quality of service to the patient.

In terms of quality, another obvious free market idea is to have warranties for surgery such as we have on cars, houses and appliances. Many are surprised to learn that about 17 percent of Medicare patients who enter a hospital re-enter within 30 days—usually because of a problem connected with the initial surgery—with the result that the typical hospital makes money on its mistakes. In order for a hospital to make money in a system based on warranties, it must lower its mistake rate. Again, the goal of our policy should be to generate a market in which doctors and hospitals compete with each other to improve quality and cut costs.

We won't be able to make any of this work in the long run, however, unless we pre-fund the system. Today's teenagers are unlikely to receive medical care during retirement if they must rely on future taxpayers, because taxpayers of the future are unlikely to be agreeable to living in poverty in order to pay their elders' medical bills. This means that everyone must start saving now for post-retirement health care. I would propose that everyone in the workforce put a minimum of four percent of his or her income—perhaps two percent from the employer and two percent from the employee—into a private account, invested in the marketplace, that would grow through time. These private accumulations would eventually replace taxpayer burdens.

In summary, if health care consumers are allowed to save and spend their own money, and if doctors are allowed to act like entrepreneurs—in other words, if we allow the market to work—there is every reason to believe that health care costs can be prevented from rising faster than our incomes.

## The Market in Action

Let me offer a few examples of how the free market is already working on the fringes of health care. Cosmetic surgery is a market that acts like a real market—by which I mean that it is not covered by insurance, consumers can compare prices and services, and doctors can act as entrepreneurs. As a result, over the last 15 years, the real price of cosmetic surgery has gone down while that of almost every other kind of surgery has been rising faster than the Consumer Price Index—and even though the number of people getting cosmetic surgery has increased by five- or six-fold.

In Dallas there is an entrepreneurial health care provider with two million customers who pay a small fee each month for the ability to talk to a doctor on the telephone. Patients must have an electronic medical record, so that whichever doctor answers the phone can view the patient's electronic medical record and talk to the patient. This company is growing in large part because it provides a service that the traditional health care system can't provide. Likewise, walk-in clinics are becoming more numerous around the country. At most of these clinics a registered nurse sits in front of a computer terminal, the patient describes his symptoms, and the nurse types in the information and follows a computerized protocol. The patient's record is electronic, the nurse can prescribe electronically, and the patient sees the price in advance.

We're also seeing the rise of concierge doctors—doctors who don't want to deal with third-party insurers. When this idea started out in California, doctors were charging 10-15 thousand dollars per year. But the free market has worked and the price has come down radically. In Dallas, concierge doctors charge only $40 per employee per month. In return, the patient receives access to the doctor by phone and e-mail, and the doctor keeps electronic medical records, competes for business based on lowering time costs as well as money costs, and is willing to help with patient education.

Finally, consider the international market for what has become known as medical tourism. Hospitals in India, Singapore and Thailand are competing worldwide for patients. Of course, no one is going to get on a plane without some assurances of low cost and high quality—which means that, in order to attract patients, these hospitals have to publicize their error rates, their mortality rates for certain kinds of surgery, their infection rates, and so on. Their doctors are all board-certified in the United States, and they compete for patients in the same way producers and suppliers compete for clients in any other market. Most of their patients come from Europe, but the long-term threat to the American hospital system can't be denied. Leaving the country means leaving bureaucratic red tape behind and dealing instead with entrepreneurs who provide high-quality, low-cost medicine.

As these examples suggest, liberating the medical market by freeing doctors and patients is the only way to bring health care costs under control without sacrificing quality. Continuing on our current path—allowing health care costs to rise at twice the rate of income under the aegis of an unworkable government Ponzi scheme—is by comparison unreasonable.

# How Detroit's Automakers Went from Kings of the Road to Roadkill
## Joseph B. White (2009)

---

*Joseph B. White is a senior editor for* The Wall Street Journal. *A graduate of Harvard University, he has worked for the* Journal *since 1987, and for most of that time he covered the auto industry, serving as Detroit bureau chief from 1998-2007. He won the Pulitzer Prize for reporting in 1993. At the time of this speech in January 2009, General Motors had not yet declared bankruptcy, which it did later in the year.*

February 2009 *Imprimis*

I'd like to start by congratulating all of you. You are all now in the auto business, the Sport of Kings—or in our case, presidents and members of Congress. Without your support—and I assume that most of you are fortunate enough to pay taxes—General Motors and Chrysler would very likely be getting measured by the undertakers of the bankruptcy courts. But make no mistake. What has happened to GM is essentially bankruptcy by other means, and that is an extraordinary event in the political and economic history of our country.

GM is an institution that survived in its early years the kind of management turbulence we've come to associate with particularly chaotic Internet startups. But with Alfred P. Sloan in charge, GM settled down to become the very model of the modern corporation. It navigated through the Great Depression, and negotiated the transition from producing tanks and other military materiel during World War II to peacetime production of cars and trucks. It was global before global was cool, as its current chairman used to say. By the mid-1950s the company was the symbol of American industrial power—the largest industrial corporation in the world. It owned more than half the U.S. market. It set the trends in styling and technology, and even when it did not it was such a fast and effective follower that it could fairly easily hold its competitors in their places. And it held the distinction as the world's largest automaker until just a year or so ago.

How does a juggernaut like this become the basket case that we see before us today? I will oversimplify matters and touch on five factors that contributed to the current crisis—a crisis that has been more than 30 years in the making.

First, Detroit underestimated the competition—in more ways than one.

Second, GM mismanaged its relationship with the United Auto Workers, and the UAW in its turn did nothing to encourage GM (or Ford or Chrysler) to defuse the demographic time bomb that has now blown up their collective future.

Third, GM, Ford, and Chrysler handled failure better than success. When they made money, they tended to squander it on ill-conceived diversification schemes. It was when they were in trouble that they often did their most innovative work—the first minivans at Chrysler, the first Ford Taurus, and more recently the Chevy Volt were ideas born out of crisis.

Fourth, GM (and Ford and Chrysler) relied too heavily on a few, gas-hungry truck and SUV lines for all their profits—plus the money they needed to cover losses on many of their car lines. They did this for a good reason: When gas was cheap, big gas-guzzling trucks were exactly what their customers wanted—until they were not.

Fifth, GM refused to accept that to survive it could not remain what it was in the 1950s and 1960s—with multiple brands and a dominant market share. Instead, it used short-term strategies such as zero percent financing to avoid reckoning with the consequences of globalization and its own mistakes.

## Competition from Overseas

In hindsight, it's apparent that the gas shocks of the 1970s hit Detroit at a time when they were particularly vulnerable. They were a decadent empire—Rome in the reign of Nero. The pinnacles of the Detroit art were crudely engineered muscle cars. The mainstream products were large, V8-powered, rear-wheel-drive sedans and station wagons. The Detroit marketing and engineering machinery didn't comprehend the appeal of cars like the Volkswagen Beetle or the Datsun 240Z.

But it took the spike in gas prices—and the economic disruptions it caused—to really open the door for the Japanese automakers.

Remember, Toyota and Honda were relative pipsqueaks in those days. They did not have much more going for them in the American market prior to the first Arab oil embargo than Chinese automakers have today, or Korean automakers did 15 years ago. The oil shocks, however, convinced a huge and influential cohort of American consumers to give fuel-efficient Japanese cars a try. Equally important, the oil shocks persuaded some of the most aggressive of America's car dealers to try them. The Detroit automakers believed the Japanese could be stopped by import quotas. They initially dismissed reports about the high quality of Japanese cars. They later assumed the Japanese could never replicate their low-cost manufacturing systems in America. Plus they believed initially that the low production cost of Japanese cars was the result of automation and unfair trading practices. (Undoubtedly, the cheap yen was a big help.) In any case, they figured that the Japanese would be stuck in a niche of small, economy cars and that the damage could be contained as customers grew out of their small car phase of life.

They were wrong on all counts.

There were Cassandras—plenty of them. At GM, an executive named Alex Mair gave detailed presentations on why Japanese cars were superior to GM's—lighter, more fuel efficient, and less costly to build. He set up a war room at GM's technical center with displays showing how Honda devised low-cost, high-quality engine parts, and how Japanese automakers designed factories that were roughly half the size of a GM plant but produced the same number of vehicles.

Mair would hold up a connecting rod—the piece of metal in an engine that connects the piston to the crankshaft. The one made by GM was bulky and crudely shaped with big tabs on the ends. Workers assembling the engines would grind down those tabs so that the weight of the piston and rod assembly would be balanced. By contrast, the connecting rod made by Honda was smaller, thinner, and almost like a piece of sculpture. It didn't have ugly tabs on the end, because it was designed to be properly balanced right out of the forge.

Mair's point was simple: If you pay careful attention to designing an elegant, lightweight connecting rod, then the engine will be lighter and quieter, the car around the engine can be more efficient, the brakes will have less mass to stop, and the engine will feel more responsive because it has less weight to move.

Another person who warned GM early on about the nature of the Japanese challenge was Jim Harbour. In the early 1980s, he took it into his head to try to tell GM's executives just how much more efficient Japanese factories really were, measured by hours of labor per car produced. The productivity gap was startling—the Japanese plants were about twice as efficient. GM's president at the time responded by barring Jim Harbour from company property.

By the late 1980s, GM's chairman, Roger Smith, had figured out that his company had something to learn from the Japanese. He just didn't know what it was. He poured billions into new, heavily automated U.S. factories—including an effort to build an experimental "lights out" factory that had almost no hourly workers. He entered a joint venture with Toyota to reopen an old GM factory in California, called New United Motor Manufacturing, Inc., or NUMMI. The idea was that GM managers could go to NUMMI to see up close what the "secret" of Toyota's assembly system was. Smith also launched what he promoted as an entirely new car company, Saturn, which was meant to pioneer both a more cooperative relationship with UAW workers and a new way of selling cars. None of these was a bad idea. But GM took too long to learn the lessons from these experiments—good or bad. The automation strategy fell on its face because the robots didn't work properly, and the cars they built struck many consumers as blandly styled and of poor quality. NUMMI did give GM managers valuable information about Toyota's manufacturing and management system, which a team of MIT researchers would later call "lean production." But too many of the GM managers who gained knowledge from NUMMI were unable to make an impact on GM's core North American business. Why? I believe it was because the UAW and GM middle managers quite understandably focused on the fact that Toyota's production system required only about half the workers GM had at a typical factory at the time. That was an equation the union wouldn't accept. The UAW demanded that GM keep paying workers displaced by new technology or other shifts in production strategy, which led to the creation of what became known as the Jobs Bank. That program discouraged GM from closing factories and encouraged efforts to sustain high levels of production even when demand fell.

## GM and the UAW

This brings me to the relationship between Detroit management and the UAW.

It is likely that if no Japanese or European manufacturers had built plants in the U.S.—in other words if imports were still really imports—the Detroit carmakers would not be in their current straits, although we as consumers would probably be paying more for cars and have fewer choices than we do. The fact is that the Detroit Three's post-World War II business strategies were doomed from the day in 1982 when the first Honda Accord rolled off a non-union assembly line in Ohio. After that it soon became clear that the Japanese automakers—and others—could build cars in the U.S. with relatively young, non-union labor forces that quickly learned how to thrive in the efficient production systems those companies operated.

Being new has enormous advantages in a capital-intensive, technology-intensive business like automaking. Honda, Toyota, Nissan, and later BMW, Mercedes, and Hyundai, had new factories, often subsidized by the host state, that were designed to use the latest manufacturing processes and technology. And they had new work forces. This was an advantage not because they paid them less per hour—generally non-union autoworkers receive about what UAW men and women earn in GM assembly plants—but because the new, non-union companies didn't have to bear additional costs for health care and pensions for hundreds of thousands of retirees.

Moreover, the new American manufacturers didn't have to compensate workers for the change from the old mass production methods to the new lean production approach. GM did—which is why GM created the Jobs Bank. The idea was that if UAW workers believed they wouldn't be fired if GM got more efficient, then they might embrace the new methods. Of course, we know how that turned out. The Jobs Bank became little more than a welfare system for people who had nothing more to contribute because GM's dropping market share had made their jobs superfluous.

Health care is a similar story. GM's leaders—and the UAW's—knew by the early 1990s that the combination of rising health care costs and the longevity of GM's retired workers threatened the company. But GM management backed away from a confrontation with the UAW over health care in 1993, and in every national contract cycle afterwards until 2005—when the company's nearness to collapse finally became clear to everyone.

In testimony before Congress this December, GM's CEO Rick Wagoner said that GM has spent $103 billion during the past 15 years funding its pension and retiree health-care obligations. That is nearly $7 billion a year—more than GM's capital spending budget for new models this year. Why wasn't Rick Wagoner making this point in 1998, or 1999, or even 2003? Even now, GM doesn't seem willing to treat the situation like the emergency it is. Under the current contract, the UAW will pay for retiree health-care costs using a fund negotiated in last year's contract—but that won't start until 2010. GM is on the hook to contribute $20 billion to that fund over the next several years—unless it can renegotiate that deal under federal supervision.

## Quality is Job One

Rick Wagoner told Congress: "Obviously, if we had the $103 billion and could use it for other things, it would enable us to be even farther ahead on technology or newer equipment in our plants, or whatever." Whatever, indeed.

This is a good place to talk about the Detroit mistake that matters most to most people: quality. By quality, I mean both the absence of defects and the appeal of the materials, design, and workmanship built into a car. I believe most people who buy a car also think of how durable and reliable a car is over time when they think of quality.

The failure of the Detroit automakers to keep pace with the new standards of reliability and defect-free assembly set by Toyota and Honda during the 1980s is well known, and still haunts them today. The really bad Detroit cars of the late 1970s and early to mid-1980s launched a cycle that has proven disastrous for all three companies. Poor design and bad reliability records led to customer dissatisfaction, which led to weaker demand for new Detroit cars as well as used ones. Customers were willing to buy Detroit cars—but only if they received a discount in advance for the mechanical problems they assumed they would have.

During the 1990s and the 2000s, a number of the surveys that industry executives accept as reliable guides to new vehicle quality began to show that the best of GM's and Ford's new models were almost as good—and in some cases better—in terms of being free of defects than comparable Toyotas, Hondas, or Nissans. But the Detroit brands still had a problem: They started $2,000 or more behind the best Japanese brands in terms of per-car costs, mainly because of labor and legacy costs, with a big helping of inefficient management thrown in. To overcome that deficit, GM and Ford (and Chrysler) resorted to aggressive cost-cutting and low-bid purchasing strategies with their materials suppliers. Unfortunately, customers could see the low-bid approach in the design and materials used for Detroit cars. So even though objective measures of defects and things gone wrong showed new Detroit cars getting better and better, customers still demanded deep discounts for both new and used Detroit models. This drove down the resale value of used Detroit cars, which in turn made it harder for the Detroit brands to charge enough for the new vehicles to overcome their cost gap.

*An Elderly Washingtonian in His 1921 Model T in Front of the White House, 1938*

GM, Ford, and Chrysler compounded this problem by trying to generate the cash to cover their health care and pension bills by building more cars than the market demanded, and then "selling" them to rental car fleets. When those fleet cars bounced back to used car lots, where they competed with new vehicles that were essentially indistinguishable except for the higher price tag, they helped drive down resale values even more.

So the billions spent on legacy costs are matched by billions more in revenue that the Detroit automakers never saw because of the way they mismanaged supply and demand. This is why the Detroit brands appear to be lagging behind not just in hybrids—and it remains to be seen how durable that market is—but also in terms of the refinement and technology offered in their conventional cars.

## What to Build?

The recent spectacle of the Diminished Three CEOs and the UAW president groveling before Congress has us focused now on how Detroit has mishandled adversity. A more important question is why they did so badly when times were good.

Consider GM. In 2000 Rick Wagoner, his senior executive team, and a flock of auto journalists jetted off to a villa in Italy for a seminar on how the GM of the 21st century was going to look. Wagoner and his team talked a lot about how GM was going to gain sales and profit from a "network" of alliances with automakers such as Subaru, Suzuki, Isuzu, and Fiat—automakers into which GM had invested capital. They talked about how they were going to use the Internet to turbocharge the company's performance. And so on. But five years later, all of this was in tatters. Much of the capital GM invested in its alliance partners was lost when the company was forced to sell out at distressed prices. Fiat was the worst of all. GM had to pay Fiat $2 billion to get out of the deal—never mind getting back the $2 billion it had invested up front to buy 20 percent of Fiat Auto. GM said it saved $1 billion a year thanks to the Fiat partnership. Obviously, whatever those gains were, they didn't help GM become profitable.

At least GM didn't use the cash it rolled up during the 1990s boom to buy junkyards, as Ford did. But GM did see an opportunity in the money to be made from selling mortgages, and plunged its GMAC financing operation aggressively into that market. Of course, GM didn't see the crash in subprime mortgages coming, either, and now GMAC is effectively bankrupt.

GM's many critics argue that what they should have done with the money they spent on UAW legacy costs and bad diversification schemes was to develop electric cars and hybrids, instead of continuing to base their U.S. business on the same large, V8-powered, rear-wheel-drive formula they used in the 60s—except that now these vehicles were sold as SUVs instead of muscle cars. And indeed, Detroit did depend too heavily on pickup trucks and SUVs for profits. But they did so for understandable reasons. These were the vehicles that consumers wanted to buy from them. Also, these were the vehicles that government policy encouraged them to build.

When gas was cheap, big gas-guzzling trucks were exactly what GM customers wanted. Consumers didn't want Detroit's imitation Toyota Camrys. Toyota was building more than enough real Camrys down in Kentucky. GM made profits of as much as $8,000 per truck—and lost money on many of its cars. Federal fuel economy rules introduced in 1975 forced GM to shrink its cars so that they could average 27.5 miles per gallon. GM did this poorly. (Remember the Chevy Citation or the Cadillac Cimarron?) But federal laws allowed "light trucks" to meet a lower mileage standard. This kink in federal law allowed GM, Ford, and Chrysler to design innovative products that Americans clamored to buy when gas was cheap: SUVs. When Ford launched the Explorer, and GM later launched the Tahoe and the upgraded Suburban, it was the Japanese companies that were envious. In fact, one reason why Toyota is on its way to a loss for 2008—its first annual loss in 70 years—is that it built too many factories in the U.S. in order to build more SUVs and pickups.

One irony of the current situation is that the only vehicles likely to generate the cash GM and the others need right now to rebuild are the same gas-guzzlers that Washington no longer wants them to build. Even New York Times columnist Thomas Friedman has now come to realize that you can't ask Detroit to sell tiny, expensive hybrids when gasoline is under $2 a gallon. We have two contradictory energy policies: The first demands cheap gas at all costs. The second demands that Detroit should substantially increase the average mileage of its cars to 35 or even 40 miles per gallon across the board. How the Obama administration will square this circle, I don't know.

### Thinking Anew

So now, where are we? GM has become Government Motors. With the U.S. Treasury standing in for the DuPonts of old, GM is going to try to reinvent itself. One challenge among many for GM in this process will be coming to terms with the reality that the U.S. market is too fractured, and has too many volume manufacturers, for any one of them to expect to control the kind of market share and pricing power GM had in its heyday. Today, according to Wardsauto.com, there are ten foreign-owned automakers with U.S. factories that assembled 3.9 million cars, pickups, and SUVs in 2007, before auto demand began to collapse. That's more than Ford's and Chrysler's U.S. production combined.

GM's efforts to cling to its 1950s self—with the old Sloanian ladder brands of Chevy, Pontiac, Buick, and Cadillac, plus Saturn, Saab, Hummer, and GMC—have led its management into one dark wood of error after another. Since 2001, GM's marketing strategy has come down to a single idea: zero percent financing. This was the automotive version of the addictive, easy credit that ultimately destroyed the housing market. Cut-rate loans, offered to decreasingly credit-worthy buyers, propped up sales and delayed the day of reckoning. But it didn't delay it long enough. The house of cards began tumbling in 2005, and I would say it has now collapsed fully.

Between 1995 and 2007, GM managed to earn a cumulative total of $13.5 billion. That's three-tenths of one percent of the total revenues during that period of more than $4 trillion—and those are nominal dollars, not adjusted for inflation. Between 1990 and 2007, GM lost a combined total of about $33 billion. The six unprofitable years wiped out the gains from 12 profitable years, and then some. But old habits die hard. Within hours of clinching a $6 billion government bailout last month, GMAC and GM were back to promoting zero-interest loans.

During the 1980s and 1990s, GM's leaders refused—and I believe some still refuse—to accept the reality of the presence of so many new automakers in the U.S. market, more than at any time since the 1920s. This hard truth means the company's U.S. market share going forward isn't going to return to the 40 percent levels of the mid-1980s, or the 30 percent levels of the 1990s, or even the mid-20 percent levels we have seen more recently. One thing to watch as GM tries to restructure now will be what assumptions the company makes about its share of the U.S. market going forward. If they call for anything higher than 15 percent, I would be suspicious.

Since all of you are now part owners of this enterprise, I would urge all of you to pay close attention, since what's about to unfold has no clear precedent in our nation's economic history. The closest parallels I can see are Renault in France, Volkswagen in Germany, and the various state-controlled Chinese automakers. But none of these companies is as large as GM, and none of these companies is exactly a model for what GM should want to become.

As I have tried to suggest, it's hard enough for professional managers and technicians—who have a clear profit motive—to run an enterprise as complex as a global car company. What will be the fate of a quasi-nationalized enterprise whose "board of directors" will now include 535 members of Congress, plus various agencies of the Executive Branch? As a property owner in suburban Detroit, I can only hope for the best.

# Ecology and the Economy: The Problems of Coexistence
## James L. Buckley (1980)

*James L. Buckley (born 1923) is a graduate of Yale and of Yale Law School. For many years he worked with a company that performed oil and gas exploration. In 1970 he was elected to the U.S. Senate from New York on the Conservative Party ticket in that state, and he served one term. He later was an Undersecretary for Security, Science, and Technology in the Department of State (1981-1982); president of Radio Free Europe (1982-1985); and then a judge on the U.S. Court of Appeals for the District of Columbia (1985-1996). Thus Mr. Buckley served in all three branches of the Federal government. He is the brother of the late conservative writer William F. Buckley Jr. This speech was given many years ago as environmental policy was in its early stages. Some of the specific questions he discussed have changed or been resolved, but the speech does a good job of presenting the issues involved in balancing economic growth with environmental responsibility.*

February 1980 *Imprimis*

I come before you as a conservationist who is also a political conservative. I try to make up for this apparent anomaly (and I haven't yet given up hope for my philosophical brethren) by being at the same time what might be styled a conservative conservationist; by

which I mean to say that I see no particular virtue in turning the American environmental clock back to the year 1491. I am among those who view man as part of nature, with natural imperatives of his own which are not necessarily at odds with the rest of creation.

Over the centuries, in most parts of the world, man managed to live in a state of essential balance with nature, adjusting his agricultural practices by trial and error to meet the natural requirements of the land he tilled. Such pollution as his industries produced could usually be dissipated or reabsorbed into the environment without doing lasting harm. But over the past few decades, we have seen a dramatic change in the qualitative nature of man's impact on the world he lives in and on which he depends for his biological survival.

We are now producing vast varieties and volumes of exotic new chemicals which when released in the air and water as industrial wastes, or spread on the land as insecticides and pesticides, can inflict damage on a scale that no one could have anticipated a generation or so ago.

Unlike man's earlier wastes, which were derived from nature and in due course would be broken down by natural processes and recycled back into the soil, water or atmosphere, many of today's synthetics are proving virtually indigestible. We have learned that when such substances are used on any scale, there may be no such thing as "safe" concentrations. Radioactive materials and D.D.T., for example, are subject to biological concentration as they move up the food chain, and once injected into the environment they cannot be reclaimed.

In sum, our technology has propelled us into a new era where we have achieved an awesome power to disrupt the very rhythms of life and to inflict costs on society the full extent of which we have not yet learned to assess, costs that are no less real for having so long been either unsuspected or ignored.

It was a perception of the accelerating scale of the damage we were inflicting on the environment, and hence on ourselves, that sparked the environmental revolution of the past decade. One can question the appropriateness of the regulatory mechanisms we have set in place; one can question whether the costs exacted by them bear a rational relationship to the benefits gained; one can argue over the relative priority to be placed on certain environmental values whose importance few deny, but which no one has yet determined how to quantify; but no dispassionate person in possession of the facts, no one with an elementary grasp of biological cause and effect, can any longer deny that man has achieved the power to abuse his environment on a massive scale, or that there are formidable economic costs that flow from that abuse.

The challenge facing mankind, then, is not one of having to make a choice between economic welfare and ecological preservation, because our economic wellbeing ultimately depends on the health of our environment. The challenge, therefore, is to develop more effective techniques for bringing man's economic activities into equilibrium with the natural world of which he is an inescapable part.

As the saying goes, this is easier said than done. There is almost universal agreement on the need to do something about pollution. It is when one tries to suggest what should be done and at what cost that the discussion tends to degenerate into a brawl. Part of the problem is that the costs of implementing our existing anti-pollution laws are huge, and they fall on relatively few backs.

Until relatively recently public waters and the atmosphere were routinely considered to be available to all comers—industry, municipalities, individual households—as cost-free "dispos-alls." Thus the disposition of waste did not constitute a cost of production, and was not reflected in the price of goods. But the wastes discharged into our air and water nevertheless give rise to very real costs—costs measured in terms of corrosion, crop losses, doctor's bills, declines in fisheries, loss of recreational values, industrial absenteeism, and the like—that society as a whole has had to absorb.

Properly designed anti-pollution strategies will result not so much in added burdens on society as in what economists call the "internalizing" of external costs. This comes about as manufacturers incorporate the expense of cleaning up their wastes into the prices they charge for their products. Thus the ultimate consumer is required to pay the full cost of what he elects to use. Viewed from another perspective, if polluting is recognized as a form of public nuisance in which environmental freeloaders impose real costs on their downwind or downstream neighbors, then it is not entirely unreasonable for the neighbors to ask that the polluters be required to absorb those costs.

Therefore, what we ought to be asking ourselves is not whether we can afford a cleaner environment, but how we can best go about achieving one. Specifically, we need to determine whether the costs associated with our current pollution abatement strategies bear a reasonable relationship to the benefits to be derived from them. This, I admit, is a proposition far easier to state than to apply because of the exquisite difficulty of identifying all of the adverse effects of pollution in the first place, and of quantifying so many of them in the second.

Nevertheless, this is the rational context within which the current debate over our environmental laws ought to proceed. In comparing current costs with current benefits, however, one must keep in mind that our environmental effort today is rather like a football team that remains several touchdowns behind. It has to catch up before it can think of winning. As we have only recently awakened to the need for environmental protection, we are faced with a formidable backlog of pollution problems requiring immediate attention.

And make no mistake, the backlog is a massive one. Just the other day, the Environmental Protection Agency estimated that Federal programs to control environmental pollution will cost society some $360 billion in the decade between 1977 and 1986. That is an enormous figure—an average of some $36 billion for each of 10 years: and much of it will be required for the construction of such things as mutual sewerage treatment facilities that ought to have been in place years ago.

That figure reflects the fact that we have a lot of catching up to do, catching up that must be done sooner or later; but once we have caught up, once the capital investments required to achieve our stated goals have been completed, we can expect the annual cost of pollution abatement to decline. Furthermore, in assessing the E.P.A.'s estimates, we should keep in mind that they assume a continuation of the present system of control by regulation rather than through an alternative system of economic incentives that I shall discuss later; and they assume that no technological breakthroughs in pollution control will be achieved, which is certainly unrealistic—especially if such an alternative is adopted.

Perhaps our major problem in examining the environmental equation is in the assumption that both the benefits and the costs can be estimated with any degree of precision. I have seen enough cost-benefit analyses on dam and harbor projects to know that even when trying to compute so simple a benefit as flood protection for a particular town, the attempt to place a monetary value on that protection is anything but an exercise in precision; and it is apt to do little more than reflect the prejudice of the calculator. Time, however, seems to be on the side of those who argue the extent of the real economic costs that result from the indiscriminate discharge of manmade wastes. Too many examples are now surfacing where an ounce of pollution prevention could have saved a ton of environmental costs.

Our experience with the now notorious Love Canal in Niagara Falls, New York, is a case very much in point. This ironically-named ditch was originally intended to provide hydroelectric power for some nearby homes, but in the 1920s it was converted into a dumpsite. Over the years, dozens of chemicals—eleven suspected of producing cancer— were discovered to have oozed from their containers in the canal and percolated through the soil and into the basements of nearby homes, with a disastrous impact on the health of their inhabitants. The history of their illnesses included unusually high rates of miscarriages, abnormal births, and chronic illnesses.

At the time the Congress began work on the Clean Air Act of 1970, relatively little was known about the exact nature and extent of the harm done to human health by air pollution, although the fact of such harm was apparent to any one who had coughed and wheezed his way through a Los Angeles smog. Nor was much known about the probable cost of doing something about it or of the exact nature of the technology that would be required to bring air pollution under control. All that was known was that the situation was rapidly deteriorating, the costs to health undoubtedly soaring, and that something had to be done. But what?

Under Senator Edmund Muskie's leadership, the Congress came up with a strategy and a standard which at the time were entirely reasonable, especially as no one could have anticipated that they would take on something of the aura of the tablets handed down by a higher authority some millennia ago on Mount Sinai.

The strategy was to force the development of antipollution technology by legislative fiat; in the case of automobile emissions, by legislating stepped decreases in the principal pollutants—carbon monoxide, hydrocarbons, and nitrogen oxides over a specified period.

This was an admittedly crude approach; and it was acknowledged at the time to be nothing more than the initiation of a process that would have to be reassessed from time to time in the light of new knowledge and experience. The impact of this legislation has been formidable; and insofar as its initial goals are concerned, it has proven enormously effective.

Research conducted by the Council on Environmental Quality and others suggests that the achievement of current ambient air standards would result in savings of between $20 billion and $25 billion a year. This compares with a cost (as estimated by the E.P.A. in 1978) of $12 billion per year for the air pollution controls required to achieve those standards. And these studies have not taken into full account some of the unsuspected consequences of air pollution that are just now beginning to be perceived.

A few years ago, one of the popular proposals for handling emissions of sulfur dioxide was to build very tall stacks that would protect surrounding areas by dissipating the gas into the atmosphere. The strategy was first tested in England, where it achieved local miracles. Shortly thereafter, however, German and Swedish scientists hundreds of miles to leeward began to notice a sharp increase in the sulphuric acid content of their rain water. Thus did the phrase "acid rains" enter our vocabulary.

Foresters working in our northeastern states subsequently noticed the same phenomenon and began to speculate as to the possible impact of changes in soil acidity on the rate of growth of timber. But hard evidence of the adverse environmental impact of acid rain is now coming to the fore. Just a few months ago, Canadian biologists found that over two hundred lakes in the province of Ontario have been rendered sterile; and the E.P.A. has now identified between ninety and one hundred lakes in the Adirondacks which no longer can support fish life. Apparently the acidity of their waters has reached levels where the fish fail to reproduce. In short, we have not yet reached the end of the catalog of damage attributable to air pollution. . . .

[We have learned some things about the marginal costs of pollution control] since our original landmark environmental laws were enacted. Whereas the great majority of our air and water pollutants can be brought under control at costs that most people will consider reasonable, it can become incredibly expensive to remove the last few percentages that existing legislation require to be removed within stated periods. Furthermore, the cost of such removal will vary by enormous margins depending on the particular industrial processes involved. Finally, there is increasing question as to whether the achievement of our necessary environmental goals really requires the uniform application of statutory standards irrespective of cost in specific localized instances; or for that matter whether it is possible to impose programs that will disrupt entire communities.

Let me illustrate by taking the celebrated case of Los Angeles and the ambient air goals legislated by Congress in 1970. Given the facts of the Los Angeles situation and the dependence of its people on the automobile, given the state of emission control technology, given the lack of adequate public transportation facilities and the impossibility of conjuring them up overnight, it became apparent by 1973 that there was no possible way of meeting statutory deadlines without closing down the city. When the E.P.A. decided to handle this dilemma by simply ignoring the explicit requirements of the law, environmentalists took the agency to court and a judge issued a decision which required the agency to promulgate a plan for the city that could in effect have declared a moratorium on the use of private automobiles during much of the year. This in turn left the Congress with little choice but to enact legislation extending the deadlines.

What becomes increasingly clear is the need for a greater flexibility in the application of our environmental laws so as to enable us to cope with the exceptional situation, but always under carefully defined safeguards. For example, if it should prove impossible, except at exorbitant cost, to achieve the incremental improvements in air pollution controls required to keep pollutants in the Los Angeles basin at national ambient standards during the periods of atmospheric inversions to which the city is prone, then perhaps we ought to allow Los Angeles the option to suffer under less than optimum conditions, perhaps requiring them to post signs along highways leading into the city warning travelers that "Breathing Los Angeles air may be dangerous to your health."

None of this suggests that we should back away from our broadly-defined environmental objectives; rather, we should recognize that the time has come to take advantage of the substantial experience we have accumulated over the past decade and see how we can better achieve those objectives with a special eye to cost efficiency. Without pretending to cover the universe, let me suggest a few modifications in our present approach that I believe would go a long way toward dispelling the idea that there is a necessary conflict between environmental and economic goals.

The first and foremost problem posed by our environmental laws is the way they are structured—their almost total reliance on regulation for the achievement of stated goals. Because the regulatory approach to the implementation of public policy in any complex area requires the drafting of hundreds of detailed rules; because these in turn require the exercise of thousands of individual judgments by those charged with enforcing them; because our anti-pollution laws have tended to describe their policy objectives in the broadest terms; because of all these factors, the regulations drawn up and administered by the E.P.A. have proven in case after case to be inordinately complicated, their implementation needlessly costly, and the decisions made by individual E.P.A. administrators subject to infinite challenge.

And this in turn has converted our environmental laws into instruments for protracted litigation often entered into by environmentalist diehards whose primary goal is simply to obstruct. And so economically-important projects that have been cleared by all the relevant state and federal environmental agencies can nevertheless be delayed year after costly year until many of them are simply abandoned.

The answer to this regulatory morass is not to create an Energy Mobilization Board with the power to override the most important environmental safeguards by simple fiat, as the Congress is now in the process of doing. Such an approach is not only irresponsible, but it is apt to delay the kinds of revisions in our environmental laws and procedures which are so clearly needed.

We need, for example, to enact procedural reforms that will allow specific proposals to be submitted, considered, ruled upon, the rulings challenged, and the challenges adjudicated with an eye to achieving as expeditious a final determination of a particular matter as prudence will allow. We cannot permit the endless second guessing that is creating unconscionable delays and giving rise to confrontations and public frustration which in the end can only harm the environmental cause.

We should also move away from a reliance on regulations toward a strategy of economic incentives for the achievement of specific environmental goals. The fact is that no mechanism has yet been discovered that is as effective as the marketplace in harnessing human energy and ingenuity. Such a strategy offers the surest way to make pollution control less arbitrary, less costly, and less bureaucratic. Regulations are too often framed in terms of immutable standards to be universally applied, rather than in terms of innovative, cost effective, flexible controls.

We need to encourage the development of improved ways to control pollution; and the most promising way to do this is to move away from the present system of plant-by-plant regulation toward one that will rely on such incentives to innovation as taxes on specific pollutants or pollution permits that will encourage the marketplace to determine the most cost-effective ways to control pollution.

Before I left the United States Senate, I introduced an amendment to a revision of the Clean Air Act that would require the E.P.A. to study various ways of harnessing economic incentives for the abatement of nitrogen oxide emissions from stationary sources as a test of this approach to pollution control. Nitrogen oxides are produced in all combustion processes; but up to that time, efforts to control this particular pollutant had been limited to automobile emissions. My amendment survived my own tenure in the Senate, and became law in 1977.

The E.P.A. report mandated by the amendment is now close to completion, and its conclusions are more favorable than even I had anticipated. They show that such economic alternatives to regulation as a system of emission charges or pollution permits are likely to produce the same degree of nitrogen oxide control at anywhere from one-tenth to one-fourth the cost of the present system of regulation. In the words of the study: "Perhaps the greatest strength of economic approaches relative to the regulatory approaches is that they tend to locate decision-making responsibility with those who possess the information needed to make the best decision."

Another concept that I believe holds merit is what the E.P.A. terms its "offset" policy. Under this approach, a corporation wishing to locate or expand its operations in a polluted area may buy and retire the existing pollution from another company. An oil refinery, for example, might buy out a local dry cleaning plant and close it down rather than install a highly expensive, stringent pollution control system of its own. The refinery would thus obtain the degree of pollution reduction required to offset the pollution that its proposed facilities would generate.

Obviously, an offset purchase would only occur when it proved less costly than the alternative. Furthermore, this approach does not necessarily mean that the dry cleaning establishment would vanish from the area. If dry cleaners can handle their own pollution at a far lower cost per unit of pollutant than a refinery, then they can utilize the funds received from the refinery to install the necessary hardware and continue in operation at no net increase of pollution in the area. Thus flexibility replaces rigidity, and pollution abatement dollars are focused where they can achieve the greatest good.

Perhaps most important, these economic alternatives appear to be more likely than any other system to motivate the development of new pollution control technology. Under the present regulatory strategy, industry often balks at investing large sums in developing new technology because success is likely to mean that the industry will have to install that new technology even when to do so will significantly raise the overall costs of its operations. Under a system of economic incentives, however, the development of cost-efficient technology becomes a logical goal. In short, a move toward market incentives seems a far surer way of marrying economic and environmental objectives than the existing strategy of forcing technology to achieve fixed statutory goals.

Which brings me to another area for reform which would deal with what might be called the problem of environmental holy writ. The decision nine years ago to decrease each component of automotive pollution by 90% over a five- to six-year period was acknowledged at the time to be wholly arbitrary. Yet, it has fixed some totemic numbers in the statute books.

Nitrogen oxide must be reduced to 0.4 parts per million because that was what was decreed in 1970 irrespective of what later studies may tell us as to the merits of such an objective.

If the necessary coexistence between economics and the environment is to be achieved, it is essential that specific goals be reviewed periodically in the light of developing knowledge, so that we may always be sure that the costs imposed by them are justified. Such reviews, of course, will apply the disciplines of cost-benefit analysis to the evaluation of pollution abatement strategies. But here I think we should keep in mind certain inherent limitations of this kind of exercise when applied to environmental problems. Reasonably reliable values can be assigned to the more obvious kinds of damage done by specific pollutants; and as I have suggested, I believe the case can be made that once in place, the costs of properly-structured pollution controls will more than pay for themselves in savings of a kind that the least imaginative cost accountant can recognize.

But inevitably there will be the cases at the margin, some of them involving substantial sums or important economic objectives, where the value to be placed on specific environmental benefits becomes more difficult or even impossible to quantify; and, of course, these are the cases that tend to become the focus of the most heated controversy. I do not suggest that the case for environmental protection is necessarily the weaker for having to deal at times with intangible values; only that at times this case may be more difficult to present and to understand. What value, for example, does one place on the Parthenon, whose facade is now being eaten away by the pollutants generated in modern Greece; what value on a pristine Grand Canyon, given its hydroelectrical potential; what value on the last great herd of migratory mammals left on earth, the protection of whose calving grounds would deny us access to potential oil reserves equivalent to perhaps five or ten days' consumption?

No legislation has focused more clearly on these less easily quantified aspects of environmental concern, and none in recent years has caused such apoplexy among so-called practical men of affairs, as the Endangered Species Act of 1973. This bill first burst upon the public consciousness two years ago when it was invoked to scuttle projected dams in Tennessee and Maine; the first to save a nondescript little fish called the snail darter and the other, an inconspicuous flower called the furbish lousewort.

It is idiotic, cry the practical men of affairs, to allow sentimentality over a few hundred weeds or minnows to stand in the way of progress. It is irresponsible, reply the conservationists, to destroy forever a unique pool of genetic material; and the conservationists can marshal a host of non-sentimental arguments in support of what many consider to be the most important environmental legislation of the decade.

Having said this, I can hear the P.M.O.A.'s swallow in disbelief as they ask, "Of what possible dollars-and-cents value is the snail darter?" To which conservationists will have to reply, "None that we know of." And that, paradoxically, is one of the major scientific justifications for the Endangered Species Act.

Our biological knowledge is still so pitifully small that it is less than likely that science can identify the immediate worth of any given species. It is therefore imprudent to allow such an estimate, as perceived by men trained to think in terms only of near-term goals, to be the basis for deciding whether a given species is to be preserved.

What good is a snail darter? As practical men measure "good," probably none; but we simply don't know. What value would have been placed on the cowpox virus before Jenner; or on penicillium molds before Fleming; or on wild rubber trees before Goodyear learned to vulcanize their sap? Yet the life of most Americans has been profoundly affected by these species.

Fully 40% of modern drugs have been derived from nature. Most of the food man eats comes from only about twenty out of the thousands of plants known to be edible. And even those currently being cultivated require the preservation of large pools of genetic material on which plant scientists can draw in order to produce more useful strains or to restore the vigor of the highly inbred varieties that have revolutionized agriculture in recent years.

Just a few months ago a front-page story in the *New York Times* announced: "In a remote mountain region in Mexico, a perennial plant that crossbreeds with corn has been discovered, awakening hopes for producing a perennial variety of that food crop with revolutionary implications for agriculture." This wild grass offers the prospect of a dramatic reduction in the cost of producing one of the world's most important foods. Had practical men of affairs been in charge of building dams in the Mexican Sierras, however, it might have been lost—forever.

This century has witnessed over half the extinctions of animal species known to have occurred during recorded history; and, largely because of the vast scale on which tropical rain forests are being cut around the world, it is estimated that by the year 2000 upwards of a million additional species—about 20% of those now in existence—may become extinct.

The Endangered Species Act was passed in order to slow down this accelerating rate of man-caused extinctions. Its purpose is not only to help save species that might prove of direct value to man, but to help preserve the biological diversity that, in America and on the rest of our planet, provides the fundamental support system for man and other living things.

As living creatures, the more we understand of biological processes, the more wisely we will be able to manage ourselves. Thus the deliberate extermination of a species can be an act of recklessness. By permitting high rates of extinction to continue, we are limiting the potential growth of biological knowledge. In essence, the process is tantamount to book-burning; but it is even worse, in that it involves books yet to be deciphered and read.

One might contend, of course, that our country's biological diversity is still so great and the land so developed—so criss-crossed with the works of man—that it will soon be hard to locate a dam anywhere without endangering some species. But as we develop a national inventory of endangered species, we certainly can plan our necessary developments so as to exterminate the smallest number possible, if not to preclude man-caused extinctions altogether. This, of course, is what the legislation is intended to accomplish.

This objective represents a quantum jump in man's acknowledgement of his moral responsibility for the integrity of the natural world he passes on to succeeding generations.

It is this which lends the Endangered Species Act its special significance. It recognizes values, be they ethical or aesthetic, that transcend the purely practical and admit to awe in the face of the diversity of creation. Not everyone will be moved by them, and they no more lend themselves to a cost-effective calculus than does a Bach chorale. But surely it is an act of unseemly arrogance to decree the extinction of a unique form of life without compelling justification.

Unfortunately, the Congress recently voted to override the procedures it itself had established for determining when such justification exists, and ordered the completion of the Tellico Dam despite detailed economic studies demonstrating it to be a costly boondoggle, a classic case of pork barrel legislation.

Nevertheless, I do believe that the history of the Endangered Species Act illustrates a growing awareness of the interrelationship between ecological preservation and economic well-being as well as the need for establishing mechanisms for mediating decisions in what I believe will in time be recognized as the relatively rare instances where the two are in genuine conflict.

I firmly believe that when all the facts are placed in their proper perspective, when we truly come to understand the full consequences of abusing the natural systems on which life depends, then it will be generally accepted that man cannot conduct his economic

activities in an ecological void except at tremendous ultimate cost. If we care about the economic well-being of the next generation, then we must care more than we have in the past about the quality of the physical and biological world they will inherit.

As Edmund Burke reminded us years ago, the men and women of each generation are but "temporary possessors and life-renters" who "should not think it among their rights to cut off the entail or commit waste on the inheritance," lest they "leave to those who come after them a ruin instead of a habitation." I can think of no more appropriate perspective than Burke's as we work to establish a new harmony between man and the natural world he lives in.

# I Must See the Things; I Must See the Men
## One Historian's Recollections
## of the 1930s and 1940s
## Russell Kirk (1987)

*Russell Kirk (1918-1994) was a leading conservative writer for decades whose work was widely respected and frequently honored. He wrote over thirty books and hundreds of articles. One of his books was the text* Economics: Work and Prosperity *(1989). This speech is included as a reminder that, behind the theories, statistics, and debates in economics are real human beings, all of whom have value before God and most of whom want to live well and responsibly.*

October 1987 *Imprimis*

## Introduction

The Greek historian Polybius gave us what is called the "pragmatic method" of historical study, dealing accurately with important events and offering explanations for them; ascertaining, so far as possible, the how and the why of those events; thus providing instruction to seekers after prudence, pointing the way toward right conduct through knowledge of both the blunders and the successes of the past. Writing principally about his own time during the third and second centuries before Christ, Polybius traveled at an advanced age from the Pillars of Hercules to the shores of the Black Sea, seeking out monuments and inspecting archives and battle sites, so that he might get at the truth of reports of events.

To write a truthful history, as Hilaire Belloc reminds us, one must know the towns, the country houses, the landscape, the whole physical setting, of the country of one's studies; one must talk with old men and women, besides reading other people's books; one must peer imaginatively behind the veil of yesteryear. As Edmund Burke said concerning a prudent statesman's attention to grand policies, "I must see the things; I must see the men."

In particular, the New Deal needs to be examined afresh, with candor, now that people no longer are roused to partisan political passions by discussion of the Roosevelt era. For some years the majority of publications about the New Deal were written without much judicious criticism; but in the fullness of time there were counterblasts, often on radical premises, from writers no more impartial. Temperate treatments of the subject also have been published, true; yet too often the "neutral" authors seem content with generalizations, as if they lacked close personal knowledge of the people and events that they discuss.

Neither will it do to rely altogether upon the memoirs of leading men of the period, few of whom were perfectly ingenuous; nor upon "court histories" of that period. For in a democracy, the beliefs, interests, moods, and passions of the mass of the people are more powerful causes of historical events than are the polemics of eminent politicians and publicists.

A decade from now, surviving men and women who were even children when Herbert Hoover lost the Presidency will be few enough. So, with a view to a truthful art of history, it is well for some of us to set down our own recollections of the events of the Twenties and Thirties and Forties, and of the circumstances and notions behind those events. This is my apology for presenting to you here a pragmatic description of certain events and opinions in this state of Michigan, during the Thirties, as seen and experienced by a very young man of a reflective turn of mind.

I offer you, in short, a microcosmic glimpse of American life and opinion in the times of Presidents Hoover and Roosevelt—not in New York or Washington, but mostly in the neighborhood of Detroit, hard hit by the Great Depression; and not among the prosperous, but among what the British would call the working class, and American journalists today call blue-collar people. I will confine myself principally to this question: Did the New Deal avert a violent revolution in the United States?

## One Youth's Recollection

Sometime in 1928, at the age of ten, I begin to read the *Detroit News*, *Detroit Times*, and *Detroit Free Press*. I took a precocious interest in political news, but ignored the financial pages—as, indeed, I ignore financial pages still. Thus I was vexed when on the front page of the paper appeared a lengthy boring account of the suicide of Ivar Kruger, the Swedish "match king," and the consequences of his death; thus I was still more annoyed when the papers devoted their headlines to fluctuations on the New York Stock Exchange. Yet in the fullness of time I was made aware that such financial transactions did indeed concern the material interests and the social prospects of even a ten-year-old boy in the town of Plymouth, Michigan, twenty miles west of Detroit's city hall.

My father was a locomotive engineman, and we lived very close to the Pere Marquette depot, the spreading railway yards, the roundhouse, and the riptrack; the steam locomotives hooted and thundered past our house round the clock. For us boys of the Lower Town, literally on the wrong side of the tracks, the yards were our playground for games of Prisoners' Base and other sports including miniature wars with defective discarded B.B. guns pilfered from the scrap-heap of the Daisy Air Rifle Company. In 1928-29, we had no bathroom in our house, and no automobile; ours were Gray's "short and simple annals of the poor." We Kirks were not of the number of FDR's "malefactors of great wealth." Neither were we Marchers in the Dawn toward some terrestrial Zion.

Upon us there descended, by degrees, the Great Depression. On the Pere Marquette Railroad the volume of freight diminished. Under the seniority system of the Railway Brotherhood, my father was "bumped" repeatedly from the more desirable assignments, so that presently he was working only half-time. We could not pay our accustomed rent; the landlord, pleasantly named Doomstrike, reduced it. A few months later we could not afford even the reduced rent; Mr. Doomstrike reduced it yet more. Still my father's wage-packet shrank, so that we decided to move in with my widowed grandmother, who had a biggish house. Mr. Doomstrike begged us to stay on, paying no rent at all until better times, not wishing his rental property to stand empty and defenseless; but we deserted him and shifted to my grandmother's house—yet closer to the tracks. If this narration seems digressive—why, I am suggesting that the circumstances of people with much-reduced incomes between 1929 and 1933 were not nearly so desperate as certain school textbooks would have us believe.

Railwaymen, somewhat fulsomely called "the aristocracy of labor," were fairly resourceful in adversity. When our family friend Eddie Ebert, the yardmaster, was bumped from his post by an older man from Detroit, he took a job as an ordinary section-hand, swinging a pick along with the Mexican laborers—and gradually worked his way back up. Having sometime to spare, Eddie and my father enrolled in a course in bricklaying at a proprietary trade-school in the city, paying scarce cash for instruction; my father never actually obtained work as a bricklayer in consequence, but Eddie did. President Hoover's much-ridiculed anecdote about folk who kept themselves off relief by selling apples on street corners did not seem patently absurd to us Kirks—not that we were especial admirers of Mr. Hoover. One of my uncles, who had been foreman in a foundry, on losing his job took up selling magazine subscriptions—and did rather well out of it. Another uncle who ran a small dry-cleaning business kept his doors open when he could pay his help no longer by enrolling his employees in a profit-sharing plan. It succeeded.

The hardest knocks of the Depression did not hit Plymouth, indeed, until President Roosevelt, so soon after taking office, proclaimed his national bank moratorium. That measure dismayed and much inconvenienced the people with some small savings; but it did not ruin many of them. One such family in Plymouth, who raised chickens on a small farm, were reduced to eating little but eggs, chicken in a variety of forms and their own vegetables for three years; their health did not suffer.

Across Mill Street from my grandmother's house stood the Hotel Anderine, Italian-operated, where drink could be obtained, Volstead Act or no Volstead Act. (The town marshal lived next door.) Some rough customers were to be encountered there—all of them, though, in justifiable awe of my formidable grandmother's huge bulldog, Towser. In Italy, say, the Hotel Anderine might have hung out the sign "Albergo Karl Marx;" in Plymouth, the American flag was displayed from the hotel's cornice on every possible occasion, and now and again the strains of a patriotic melody of the First World War might issue from the barroom.

During those late years of Hoover and early years of Roosevelt, I was no political ignoramus. As a junior in high school, I read with much interest Trotsky's *History of the Russian Revolution*, with Rostovtzeff's *Social and Economic History of the Roman Empire* as antidote. (These studied privately, of course, not as a general classroom exercise.) I was alert to tones of political opinion. My principal school chum, Jack Sessions, thought of himself as a socialist. Years later, when director of political education for the International Ladies' Garment Workers Union in Manhattan, he would become a most effective and intelligent opponent of Communist influence, abroad and in the United States. With Comrade Trotsky at the back of my mind, I kept an ear open for whisperings of sedition.

A great storm cloud of public disapproval menaced President Hoover by 1932; and General Douglas MacArthur's dispersal of the Bonus Marchers at Anacostia Flats undid the Hoover Administration altogether. The newspapers fulminated steadily against Mr. Hoover. For my part, in the principal radical act of my life, I pulled down a big photograph of the President that our school superintendent had posted on the chief bulletin board, tore it in half, and flung it in the trash can. (I refrained from telling of this episode to Mr. Hoover himself, when long later I breakfasted with him in his suite at the Waldorf-Astoria.) It became clear that Mr. Hoover and his cabinet were on the way out.

An iron-jawed elderly spinster teacher of English took Jack Sessions, me, and some classmates to meetings in Ann Arbor of the Leagues Against War and Fascism, and that sort of thing; but we joined nothing and demonstrated against nothing. In Detroit, riots broke out downtown, and the rioters were dispersed by mounted police. I called the police Cossacks, but my mother laughed, and said that the horses merely danced toward the mob without stepping on anybody's toes, and that I ought to go watch them some time. My mother was an optimist, a progressive, conscious of being poor, suspicious of the rich; but no thought of serious social upheaval ever entered her kindly mind. At one time our family funds sank to a single twenty-dollar bill, concealed in my mother's copy of Kipling's novel *The Light That Failed*. To small Russell A. Kirk Jr., that sum seemed wealth beyond the dreams of avarice.

There arrived weekly in our mailbox copies of the Railway Brotherhood's newspaper *Labor*. The editors rejoiced in cartoons representing the villain Capitalist as a very rotund person perpetually in evening dress, with a silk top-hat, puffing at a cigar fat as himself. The paper's editorials regularly reviled the wicked owners of the nation's railroads, though by this time many lines had gone into receivership, the stockholders having lost their investment and the bondholders having taken over. I read avidly the joke-column in *Labor*, that being rather good, but my father scarcely glanced at the paper. It printed pretty much the same abuse from week to week. Clearly the paper's editors fancied it their moral obligation to denounce capitalism root and branch, without cessation; but they did not expect any rising against this infamy to occur, ever. They knew perfectly well that railwaymen desired no overturn; their radicalism resembled the compassion of butchers, in the witticism of Samuel Johnson: "When a butcher says his heart bleeds for you, he means nothing by it." By reading *Labor* in those years, I learned to abjure cant.

My strong father, reared as a farm boy, had been apprenticed to a veterinary; but as horses vanished from the roads, the elder Russell Kirk had been claimed by the iron horse. Although a reliable worker, sober and punctual, he resented industrial discipline, intensely disliked the inhumane scale of modern industry, and (though a very mild-mannered, good-natured man) was hot against speculators in stocks and bonds, and against the New York Stock Exchange in particular. He knew avarice for the deadly sin of the twentieth century, and very right he was. There was in him, nevertheless, no spark of political radicalism. So far as he thought about socialism at all, he thought it silly. He was a reactionary, rather, in that he would have shifted Wayne County and the neighboring counties of Michigan back into the rural life of 1890, had he enjoyed magical power.

The swelling spirit of public unrest did not spare him, for all that, by the summer of 1932. He said to my mother and me, with some emphasis, "If something isn't done, there's going to be a revolution."

Though I had rent Mr. Hoover's photograph asunder, I was not disposed even then to turn radical. "Who is going to fight in this revolution, Daddy?" I inquired skeptically. "Are you?"

"Oh, no," he replied. "I don't want any revolution. I'm just saying that there are people who would start a revolution."

He had read hints of that sort not merely in *Labor*, but in the daily papers, particularly in the Hearst paper, *The Detroit Times*, then ardently Democratic. Mr. William Randolph Hearst was bound and determined to expel Mr. Herbert Hoover from the White House. There was appearing in the newspapers of the Hearst chain, read chiefly by blue-collar families, an ominous serial romance entitled Gabriel Over the White House (which was soon made into a film, still available today) that foretold the coming of an angel-inspired dictator of the United States, who would put down crime, disorder, and malefactors of great wealth, not scrupling to overturn civil rights in the performance of his appointed mission.

Newspaper editors, radio commentators, voters economically hard pressed and the popular rhetoric of Franklin Delano Roosevelt proceeded to pull President Hoover down from the seats of the mighty. If this had not occurred, and if Mr. Roosevelt's New Deal had not been unfolded very swiftly thereafter, might there have come to pass a violent revolution in the United States of America? Let us examine that question.

It has been argued quite sincerely that had no New Deal been contrived, the Constitution of the United States, the American competitive economy, and, indeed, the whole pattern of American society, would have been swept away by a rising of the indignant masses against an inhumane domination that had thrust them into want. One still encounters declarations of this sort today. Only recently, a Michigan journalist of my acquaintance, in the course of criticizing certain publications of a conservative organization, reaffirmed this theory: "Half a century and more after FDR gave the nation his own lifesaving 'new deal,' these people are still preaching Hooverism. A real threat of armed revolution was on America's doorstep in Flint and Detroit in the '30s, and it took the foresight of federal assistance to the working class to avert it."

But who would have worked this "armed revolution"? Not my father, with his Marlin carbine for deer-hunting; not Eddie Ebert, the pistol-packing yardmaster; not the Mexican section-hands with their picks; not anybody I ever encountered in the railroad and manufacturing town of Plymouth. The labor unions of Detroit were not nearly so strong in 1932 as they became after passage of the Wagner Act, and anyway, even the most radical leading spirits among them, Walter Reuther and his comrades, had not the slightest intention of taking up arms to march on Washington. There were then no organized ideological fanatics in the United States except the little bank of Communists—who, indeed, attempted to provoke confrontations between police and strikers, or Bonus Marchers and the military; but they were no more than irritating, and their chief functions were to serve as an espionage apparatus for the Soviet Union and to try to weaken American foreign policy.

Might the Communists, or some other set of ideologues, have incited the Negroes to rebellion? No task would have been more difficult, in 1932. In the national elections of that year, Negro voters were faithful to their Republican affiliation that had grown up in Reconstruction days. The only ethnic group in Detroit that gave the Republican ticket a majority of their votes in November, 1932, were the Negroes of the precincts centering upon Paradise Valley. Two years later, the Detroit Negroes still gave the majority (though a reduced majority) of their votes to Republican candidates. By 1936, true, the flood of welfare checks into their neighborhoods had shown local Negro leaders in Detroit on what side their bread was buttered; so the Negro voters shifted to the Democratic ticket, and have remained there ever since. But in 1932 there existed few Negro radicals, and certainly none with revolutionary aspirations.

Are we to suppose that the worried farmers, north or south or west, would have risen up for some devastating demagogue as disgruntled farmers followed Daniel Shays in the rebellion which bears his name? Anyone who knows twentieth-century rural America would laugh at such a vision; and in any event, by 1932 the agricultural interest was too few in numbers, relatively, to dream of dominating the country through force. Or are we to fancy that the Army of the United States, under command of some radical, might have seized power from Mr. Hoover? What radical—Douglas MacArthur? The Republic of the United States is not the Republic of Bolivia.

No, to make a violent revolution in a great modern state, there must exist a vast sullen class of the discontented and unfortunate, their circumstances seemingly desperate. They must be led by able unscrupulous men, so many Dantons; and they must count on neutrality, at the very least, from the military establishment. An elaborate propaganda must have subverted the loyalty, over a period of years, of many people whose stake in the existing society would incline them to support an existing political order.

Such circumstances did not exist in 1932. Indeed something resembling those circumstances did come to pass toward the close of Lyndon Johnson's administration; but we find nobody claiming that if the reforms of President Nixon had not undone the follies of the Johnson Administration, America would have suffered a violent revolution. The broad-based American republic is virtually impossible to overthrow, under any circumstances except conceivably an overwhelming military defeat abroad that should result in domestic ruin. These people who were naive, pretentious radicals in their youth, during the late Sixties and the early Seventies, now acknowledge that hard truth.

## Lansing, 1937

It was possible, twenty years ago and less, to assemble campus mobs that would oppose all order, political or academic. But even such affectation would not have been possible in 1932, or for a good while thereafter. College students of the Thirties, a group somewhat more select than their counterparts today, were not attracted by revolutionary doctrines. In my undergraduate days and later, I knew personally, on rather friendly terms, the tiny handful of professed Marxists at Michigan State University. They were forlorn folk, perfectly incapable of proletarian heroism.

A sufficient illustration of the campus Toryism of the Thirties—particularly at the big institutions—was the violent confrontation that occurred in the spring of 1937 at Michigan State College, East Lansing, along Grand River and Michigan Avenues. I, a freshman then, was a participant. That was the year of the United Automobile Workers' sit-down strikes at Michigan factories, distressing even to President Roosevelt. We undergraduates won a battle.

In Lansing, illegal picketing by union members had been occurring at the premises of Capitol Wrecking. The union had ignored a judge's order to cease and desist; therefore some union members were arrested at night and jailed.

In wrath, and prideful because of their recent successes in the Flint and Detroit sit-down strikes, the UAW members turned out in strength the following morning. As if they were playing at revolution, they drove their cars downtown and parked them to block the principal streets to any traffic; they invaded radio stations; they tramped into the jail, but did not venture to lay hands on the armed police who barred the way to the cells where the union members were kept. In short, they shut down the municipality of Lansing for most purposes.

Toward evening, union zealots—vulgarly denominated "goons," a term derived from the comic strip that featured Popeye the Sailor—sped out to East Lansing on motorcycles, meaning to close down the places of business in that college suburb. Unhappily for the goons, they arrived at supper time; and when they attempted to shut the restaurants, the more athletic undergraduates seized upon the goons and flung them and their motorcycles into the shallow Red Cedar River.

When dripping union zealots, crestfallen, carried back to union headquarters in Lansing these tidings of disaster, the UAW stalwarts came buzzing and fuming down Michigan Avenue, crying for vengeance upon the student body. Hundreds of them advanced on the campus; but they were met by hundreds of students, myself among them, some students armed with sticks and pipes snatched from a construction site ready to hand. At this prospect of a yet more humiliating and overwhelming defeat, and after some wrestling and shouting, the union stewards prevailed upon their rank and file to turn tail and make their way back in disorderly fashion to their Lansing fastnesses. Some students pursued them to their lairs later in the evening, but were badly thrashed for their pains. The ROTC cavalry students had hoped to charge the UAW rabble on horseback, and had so implored Governor Frank Murphy, who at the moment of the riot happened to be riding on the campus in company with the college president's daughter: would he not let them take the ROTC mounts to put down civil order? Doubtless Governor Murphy had thought he was escaping hard decisions by forsaking his capitol office to canter by the river with Miss Shaw; but he was compelled to restrain the student cavalry in the interest of his political adherents of the UAW.

The college students of the Thirties, on a good many campuses, were more Jacobite than Jacobin. There could be found no SDS enthusiasts or Weatherman fanatics, in 1932 or 1937, to make the world over new by violence, and there were no American counterparts of the passionate student ideologues of Germany or Latin America.

## "The Things" and "The Men"

If the actual peril of armed revolution was so slight in 1932 or later, how is it that some people have stoutly affirmed otherwise—even some historians? I discern two reasons for this assertion of a radical discontent that could have been assuaged only by the measures of the New Deal.

The first is the facile drawing of a parallel between the totalist revolutions of Europe from 1917 down to Hitler's triumph and American circumstances during the Thirties. But such superficial comparisons ignore the huge differences of social structure, political organization, and economic circumstances between European nations and American society. The United States in 1932 had scarcely any proletariat, strictly speaking, and no coherent mischievous class of intellectual ideologues to organize a violent transformation of the American republic. If a class struggle had arisen literally in the United States, the yardmaster and the engine driver would have adhered to things established.

The second reason for the allegation, in 1932, that either the Hoover Administration must go or else the fabric of American society would be torn in shreds was merely an argument which had its uses for the partisans of FDR. Dread of ruinous violence strongly moves those citizens who have been called "shop-and-till" conservatives: better the genteel reformer than the anarchist, their reasoning runs. Under circumstances of disorder much more alarming than American discontents of 1932, Mussolini had represented himself as the protector of the Italian civil social order in 1922, and so had been granted power; Hitler would so pose and so succeed in 1933. In a materialistic democracy, the promise that any great possible change will be averted, and economic prosperity restored by ingenious measures, will assure a candidate's success in an hour of crisis—supposing the candidate has command of the art of popular rhetoric. It was so with Franklin Delano Roosevelt. The first New Deal neither averted a revolution nor made one: the scheme was falling apart four years later. But the promises of the first New Deal did restore hope to many Americans, and in that sense served a conservative function.

Having seen something of the things and the men of 1932 and later, I offer you the considered judgment of mine, on what I hope is the pragmatic method of the historian. If this be treason to the historical establishment of which my friendly adversary Mr. Arthur M. Schlesinger Jr., is pontifex maximus—why, make the most of it. Swearing fealty to old Polybius, I try to see clearly both "the things" and "the men."

# Speech on the Economic Bailout Proposal
## George W. Bush (2008)

*President George W. Bush delivered this televised address on September 24, 2008, outlining the economic crisis that the country faced and the bailout legislation that he was proposing to Congress.*

Good evening. This is an extraordinary period for America's economy. Over the past few weeks, many Americans have felt anxiety about their finances and their future.

*George W. Bush*

I understand their worry and their frustration. We've seen triple-digit swings in the stock market. Major financial institutions have teetered on the edge of collapse, and some have failed. As uncertainty has grown, many banks have restricted lending. Credit markets have frozen. And families and businesses have found it harder to borrow money.

We're in the midst of a serious financial crisis, and the federal government is responding with decisive action. We've boosted confidence in money market mutual funds, and acted to prevent major investors from intentionally driving down stocks for their own personal gain.

Most importantly, my administration is working with Congress to address the root cause behind much of the instability in our markets. Financial assets related to home mortgages have lost value during the housing decline. And the banks holding these assets have restricted credit. As a result, our entire economy is in danger. So I've proposed that the federal government reduce the risk posed by these troubled assets, and supply urgently-needed money so banks and other financial institutions can avoid collapse and resume lending.

This rescue effort is not aimed at preserving any individual company or industry—it is aimed at preserving America's overall economy. It will help American consumers and businesses get credit to meet their daily needs and create jobs. And it will help send a signal to markets around the world that America's financial system is back on track.

I know many Americans have questions tonight: How did we reach this point in our economy? How will the solution I've proposed work? And what does this mean for your financial future? These are good questions, and they deserve clear answers.

First, how did our economy reach this point?

Well, most economists agree that the problems we are witnessing today developed over a long period of time. For more than a decade, a massive amount of money flowed into the United States from investors abroad, because our country is an attractive and secure place to do business. This large influx of money to U.S. banks and financial institutions—along with low interest rates—made it easier for Americans to get credit. These developments allowed more families to borrow money for cars and homes and college tuition—some for the first time. They allowed more entrepreneurs to get loans to start new businesses and create jobs.

Unfortunately, there were also some serious negative consequences, particularly in the housing market. Easy credit—combined with the faulty assumption that home values would continue to rise—led to excesses and bad decisions. Many mortgage lenders approved loans for borrowers without carefully examining their ability to pay. Many borrowers took out loans larger than they could afford, assuming that they could sell or refinance their homes at a higher price later on.

Optimism about housing values also led to a boom in home construction. Eventually the number of new houses exceeded the number of people willing to buy them. And with supply exceeding demand, housing prices fell. And this created a problem: Borrowers with adjustable rate mortgages who had been planning to sell or refinance their homes at a higher price were stuck with homes worth less than expected—along with mortgage payments they could not afford. As a result, many mortgage holders began to default.

These widespread defaults had effects far beyond the housing market. See, in today's mortgage industry, home loans are often packaged together, and converted into financial products called "mortgage-backed securities." These securities were sold to investors around the world. Many investors assumed these securities were trustworthy and asked few questions about their actual value. Two of the leading purchasers of mortgage-backed securities were Fannie Mae and Freddie Mac. Because these companies were chartered by Congress, many believed they were guaranteed by the federal government. This allowed them to borrow enormous sums of money, fuel the market for questionable investments, and put our financial system at risk.

The decline in the housing market set off a domino effect across our economy. When home values declined, borrowers defaulted on their mortgages, and investors holding mortgage-backed securities began to incur serious losses. Before long, these securities became so unreliable that they were not being bought or sold. Investment banks such as Bear Stearns and Lehman Brothers found themselves saddled with large amounts of assets they could not sell. They ran out of the money needed to meet their immediate obligations. And they faced imminent collapse. Other banks found themselves in severe financial trouble. These banks began holding on to their money, and lending dried up, and the gears of the American financial system began grinding to a halt.

With the situation becoming more precarious by the day, I faced a choice: To step in with dramatic government action, or to stand back and allow the irresponsible actions of some to undermine the financial security of all.

I'm a strong believer in free enterprise. So my natural instinct is to oppose government intervention. I believe companies that make bad decisions should be allowed to go out of business. Under normal circumstances, I would have followed this course. But these are not normal circumstances. The market is not functioning properly. There's been a widespread loss of confidence. And major sectors of America's financial system are at risk of shutting down.

The government's top economic experts warn that without immediate action by Congress, America could slip into a financial panic, and a distressing scenario would unfold:

More banks could fail, including some in your community. The stock market would drop even more, which would reduce the value of your retirement account. The value of your home could plummet. Foreclosures would rise dramatically. And if you own a business or a farm, you would find it harder and more expensive to get credit. More businesses would close their doors, and millions of Americans could lose their jobs. Even if you have good credit history, it would be more difficult for you to get the loans you need to buy a car or send your children to college. And ultimately, our country could experience a long and painful recession.

Fellow citizens: We must not let this happen. I appreciate the work of leaders from both parties in both houses of Congress to address this problem—and to make improvements to the proposal my administration sent to them. There is a spirit of cooperation between Democrats and Republicans, and between Congress and this administration. In that spirit, I've invited Senators McCain and Obama to join congressional leaders of both parties at the White House tomorrow to help speed our discussions toward a bipartisan bill.

*U.S. Capitol*

I know that an economic rescue package will present a tough vote for many members of Congress. It is difficult to pass a bill that commits so much of the taxpayers' hard-earned money. I also understand the frustration of responsible Americans who pay their mortgages on time, file their tax returns every April 15th, and are reluctant to pay the cost of excesses on Wall Street. But given the situation we are facing, not passing a bill now would cost these Americans much more later.

Many Americans are asking: How would a rescue plan work?

After much discussion, there is now widespread agreement on the principles such a plan would include. It would remove the risk posed by the troubled assets—including mortgage-backed securities—now clogging the financial system. This would free banks to resume the flow of credit to American families and businesses. Any rescue plan should also be designed to ensure that taxpayers are protected. It should welcome the participation of financial institutions large and small. It should make certain that failed executives do not receive a windfall from your tax dollars. It should establish a bipartisan board to oversee the plan's implementation. And it should be enacted as soon as possible.

In close consultation with Treasury Secretary Hank Paulson, Federal Reserve Chairman Ben Bernanke, and SEC Chairman Chris Cox, I announced a plan on Friday. First, the plan is big enough to solve a serious problem. Under our proposal, the federal government would put up to $700 billion taxpayer dollars on the line to purchase troubled assets that are clogging the financial system. In the short term, this will free up banks to resume the flow of credit to American families and businesses. And this will help our economy grow.

Second, as markets have lost confidence in mortgage-backed securities, their prices have dropped sharply. Yet the value of many of these assets will likely be higher than their current price, because the vast majority of Americans will ultimately pay off their mortgages. The government is the one institution with the patience and resources to buy these assets at their current low prices and hold them until markets return to normal. And when that happens, money will flow back to the Treasury as these assets are sold. And we expect that much, if not all, of the tax dollars we invest will be paid back.

A final question is: What does this mean for your economic future?

The primary . . . purpose of the steps I have outlined tonight is to safeguard the financial security of American workers and families and small businesses. The federal government also continues to enforce laws and regulations protecting your money. The Treasury Department recently offered government insurance for money market mutual funds. And through the FDIC, every savings account, checking account, and certificate of deposit is insured by the federal government for up to $100,000. The FDIC has been in existence for 75 years, and no one has ever lost a penny on an insured deposit—and this will not change.

Once this crisis is resolved, there will be time to update our financial regulatory structures. Our 21st century global economy remains regulated largely by outdated 20th century laws. Recently, we've seen how one company can grow so large that its failure jeopardizes the entire financial system.

Earlier this year, Secretary Paulson proposed a blueprint that would modernize our financial regulations. For example, the Federal Reserve would be authorized to take a closer look at the operations of companies across the financial spectrum and ensure that their practices do not threaten overall financial stability. There are other good ideas, and members of Congress should consider them. As they do, they must ensure that efforts to regulate Wall Street do not end up hampering our economy's ability to grow.

In the long run, Americans have good reason to be confident in our economic strength. Despite corrections in the marketplace and instances of abuse, democratic capitalism is the best system ever devised. It has unleashed the talents, and the productivity, and entrepreneurial spirit of our citizens. It has made this country the best place in the world to invest and do business. And it gives our economy the flexibility and resilience to absorb shocks, adjust, and bounce back.

Our economy is facing a moment of great challenge. But we've overcome tough challenges before—and we will overcome this one. I know that Americans sometimes get discouraged by the tone in Washington, and the seemingly endless partisan struggles. Yet history has shown that in times of real trial, elected officials rise to the occasion. And together, we will show the world once again what kind of country America is—a nation that tackles problems head on, where leaders come together to meet great tests, and where people of every background can work hard, develop their talents, and realize their dreams.

Thank you for listening. May God bless you.

# The Innate Power of the Individual
## Kent C. Nelson (1997)

*Kent C. Nelson (born 1938) became United Parcel Service's chairman and chief executive officer in 1989 after working for the company for three decades in a variety of positions from chief financial officer to executive vice president and vice chairman. He retired in January 1997. Mr. Nelson has also led a number of philanthropic initiatives.*

March 1997 *Imprimis*

What is the single greatest aspect of the American creed? What is responsible for the greatness we have achieved as a nation? What will guarantee the success of our generation and generations to come? I believe that the answer to all these questions is the innate power of the individual.

Back in the days of Teddy Roosevelt, Americans used to talk about the virtues of "rugged individualism." But times change, and more recently, in the 1960s and 1970s, it was: "Do your own thing." And now, on the threshold of a new century, it is: "In your face!" This is reverse evolution. Our culture is distancing itself from the high principles that guided us so well for so long, and we are all paying a heavy price for it. All three of the phrases I just cited affirm the supremacy of the individual, but with vastly different attitudes. In Roosevelt's time, the rugged individual was admired for being self-reliant, decisive, and determined. He was someone who saw each challenge as an opportunity for improvement. By the 1960s and 1970s, the economic and material success of the United States had spawned a generation that demanded—and received—a license for self-indulgence. By the 1980s and early 1990s, we had elevated self-indulgence to an art form.

"Situational ethics" and moral relativism replaced the bedrock American values of honesty and fairness. Advocates once promised that these new values would lead to unprecedented peace and tolerance. Not too surprisingly, they have brought about just the opposite. But not everywhere. Some pockets of peace and tolerance as well as civility and optimism remain. One of them is Hillsdale College. This is an institution that all Americans ought to revere for its unwavering commitment not only to independence but to traditional, time-tested values. Here is a bastion of freedom for individuals who seek truth and wisdom among competing ideas.

It hasn't been easy. Hillsdale's insistence on independence has not gone over well in Washington, D.C. There appears to be widespread resentment among bureaucrats that Hillsdale long ago achieved, through independent action, the goals of diversity and personal opportunity that still elude the government, with all its resources, tax money, and enforcement powers. It happened because the individuals who organized this college put purpose ahead of process. Their pioneer experience and religious faith taught them right from wrong, and they acted courageously to defend their beliefs.

In his book, *The Death of Common Sense*, attorney Philip K. Howard attributes many of the problems we have as a society to our willingness to subjugate purpose to process. "It once existed to help humans make responsible decisions," he writes, "[But] process has now

174

become an end in itself." As a result, pharmaceutical companies spend more on forms and paperwork than they do on all their research for cancer and other diseases. And children in the inner city miss out on badly needed educational programs for years while bureaucrats quibble over such details as room dimensions that do not conform to government guidelines.

At my former company, UPS, we know a lot about process. I don't think there is another organization anywhere that is so good at devising the best way to move something from A to B to C. But all our processes at UPS serve larger purposes—not the other way around. That's the way it is when you're in competition with other businesses. Like the pioneers who founded Hillsdale, the founders of UPS had a clear purpose in mind. One of them was Evert McCabe. His principles and ideals are honored at Hillsdale through the establishment of an endowed chair in economics that bears his name. McCabe believed that the innovative power of enterprise can lead to tremendous achievement and growth. The history of UPS proves him right. His partner, Jim Casey, saw that the real sinews of the organization would be its people—and he believed the power of the individual was limitless. "Within each of us

there is a mysterious, innate force that drives us onward," Casey once said. "It wants us to do better and be better. . . . If you utilize that inner power to the limit," Casey concluded, "nothing on earth can stop your progress."

Almost from day one, UPS operated in a competitive arena. That heritage of competition has served us well. We have been able to offer customers an alternative to the United States Post Office for nationwide small package delivery. In recent years, we have been challenged by some relative newcomers to the distribution industry. Today, we face a host of niche companies trying to nibble away at targeted segments of our business. Vigorous competition has caused UPS to transform itself over the past decade. We have virtually reinvented the company and made it the world leader in package distribution. UPS is also a highly regarded innovator in transportation logistics and information technology.

It seems that the harder we compete, the more determined, innovative, and successful we become. That's true in every field of human endeavor, not just business but sports, politics, education, music—you name it. There is no need to fear competition. Only those lacking in confidence try to erect barriers to freedom in the marketplace. If you want proof, just look at places where competition is absent and see the result. Not long ago, the president of the Michigan State Board of Education and the president of the Chrysler Corporation co-authored an article in the *Wall Street Journal* called "The Key to Better Schools." They wrote,

> Public schools too often fail because they are shielded from the very force that improves performance and sparks innovation in nearly every other human enterprise—competition.

> In business, in the professions, even in our private lives we rarely muster the courage to improve performance without external challenge.

I like to think of UPS as 330,000 rugged individualists who see opportunity in every challenge: The plane from Alaska is late getting into the UPS air hub in Louisville and misses the scheduled shipment to the west coast. Call out the charter jet to take one package that originated in Asia to its destination in California so that tomorrow morning 500 assembly workers will have material for the day's production. The freight train in New England is to depart at midnight, hours before the last UPS container shipment is expected to be loaded. Round up an emergency crew to help meet the deadline. These are examples of actions taken by UPS managers—on their own initiative—to serve the purpose of our business.

It may surprise you to hear about such striking individuality in a company with so uniform an outward appearance. Our corporate culture actually encourages our people to take personal charge of their part of the business. UPS employees are empowered; they are able to use their best judgment to make important decisions without waiting for a stamp of approval from a committee. On average, twelve million packages a day enter and flow through the UPS system in more than 200 countries and territories around the world. We have 147,000 delivery vehicles, a fleet of 218 aircraft, and 2,400 facilities all over the world—all connected to each other with very precise scheduling. When something goes wrong or a decision is needed, it is critical that the people on the scene have the authority to step in and take action. At the other end of the business, the people who are responsible for creating new service offerings have the autonomy to innovate, break with the past, and take us in new directions to give customers even more than they expect.

"Teamwork" may sound like a hackneyed term, but it really is key to everything we do at UPS. We all know that teams are only as good as the people that serve on them. I say with great pride that I believe our people are the finest in the industry. We hire the best we can find and then we train them thoroughly and continuously, reward them generously, and involve them personally in our business.

That's a formula for success in any enterprise. Our people, confident in their roles as individuals, have transformed our company by responding vigorously and imaginatively to competition from many different quarters. UPS has an outstanding corporate culture, structure, and strategy; but we truly owe our success to the innate power of the individuals who make the company work. Here is one testimonial from the thousands of letters we receive from customers:

Dear Mr. Nelson:

A few weeks ago the doorbell rang in the middle of the afternoon. Vanilla (my dog) ran to the door, and I could tell by her reaction someone she really likes was at the door.

I was surprised to see Oscar, our UPS man, standing at the door. He asked if I was okay and I told him yes. Then he asked me again and I assured him that I was fine.

He then told me that he was driving by and noticed that the screen was off the dining room window and lying on the ground. He thought that something was wrong. Oscar said he was going to call 911 if he had not gotten an answer.
I am so impressed that Oscar noticed that the screen was out of place and took the time to investigate. We are so lucky to have Oscar for our UPS deliveries.

We live in a world where we all rush through our day. It is nice to know that Oscar took the time from his busy route to investigate a potential problem.

If you ever try to take Oscar off this route, I can promise you there are several of us on this block who would protest. He is not just our delivery person, he is also our friend, and he is very much appreciated.

The letter ended with this postscript: "By the way, Oscar put the screen back on before he left!"

Every business ought to encourage the Oscars of this world—the men and women who don't just work hard every day but who put the jobs they do in the proper perspective and who live by the Golden Rule. It was Edward R. Murrow, the legendary broadcast journalist, who once observed that the competitive urge is a fine, wholesome energy, but only if the desire to win is wedded to an ideal, to an ethical way of life. Those of us who work in highly competitive industries love to win, just as professional athletes do. But during more than 35 years in the business world, I have observed that the people who care only about winning—who live and die by the numbers alone—end up losing out on the biggest prize of all. That prize is the joy of being an important part of something much larger than yourself. It is the comfort of knowing that your actions will touch the lives of others in a positive way. It is joining with other people in working toward worthwhile goals. It is a prize that has nothing to do with winning or making money. It has everything to do with life.

# What Makes for Success?
## Kemmons Wilson (1997)

*Kemmons Wilson (1913-2003) quit high school during the Depression when his mother lost her job. He began making money by selling popcorn outside theaters. In 1952, he opened the first Holiday Inn in Memphis, Tennessee. Today, Holiday Inn properties make up one of the largest hotel chains in the world. Mr. Wilson has been called "the father of the modern innkeeping industry." In this speech, Mr. Wilson shared his principles for personal and economic success.*

March 1997 *Imprimis*

I am often asked, "What makes for success?" I know that most people regard success as the attainment of wealth. But I think that the most successful people are those who take pride in their work, pride in their family, and pride in their country. It is great to attain wealth, but money is really just one way—and hardly the best way—to keep score.

As parents, we all try to share with our children the knowledge we have gained through our own experiences, which usually include many successes and failures. As an entrepreneur, I have also tried to pass on to my children the importance of business and economics and how each relates to the world in which we live. I am a very fortunate man in that my three sons are partners in my work and they appear to have learned their lessons well. My only problem now is that I have to listen to *their* advice.

That was not the case back in 1951 when I took my wife and our five children on a vacation to Washington, D.C. Those were the good old days when the children still had to mind us and listen to our advice. A motel room only cost about $8.00 a night, but the proprietors inevitably charged $2.00 extra for each child. So the $8.00 charge soon ballooned into an $18.00 charge for my family. If we could get a room with two beds, our two daughters slept in one, and Dorothy and I slept in the other. Our three boys slept on the floor in sleeping bags. Sometimes there was a dollar deposit for the key and another dollar for the use of a television. This made my Scotch blood boil, and, after a few nights, I told my wife how unfair I thought all the extra charges were. They did not encourage couples to travel, especially with their children.

I was active in the construction business at the time, so I also told her that building a motel, or even a hotel, was no more difficult than building a home. I was seized by an idea: I could build a chain of affordable hotels, stretching from coast to coast. Families could travel cross-country and stay at one of my hotels every night. Most travel in 1951 was by automobile, but without the benefit of the interstate system we are so familiar with now, so this kind of service would be unique. Dorothy asked me how many hotels I thought it would take, and I threw out the number 400. She laughed and said it couldn't be done. Now, my mother, who raised me alone after my father died, had instilled in me the belief that I could do anything if I worked hard enough and wanted it badly enough. At that moment, I wanted it desperately just so my wife wouldn't laugh at me.

I learned a lot of things on that vacation. I measured the bedrooms and bathrooms in every motel in which we stayed, and by the time we returned home, I knew exactly what kind of hotels I wanted to build. I learned a few things from my kids, too. When you travel with five children all under the age of eight, you learn, for example, about the vital importance of a swimming pool. Have you ever stopped at a motel or hotel with your children when their first words weren't, "Make sure it has a swimming pool"? I also learned about the importance of having a doctor and a dentist on call. One of our children fell ill with a toothache and another one had a high fever. We had to use the telephone book and make a number of calls in order to track down professionals who were willing to help.

Features that we take for granted today were ones I determined would be standard in my hotels: free televisions, in-room telephones, ice machines, and restaurants. And, of course, children would stay free.

At home in Memphis, I showed a draftsman named Eddy Bluestein the lists and diagrams of what I wanted. Several days later, he brought me his rough sketches. On the first, he had sketched out in script the words, "Holiday Inn," a fictional name he had seen in a Bing Crosby movie the previous evening.

I heartily approved, and the first Holiday Inn opened in Memphis in 1952. Before it was finished, there were others under construction in the three remaining corners of the city. I wanted to make sure that motorists could not drive through Memphis without passing at least one Holiday Inn. By the end of 1953, all four hotels were open for business, but I had used up my savings and credit. That is when I started dreaming of franchising. I don't believe I knew the word at that time; I just thought that I had a great idea and that I could sell it along with my plans and specifications for a flat fee of $500 plus a royalty of 5 cents per room per night.

To find buyers, I went to see my friend, Wallace Johnson. He was also in the construction business and was active in the National Association of Homebuilders. I showed him my figures and explained that all we had to do was get one homebuilder in each major city in the United States to build a Holiday Inn and we would soon have a chain of 400 across the country. We invited 100 homebuilders to a meeting and 64 showed up. We sold 12 franchises, and with the great sum of $6,000 in additional capital, we thought we were off and running.

We were wrong.

Most of the homebuilders were too busy building homes to exercise their franchise option. Only three of them actually built one of our hotels. Worse yet, we discovered that there was no way we could sell the rights to build Holiday Inns as cheaply as we planned. After the first 15 franchises, the fee was raised to $2,000 and 5 cents per night or 3 percent of the gross room sales. We also decided that we needed to attract investors. Holiday Inn's first public offering was 120,000 shares at $9.75. Expenses only amounted to about 75 cents per share, so we ended up getting a check for a little more than $1 million. This time, we really were off and running.

The 50th Holiday Inn opened in Dyersburg, Tennessee in 1958, and the 100th opened in Tallahassee, Florida in 1959. The first Holiday Inn outside the United States opened in Montreal in 1960. In 1964, we opened the 500th hotel in Johnstown, Pennsylvania. This was the idea—this was my dream. When I retired 28 years later there were 1,759 Holiday Inns in 50 different countries. Today there are over 2,000.

Sometimes the first step is the hardest: coming up with an idea. Coming up with an idea should be like sitting on a pin—it should make you jump up and do something. I have had a great many ideas over the years. Some were good, some were great, and some I would prefer to forget about. The important thing is to take your best ideas and see them through. Not all of them are going to be winners, but just remember, a person who wins success may have been counted out many times before. He wins because he refuses to give up.

My own success was attended by quite a few failures along the way. But I refused to make the biggest mistake of all: worrying too much about making mistakes. A man who never makes mistakes is the man who never does anything. I have made as many or more mistakes than most people, but I always try to learn from them and to profit from my failures. It is stupid to make the same mistake twice, but I have done it many times. What has saved me from despair is the knowledge that, as the late Norman Vincent Peale once said, "Enthusiasm makes the difference." He was right. Enthusiasm is the most contagious disease in all the world, and it is a disease that cures instead of weakens the patient. Very little in this world has ever been achieved without enthusiasm.

I also believe that hard work has helped me to overcome my mistakes. The freedom to work is second only to the freedom to worship. Work is the master key that opens the door to all opportunities. If a person truly knows what he wants out of life and is willing to work hard enough for it, life will pay its richest rewards and greatest dividends. Work is not man's doom but man's blessing. A 40-hour week has no charm for me. I'm looking for a 40-hour day.

I have worked in boom times and in recessions, in the Great Depression and in time of war. Our government has been led by Republicans and Democrats, conservatives and liberals. Through all, I have seen our free enterprise system survive and provide the economic means to build the greatest society in the history of the world. I suppose such observations make me seem like a fellow with a lot of old-fashioned, corny ideas. Indeed, that is just the kind of fellow I am. I can prove it too, by quoting one of my favorite pieces of inspirational literature. I came across it years ago, and I still think it is the best way to sum up what makes for success:

For best results, this garden should be planted every day:

Five rows of "P"eas:
Preparedness,
Promptness,
Perseverance,
Politeness,
Prayer.

Three rows of squash:
Squash gossip,
Squash criticism,
Squash indifference.

Five rows of lettuce:
Let us love one another,
Let us be faithful,
Let us be loyal,
Let us be unselfish,
Let us be truthful.

Three rows of turnips:
Turn up for church,
Turn up with a new idea,
Turn up with the determination to do a better job tomorrow than you did today.

# Index of Titles

American Free Trade Policy: Rhetoric or Reality, 85
American Small Business: The Quiet Giant, 104
Christianity, the Market, and Beyond, 29
The Deficit and Our Obligation to Future Generations, 127
Ecology and the Economy: The Problems of Coexistence, 154
Economic Justice for All (excerpts), 37
The Entrepreneur As American Hero, 61
Free to Choose: A Conversation with Milton Friedman, 79
Free Trade Under Attack: What Americans Can Do, 90
The Greatest Story Never Told: Today's Economy in Perspective, 134
High Technology and Judeo-Christian Values: Mind, Not Money, Drives the Economy, 71
How Detroit's Automakers Went from Kings of the Road to Roadkill, 147
I Must See the Things; I Must See the Men, 163
The Innate Power of the Individual, 174
I, Pencil, 1
Labor Unions in a Free Market, 115
The Legacy of the 1936 Election, 46
The Legitimate Role of Government in a Free Society, 123
Letter 4 of Letters from a Farmer in Pennsylvania, 43
The Market and Human Values, 66
Market Entrepreneurs: Building Empires of Service, 98
A Prescription for American Health Care, 143
Politics, Economics, and Education in the 21st Century, 51
Socialism, Capitalism, and the Bible, 12
Socialism, Free Enterprise, and the Common Good, 110
Solving the Problem of Poverty, 138
Speech on the Economic Bailout Proposal, 170
Three Cheers for Capitalism, 57
The Wealth of Nations (excerpts), 5
What Makes for Success? (Thomas), 18
What Makes for Success? (Wilson), 178

# Index of Authors

Brookes, Warren T., 71
Buchanan, James M., 127
Buckley, James L., 154
Bush, George W., 170
Davenport, John, 29, 66
Dickinson, John, 43
Folsom, Burton W. Jr., 98
Forbes, Steve, 57
Friedman, Milton, 79
Fund, John, 51

Goodman, John C., 143
Kirk, Russell, 163
Mariotti, Steve, 138
Nash, Ronald H., 12
Nelson, Kent C., 174
Read, Leonard, 1
Shlaes, Amity, 46
Sirico, Robert A., 110
Sloan, John E., 104
Smith, Adam, 5

Thomas, Dave, 18
Toomey, Patrick, 134
U.S. Catholic Bishops, 37
Van den Haag, Ernest, 115
White, Joseph B., 147
Wiedenbaum, Murray L., 90
Williams, Walter E., 61, 123
Wilson, Kemmons, 178

# Image Credits

**Charlene Notgrass** 17

**Free to Choose Media** 79

**Hal Paugh** 27

**JupiterImages** (© 2009 JupiterImages) 4, 5, 8, 19, 43, 55, 65, 73, 76, 95, 135, 136, 142, 148, 154, 157, 160, 162, 172

**Library of Congress Prints and Photographs Division** 10, 48, 50, 67, 87, 89, 100, 112, 117, 118, 127, 132, 138, 144, 151

**U.S. Department of State** 170

# Also by Ray Notgrass

### Exploring World History

This curriculum surveys world history from Creation to modern times. It includes the history narrative, Bible lessons, and reading and writing assignments needed to earn one year's high school credit in Bible, English, and World History.

### Exploring America

This curriculum surveys American history from Columbus to the war in Iraq. It includes the history narrative, Bible lessons, and reading and writing assignments needed to earn one year's high school credit in Bible, English, and American History.

### Exploring Government

This curriculum is a one-semester high school course that provides a half-year credit in government. Lessons cover Federal, state, and local government and also contemporary issues in government. Special emphasis is placed on the Biblical basis for government and on the U.S. Constitution.

For information about these and other resources
available from Notgrass Company,
call 1-800-211-8793 or visit our website:
www.notgrass.com

LaVergne, TN USA
21 December 2009
167605LV00002BA/1/P